Boundary Wars

Boundary Wars

Intimacy and Distance
in Healing Relationships

Edited by
Katherine Hancock Ragsdale

The Pilgrim Press
Cleveland, Ohio

The Pilgrim Press, Cleveland, Ohio 44115

© 1996 by Katherine Hancock Ragsdale

"A Brief History of Sexual Intimacy in Psychotherapy" © 1996 by Susan Baur

"Legal Issues in Clergy Sexual Boundary Violation Matters" © 1996 by Sally A. Johnson

"Out of Bounds" © 1995 by Miriam Greenspan. This essay originally appeared in the July/August 1995 issue of *Common Boundaries.*

Portions of "I-Thou: Interpersonal Boundaries in the Therapy Relationship" by Margo Rivera appear in *More Alike Than Different: Treating Severely Dissociate Trauma Survivors* (University of Toronto Press, 1996) and are used by permission of the author and University of Toronto Press.

Printed in the United States of America on acid-free paper

01 00 99 98 97 96   5 4 3 2 1

Library of Congress Cataloging-in-Publication Data

Boundary wars : intimacy and distance in healing relationships / edited by Katherine Hancock Ragsdale.
   p. cm.
  Includes bibliographical references and index.
  ISBN 0-8298-1118-4 (alk. paper)
   1. Clergy—Sexual behavior.   2. Clergy—Professional ethics.
  3. Psychotherapists—Sexual behavior.   4. Psychotherapists—Professional ethics.   5. Counseling—Moral and ethical aspects.
  I. Ragsdale, Katherine Hancock, 1958– .
  BV4392.B68 1996   95-52520
  253'.2—dc20   CIP

Contents

Acknowledgments

IT MAY BE A cliché to say, "I don't know how to begin to thank all the people who made this project possible," but it's true nonetheless. However, living in a converted boathouse on (literally) a cold New England lake, I'm slowly learning that the only way in is to hold your breath and dive. So, here goes.

First and foremost, thanks to all the contributors, who did such fine work on such short notice. And to Richard Brown of The Pilgrim Press, who dreamed up this project in the first place and was an absolute delight to work with.

Thanks also to Marie Fortune and the staff of the Center for the Prevention of Sexual and Domestic Violence for introducing me to this issue. Thanks to the members of the Center's Bi-National Advisory Committee for enduring, even encouraging, arguments between Marie and me as we all thought through these complicated issues together—their insights and experience have been invaluable.

Thanks to the faculty, staff, and students of Episcopal Divinity School in Cambridge, Massachusetts. They have been a hospitable community within which to live and do this work. They have provided opportunities to teach and so hone my own ideas; they have provided conversation to enlarge my perspective; they have told me their own stories and so fueled my passion.

Alison Cheek directs a Doctor of Ministry in Feminist Liberation Theology and Ministry program at EDS that provides a perfect setting for people to re-think and re-charge. Kwok Pui Lan, who has edited a collection of her own, knew, and tried to prepare me for, the perils. My assistant, Mary Marguerite Kohn, typed, organized, tracked down references, and endured. Thanks to you all.

Carter Heyward, Beverly Harrison, and Marie Fortune all suggested additional contributors and resources. They have, for years, been dependable (and entertaining) colleagues to me in this work.

Thanks to all my summer guests who pretended not to notice that I was ignoring them in favor of the computer—Cynthia, Becky, Liz, Ryan, Mary, and Moxa. And to Miriam and Nancy for taking me away from all this for a relaxing long weekend.

To my family of origin for making me laugh—Ann and Coleman, Harriett and Carl, Edwin and Amy. To my niece and nephews—Cameron, 4, Lauren, 3, and Nicholas, 21 months—for reminding me that the work we do today will matter for a very long time.

And finally, to Sue Sasser. She read everything—many times. She critiqued and encouraged and kept me fed. She is a superior partner in every sense of the word. Thank you, Sue.

Introduction

Katherine Hancock Ragsdale

MOST DISCUSSIONS OF intimacy and distance in healing relationships involve two intricately intertwined issues. The first concerns what constitutes abuse of power; the second concerns what standards of practice are most efficacious. The essays in this volume, which focus primarily on ministerial and psychotherapeutic relationships, will wrestle with both aspects of the intimacy/distance spectrum—abuse of power and standards of professional practice.

"Wars" may be a strange word to find in the title of a volume such as this. It seems an odd characterization of a discussion that thrives among feminists and our friends. Odd, perhaps, but in this case apt. Too often, the public discourse among proponents of differing positions has been notable more for the heat it sheds than for the light. People seem to talk *at* rather than *with* one another. This is, to some extent, the nature of public debate. Certainly it should not be understood to reflect on either the goodwill or the profound contributions of most participants in the debate. Nonetheless, the sustained, nuanced give-and-take of genuine conversation has been difficult to achieve in the midst of this very public controversy. This volume reflects the contributors' commitment to such conversation.

The dynamics of this evolving debate also resemble a war in that there are collateral casualties. As we struggle to develop a workable theory or theories, people who never chose to become involved in the debate find their lives affected. On the one hand,[1] there is the woman who goes to her pastor for counsel and finds herself repeatedly propositioned instead. Where there is no clarity about appropriate boundaries, such persons have found scant support for their efforts to call the offending pastor to account and to see that steps are taken to ensure that no other woman or man will suffer similar violation at the hands of the same offender.

On the other hand, there is the woman who leaves an emotionally abusive husband and finds herself attracted to a clergyman with whom she has had, in the past, conversations about her troubled marriage. They see a therapist together to disentangle some of the threads of their relationship, then decide to date. They understand that the relational dynamics are complex and demand work. They are happy—until the ex-husband finds out about the relationship. Making use of the clear and rigid boundary rules adopted by this pastor's denomination, the ex-husband finds a way to continue to control and hurt the woman who left him. He reports the pastor, complaining of a boundary violation. Perhaps the pastor will be exonerated; perhaps not.

There are countless tales of men and women who spent time and money they could ill afford on therapy with therapists who allowed their own needs and issues to cloud the professional relationship. The client ended up feeling that he or she had paid for therapy that was inadequate, at best, and perhaps actively abusive. And there are stories of those who have never been able to avail themselves of the potential benefits of therapy because they have been unable to find a therapist who would treat them with collegial respect—as partners in the enterprise of dealing with the client's issues—and have been unwilling to endure any other kind of arrangement.

Questions about boundaries, about intimacy and distance, have fueled raging debates in virtually every field and every locale. And while the debate rages, real lives are torn. It is, perhaps, because of this that the debate is so heated. Advocates on each side of the issue have seen the cost of ignoring their concerns. They will not sit quietly by while others pay that price—nor should they.

The contributors to this volume do not join this debate in a vacuum. They are all too aware of the lives that are, and will be, affected by the theories they support as well as by those they challenge. Our purpose is to put an end to any notion that we are at war or that we would settle for a victory of any one theory at the cost of devastated lives. We look, instead, for a conversation that takes seriously the competing needs and costs at stake and that looks for solutions that do not require the sacrifice of a single principle or life.

Such conversation requires some clarity about the complex interweave of issues and concepts that create the foundation of the debate. What follows is an effort to identify some of the threads of these arguments, to introduce the voices gathered together in this volume, and to set a context for their conversation.

Questions concerning abuse of power have claimed national attention in recent years. While power abuses can take a variety of forms (for example, the pastor who ingratiates herself to an elderly member of the congregation and is then remembered in his will, or who arranges for members of the congregation to clean his house and do his laundry), the form of abuse that is most often noticed and decried—and which, in some respects, epitomizes the problem—is sexual abuse.

During the 1990s we have seen a sea change in our understanding of what constitutes sexual abuse. No longer does this concept refer exclusively to sexual activity with minors, the mentally impaired, or those who are forcibly denied the opportunity to consent or not—as in the case of rape. Abusive sexual behavior has been reclassified in three[2] categories: (1) sexual abuse—sexual activity with minors or those deemed mentally incompetent to give consent; (2) sexual harassment—demands for sexual favors as a condition of employment or the creation of an intolerable atmosphere in the workplace[3]; and (3) sexual exploitation[4]—manipulation or coercion of vulnerable persons by professionals in whom they have put their trust, resulting in sexual relationships; or any sexual activity between a professional and someone with whom she or he has a professional relationship. While there is near universal consensus regarding the first two categories,[5] the third has been the focus of sustained debate among traditional allies.

The development of this third category of abuse is grounded in the courage of survivors. Women and men have begun to tell their stories of abuse at the hands of clergy, psychotherapists, and other professionals who have used their professional roles to prey on those who had entrusted themselves to their care. Courts and professional organizations have begun to hear and take seriously those stories, to respond to these calls for justice, and to hold abusers accountable.

The debate is rooted not in a dismissal of the category of sexual exploitation but in disagreement about how to define it. By sexual exploitation do we mean only the manipulation or coercion of vulnerable persons by professionals in whom they have put their trust? Or does the category include any sexual or romantic contact between a professional and a "client"? Is an adult woman or man ever able to give meaningful consent to a sexual or romantic relationship with someone to whom she or he has once turned for professional help?

These questions about the nature and meaning of sexual exploitation raise even more fundamental questions about the place of intimacy and distance in healing relationships in general and, in particular, in professional relationships. Is sexual intimacy in the context (or aftermath) of a professional relationship ever appropriate? How about romance? Friendship? Mutually respectful, collegial give-and-take? Can one contract with a professional for her services for a designated amount of time (e.g., one hour a week) over a designated period of time (e.g., three months) and still leave open the possibility of another type of relationship (friendship, collegiality, romance) outside the designated hour or after the termination of the professionally contracted relationship? Are clearly demarcated boundaries between professional and client essential to good care? Or are they antithetical to it? In what types of relationships is healing most likely to take place? For whom? What works?

The feminist community, united in its support for victims, its abhorrence of abuse, and its commitment to justice, has been divided in its understandings of which definition of abuse is appropriate— and of what all this means about appropriate practice for those in the helping professions and those who, paid professionals or not, take seriously their roles as active agents in healing relationships in the communities within which they live, work, play, or worship.

The debate rages. Some support laws and regulations, on the assumption that professionals always enjoy such a degree of power and influence in relation to those who come to them for help or professional services that they can never enter, or achieve, a relationship as equal participants on a level playing field.[6] Others argue that such assumptions, and the rules that derive from them, codify the clericalism feminist theologians have worked for decades to dismantle and the paternalistic, doctor-knows-best models of psychotherapy that feminist therapists have long challenged.[7]

Lost in the general outcry is the careful ethical analysis demanded by a complex situation involving competing needs and costs. Advocates choose sides, aligning themselves with one theorist or another, reducing a complex ethical dilemma to a polarized political debate, drowning out the voices of those struggling to respond to various (and sometimes conflicting) needs and concerns. In the meantime insurers, professional societies, legislatures, and courts promulgate regulations that (perhaps unintentionally) stifle the debate but that are uninformed by a thorough and critical understanding of the professional theories at stake.

This volume will not provide a definitive answer to this complex dilemma. It is intended, instead, to provide a suitably complex context for continuing the conversation, a forum for the voices of those who struggle with these issues, and a springboard for further (mutually respectful) debate. Included here are the diverse perspectives of writers from several disciplines. There are essays by psychotherapists, pastors of congregations, and a chaplain to AIDS patients; by theologians, ethicists, a lawyer, and a historian; by academics and practitioners; by women and men, lesbian/gay and straight, people of several colors or ethnic identifications. There are many common assumptions and some that are not shared. There is no consensus.

An Overview of the Collection

The two main foci of this debate are psychotherapy and ministry.[8] In "Walking the Bounds: Historical and Theological Reflections on Ministry, Intimacy, and Power," historian Fredrica Harris Thompsett warns of the dangers of patterning the theory and practice of ministry too closely and uncritically on that of psychotherapy.

While there is danger in a sloppy, uncritical failure to differentiate between the demands of psychotherapy and those of ministry, it is also true that many of the issues are similar and that those who carefully consider boundary issues in these two fields have much to say to one another. Psychologist and writer Susan Baur's "A Brief History of Sexual Intimacy in Psychotherapy" establishes a historical context for a discussion of intimacy and distance in psychotherapeutic relationships, much as the Thompsett essay does for ministerial relationships. Each author demonstrates that these are, indeed, not new questions but can be traced to the early days of the professions. Even as Thompsett worries that "psychological warrants are being applied, actually superimposed . . . on top of historical and other foundational understandings of ministry," Baur warns that it is far too early to declare the issue settled for psychotherapists, either.

In "Race and Gender Oppression Can Really Get in the Way: Ethical Concerns in the Counseling of African American Women," ethicist Traci C. West contends that questions of intimacy and distance between two people in a counseling relationship divorced from considerations of "sociopolitical realities such as race and race consciousness" are, in fact, the wrong questions.

Similarly, Leng Leroy Lim, an Episcopal clergyman, in "Exploring Embodiment," targets the historical American cultural assumptions and practices surrounding the use and understanding of boundaries. One cannot, Lim argues, explore questions of intimacy and distance without also exploring concepts of autonomy, privacy, relatedness, and experience of the sacred. It would be a mistake, he claims, to forget that these concepts and experiences are all culturally influenced and laden.

Marie Fortune, founder and executive director of the Center for the Prevention of Sexual and Domestic Violence, also notes the role of cultural norms in determining relational boundaries. In "The Joy of Boundaries" she argues that the question at hand is not "boundaries or no boundaries"; boundaries, she asserts, are integral to every human encounter. The question, then, is what sort of boundaries, and why?

The trick, according to Fortune, is to be clear about who the parties to the relationship are (individually, but, more important, in relation to one another), and what they are trying to accomplish. Applying these questions to the consideration of boundaries in ministry, Fortune argues that, while of necessity more flexible than many other professional relationships, ministerial relationships nonetheless require firmer boundaries than friendship or other intimate relationships.

In "Boundaries, Mutuality, and Professional Ethics" ethicist Karen Lebacqz and pastor Ronald G. Barton make a similar argument for counseling relationships in general. Like Fortune, they acknowledge the potential to misuse boundaries to enhance power differentials and cement hierarchies. However, those dangers notwithstanding, they insist that professional counseling relationships require firmer boundaries (more distance) than friendships or collegial relationships. To ignore this reality is to risk ignoring the vulnerability of clients. It raises the possibility of abusing them—if only by denying them the fully focused and un-self-interested attention of the professional.

Theologian Carter Heyward and ethicist Beverly Wildung Harrison, on the other hand, argue against the use of boundary language in both psychology and theology. In "Boundaries: Protecting the Vulnerable or Perpetrating a Bad Idea?" they contend that the constant casting of our perspectives on abuse within the framework of boundaries is "a bad idea." They seek to understand right and wrong dynamics of relationships in alternative ways, arguing that boundary language reflects "capitalist social relations and patriarchal spirituality."

Psychotherapist Miriam Greenspan also sees limited usefulness in the boundary metaphor. In "Out of Bounds," she challenges the "distance model" of psychotherapy, to which this boundary language is linked, and proposes instead a "connection model."

Ethicist Kasimu (Garth Baker-Fletcher), in "Just Boundaries or Mean-Spirited Surveillance? An Appeal for Neo-Victorianism as Gender Justice," reasserts the conviction that the dynamics of professional relationships render mutuality and genuine intimacy impossible. How then to negotiate these power differentials? Kasimu proposes a solution designed to address not only the question of distance and intimacy in counseling relationships, but also the problem of sexual harassment and changing and uncertain codes of social behavior between men and women in the workplace. He proposes "Neo-Victorianism," a "toning down of . . . explicitly informal and sexualized public presence," because, he says, "differentials in power and station require the purging of sexually explicit dynamics."

In "Legal Issues in Clergy Sexual Boundary Violation Matters," lawyer Sally A. Johnson summarizes legal developments in the last decade, examines the implications for religious institutions, and suggests how to deal with them.

In "I-Thou: Interpersonal Boundaries in the Therapy Relationship," psychologist Margo Rivera explains why she is "not particularly casual about boundaries." At the same time, she insists that imposing "rigid and overly general rules . . . is not a good solution to complex issues." She worries that "pre-fabricated rules" may replace the essential process of ongoing self-analysis and collegial accountability.

Pastor and activist Mari E. Castellanos, in "Barriers Not Withstanding: A *Lesbianista* Perspective," explores cultural understandings and practical realities of professional relationships in the Hispanic and lesbian communities that are her home, as well as the implications of modern boundary-talk for her congregation.

Bill Wallace offers his reflections as a chaplain to AIDS patients in "Care of the Dying: *Power Between, Power Under,* and *Powerlessness With* as Means for Valuing and Balancing Boundaries and Mutuality." What persons in crisis need, Wallace says, is the helper's willingness "to shed herself of the dead skin of professionalism and step over the boundary of authority."

In the Epilogue, I look at what is at stake in this debate; what is at risk and what are the possibilities?

Meaningful Consent

We noted earlier that there are two related but distinct questions at issue in this conversation: definitions of sexual abuse, and standards of professional practice.

Regarding sexual abuse, the question hinges on "meaningful consent." Those who favor legal and ethical code restrictions on sexual or romantic relationships argue that the inherent dynamics of professional/client relationships render meaningful consent impossible. A perception of dependence upon the professional for emotional or spiritual well-being makes it difficult, if not impossible, for the client to refuse advances made by the professional. The ability to refuse is central to the ability to give meaningful consent. Transference dynamics make the client's own advances, or disinclination to decline the professional's advances, suspect. Consequently, many advocates and theorists working in this field categorize any sexual contact between psychotherapists or clergy and those they serve as "sexual exploitation," a form of sexual abuse.[9] Fortune, Castellanos, Lebacqz and Barton, and Lim all make, or assume, this argument in their contributions to this volume.

Arguments that assert the impossibility of meaningful consent suggest fundamental practical implications apart from decisions about sex and romance. If the power imbalances between professional and client are presumed to be so extreme that meaningful consent is impossible, then are they not also so extreme as to render mutuality within the professional relationship similarly impossible? Such premises often provide the foundation for arguments supporting a rigidly boundaried, distance model as the only ethically appropriate standard of practice. Others argue that complex power dynamics, and, in fact, power imbalances, are inherent in every relationship. To insist that such power imbalances are static, insurmountable, and solely definitive of the relationship (and therefore, that adults in these relationships are unable ever to give meaningful consent) is insulting and infantalizing. Johnson notes,

> Those opposing such regulation [proscribing sexual intimacy between professionals and their current, or former, clients] argue that each relationship must be judged on its own merits and that to presume all clients are dependent and vulnerable robs then of their power and authority and destroys the possibility of healing through a mutual, rather than hierarchical, relationship.

Thompsett decries any formulation that denies agency (the ability to reach and act upon informed decisions) to any member of the community. This denial of agency, she insists, is not only a manifestation of professional arrogance but is also a barrier to full participation in the life, mission, and ministry of the church/community. It robs the laity of the means to fulfill their own responsibilities.

West warns of the dangers implicit in the too-common tendency to view those who come for healing as either victims or survivors, when, in fact, they are almost always both simultaneously. She counsels a respect for their moral agency that weighs both their wounds and their resources for coping and healing.

Transference

Freud considered transference, the projecting of the client's old "desires and longings" onto the analyst, essential to the psychoanalytical process. The place of transference in psychotherapy continues to be debated today. Even among those who view transference as an important dynamic in a therapeutic relationship there is disagreement about the practical implications.

Many argue that transference renders meaningful consent impossible and, therefore, makes any sexual contact abusive. They further argue that maintaining the therapist's presence as a blank screen upon whom the client projects other relationships in the course of transference precludes any authentic intimacy within the context of the counseling relationship.

Rivera, while asserting the value of transference in therapy, argues with those who insist that transference is insurmountable and eternal. She insists that each relationship is unique and that therapeutic dynamics play out differently in each. Similarly she notes that while some clients are never able to transcend the power inequities she sees inherent in the therapeutic relationship, others enter therapy as a period of only "temporary inequality." Therefore, she takes issue with regulations that are premised on the assumption that authentic mutuality and intimacy (and, consequently, meaningful consent) are never possible where once there has been a therapeutic relationship.

Lebacqz and Barton join Rivera in insisting that the purpose of therapy is for therapy to end—for power imbalances to be eliminated. They argue, however, that accomplishing this end requires maintaining professional boundaries during and after the therapy.

Baur points out that even where transference is assumed, it is also understood that clients are able to make some choices and take some responsibility for their actions (e.g., to pay their bills, to refuse to rob a bank). Heyward and Harrison note that transference is present in every significant human relationship. We see every friend and lover through the lenses of our histories and project onto them bits of our unfinished business. Working through these transferences, building ever more authentic connections, is the stuff of which deep relationships are made. Given these realities, Baur, Heyward, and Harrison all have to question rigid boundaries and enforced relational distance premised on the presence of transference.

Dual Relationships

In a "dual relationship," two people have two (or more) types of relationships with each other simultaneously. Such situations can be avoided in psychotherapeutic relationships where (provided the town or community is not too small) the therapist and client can avoid seeing each other in any but the therapy context. Dual relationships are impossible to avoid in ministry. As Fortune notes, every professional minister is simultaneously pastor and employee of the congregation. Furthermore, the nature of congregational life and pastoral relationships is such that the pastor and members of the congregation see one another in a variety of settings—worship services, educational events, counseling sessions, picnics, ball games, and so forth. Fortune calls this the "challenge" and the "genius" of ministry.

The notion that dual relationships should be avoided or minimized in therapeutic, ministerial, or other professional relationships has ties to modern, urban, Anglo-American culture and expectations. Rivera notes the difficulty in arranging such a compartmentalized life (even supposing one wanted to) in rural or small-town settings. Thompsett traces the recent development of this professionalization of ministry that has led to separation of the minister from the wider community. Castellanos writes of the continuing expectation in Hispanic and lesbian communities that one will do business, seek counsel and healing, and conduct one's family and social life within the community—among the people one knows.

Dual relationships, whether they involve having your mother as your elementary school principal, your lawyer as your golf buddy, your therapist as your faculty colleague or partner in a protest march, or your minister as dance partner, bring challenges and risk to the relationship. To some extent, theorists' and practitioners' tolerance of dual relationships is directly related to their attitudes toward risk.

Risk

Kasimu proposes reducing ambiguity and risk by returning to formalized manners in nonintimate social and business relationships. He argues that, since it is the less powerful participant in any relationship who pays the price for failure, the more powerful participants must assume responsibility for minimizing risk. Lebacqz and Barton insist that professionals recognize the vulnerability of their clients and avoid creating situations in which they may be further victimized. They embrace clear boundaries as vehicles for creating safe space for difficult (and risky) therapeutic work.

Wallace, on the other hand, suggests that real healing takes place only in the presence of real risk. The therapist's or pastor's ability to participate in a healing process is directly linked to his or her ability to let go of professional authority and predetermined expectations—to abandon safety and stand present to the moment—to embrace risk.

Fortune acknowledges that risk is inherent in ministry and insists that it is precisely for this reason that clarity about boundaries is important. She likens ministry to driving down a highway in a blizzard and notes that in such circumstances clear lane (i.e., boundary) markers become all the more important.

Lim, while embracing professional boundaries as markers of trustworthy space, cautions against the American tendency to strive for a perfect safety that life cannot offer. Heyward and Harrison, and West, warn against creating safe-feeling space as a substitute for the hard political work of creating a world that is truly less oppressive and dangerous.

It should not be inferred from this that Fortune is blind to the creative possibilities of risky situations or that Wallace doesn't appreciate strong guard rails on a treacherous highway. It is important to note, though, that each writer gives different weight to the many factors involved in this issue. To fail to protect is to put already hurt and vulnerable people at further risk. To overprotect is to deny adults the right to take the very risks that might set them free.

Who Decides?

People of good faith and informed judgment differ about which risks are worth taking, which are essential, and which are indefensible. The question, then, is how to decide what standards will govern our common life.

Johnson points out that where the churches and professional societies have failed to set and enforce standards, courts and legislatures have stepped in. She acknowledges that, at least in the case of the regulation of pastoral practice, statutory standards and judicial remedies often fail to reflect the full range of religious concerns and insight. Her plea is that churches take seriously their own responsibility, establish theologically grounded and pastorally sensitive standards of practice, and eliminate the need for governmental intervention.

Greenspan questions rigid standards, even those imposed from within the profession: "In my own practice, I worry that some of the most feminist and innovative aspects of my work are the most likely to be construed as unethical." Rivera fears that firm boundaries and clear rules will become a convenient substitute for the difficult and ongoing work of serious ethical reflection. Yet Johnson reminds us that we would not be facing this dilemma if there weren't numbers, numbers too large to ignore, of people who have been hurt badly enough to take their cases to the courts. Baur insists that there are stories still to be told and studied as we continue to try to learn together what works.

These are some of the many themes and questions that are woven through this conversation. Definitions of power and vulnerability, mutuality, agency, psychological health, and the place of the "illness metaphor" in healing relationships are also at issue. Understandings of ministry and the nature and mission of church vary. Contributors note (and give different weight to) different sociopolitical factors. West, for example, decries privatized therapy that fails to note and address the systemic sources of oppression. Heyward and Harrison, Greenspan, and Lim contend that notions of psychological health in normative U.S. culture correspond to the needs of capitalist patriarchy.

These questions are integral to determining what kinds of healing relationships are ethical and efficacious—at this time, in this world. Passions run high as we face the very real human costs associated with each approach. You will find here no facile answer that resolves all these concerns. You will find instead the work of ethics. You will find an ongoing conversation aimed at constantly weighing competing needs and interests, costs and benefits. This conversation relies on storytelling, reflection, and practice followed by more storytelling, reflection, and practice. It requires many voices. Listen to those that follow. Add your own.

Notes

1. *All* examples are composites of the many stories I am told each year. No example is drawn from a single case.

2. Forcible rape is usually categorized as a form of assault rather than a form of sexual abuse.

3. The U.S. EEOC defines sexual harassment as "The use of one's authority or power, either explicitly or implicitly, to coerce another into unwanted sexual relations or to punish another for his or her refusal; or the creation of an intimidating, hostile or offensive working environment through verbal or physical conduct of a sexual nature."

4. Sometimes called sexual misconduct.

5. The radical right's attacks on sexual harassment protections are, however, worthy of note.

6. "Sexual Misconduct means any . . . Sexual Exploitation, including but not limited to, the development of or the attempt to develop a sexual relationship be-

tween a cleric, employee or volunteer and a person with whom he/she has a pastoral relationship, whether or not there is apparent consent from the individual" (p. 5).

"Pastoral Relationship means: A relationship between a cleric, employee or volunteer and any person to whom such cleric, employee or volunteer provides counseling, pastoral care, spiritual direction or spiritual guidance or from whom such cleric, employee or volunteer has received confession or confidential or privileged information" (p. 9) [Source: The Church Insurance Company (Episcopal), "Sexual Misconduct Reference Materials" (New York, July 1993)].

See also notes 26–31 in Johnson essay, chapter 10 of this volume.

7. See, for example, Judith V. Jordan, Alexandra G. Kaplan, Jean Baker-Miller, Irene P. Striver, and Janet L. Surrey, *Women's Growth in Connection: Writings from the Stone Center* (New York: The Guilford Press, 1991); and Celia Kitzinger and Rachel Perkins, *Changing Our Minds: Lesbian Feminism and Psychology* (New York and London: New York University Press, 1993).

8. Although the main focuses of the debate have been psychotherapeutic and ministerial relationships, the question has also arisen regarding physicians and lawyers and their clients and professors and their students. See Johnson, pp. 152 and 153 of this volume.

9. See, for example, Marie Fortune, *Clergy Misconduct: Sexual Abuse in the Ministerial Relationship Workshop Manual* (Seattle: Center for the Prevention of Sexual and Domestic Violence, 1992), and note 18 in Johnson essay, chapter 10.

1

A Brief History of Sexual Intimacy in Psychotherapy

Susan Baur

IN THE LATE 1800s Eugen Bleuler, director of a chronic-care facility for the mentally ill in Switzerland (and originator of the term "schizophrenia"), made the surprising and altogether revolutionary discovery that even the sickest patients could sometimes be revitalized if a personal relationship were developed with them. Perhaps because his own sister was catatonic, Bleuler rejected the customary practice of keeping doctor and patient far away from each other. His long-term patients became his family. They called him "Father." They chopped wood with him, ate with him, and cared for each other during a typhoid epidemic. To everyone's astonishment, some got better. At about the same time, similar discoveries were made by a handful of other doctors, and ever since then it has been assumed that some form of mutually respectful affection is essential to serious psychotherapy. Why this should be so was not understood in the nineteenth century, and even today the reasons given are many and variable.

But to say that mutual concern is essential to good therapy is not to say much about how doctor and patient should actually behave toward each other. When Bleuler acted like a parent, he helped certain chronic schizophrenics, but to therapists in other periods, other roles seemed possible—a wise teacher, a trusted friend, a blank screen on which earlier relationships could be projected, perhaps even a lover. When men first set themselves up as scientific healers of the mind one hundred years ago it was not clear what the relationship between doctor and patient ought to be or what it would tend to be if left to develop on its own. Here then, is the story of one kind of intimacy—physical intimacy—that developed in various therapeutic settings. Individually these stories chronicle events in particular lives, but together they illustrate our progressive attempts to define the proper relationship between the helper and the helped.

In the early years of psychoanalysis Sigmund Freud had a great deal to say about doctor-patient intimacy. When his friend, Josef Breuer, first used the "talking cure" on the passionately hysterical Anna O., Freud was on hand to witness Breuer's distressing emotional involvement. So was Breuer's wife. After nearly losing his marriage over a long and dramatic treatment that culminated in Anna going through the motions of giving birth to an imaginary child fathered by Breuer, the esteemed physician noted with irritation that "it was impossible . . . to treat a case of that kind without bringing his [the doctor's] activities and mode of life completely to an end. I vowed at the time I would *not* go through such an ordeal again."[1] Freud commiserated with Breuer's ordeal, but saw no way of circumventing the possibility or even probability of intense attraction. In fact, after treating neurotic patients in Vienna, Freud came to believe that love was essential to his new method of psychoanalysis, although acting on this attraction would ruin the therapy. Freud realized that unless the patients he treated transferred many of their old longings and desires onto him—in other words, unless the patient fell in love with the analyst and developed what Freud called a transference or transference love—the patient would not "make the effort" or would not "listen when we submit our translation [interpretation] to him. Essentially," Freud continued, "one might say, the cure is effected by love."[2] Of course this posed certain obvious dangers. Freud realized that to the extent that analysis was powered by the patient's transference love for the doctor and made possible by the doctor's deep yet unexpressed concern for the patient, practitioners of psychoanalysis would always be at risk of being "slandered and scorched by the love with which we operate—such are the perils of our trade."[3] The slander part of the danger arose when a patient like Anna O. publicly proclaimed her love for her doctor. The scorch part referred to the doctor's own temptation to accept the passionate invitations that were offered by attractive young women.

Freud himself received such invitations, and although he admitted to his biographer that he was not much interested in sex, he was sufficiently attracted to claim that he had come "very close to it [an indiscretion] a number of times and had a narrow escape."[4] Among his disciples, such analysts as Carl Jung, Sandor Ferenczi, Otto Gross, Oskar Pfister, Wilhelm Stekel, Ernest Jones, Otto Rank, Victor Tausk, and Sandor Rado also came very close to it a number of times—and did not escape. Even for analysts who managed to stay in their chairs, erotic love posed a delicate problem. In these early days of psychoanalysis, most people were shocked by the idea that sexual longings and fantasies were discussed with young lady patients at all, much less made the focus of treatment. Critics condemned the new treatment as "morally dangerous," and labeled its more flamboyant practitioners "pigs."[5]

C. G. Jung and Sabina Spielrein

One of the earliest and most fascinating stories of erotic entanglement began in 1904, and involved C. G. Jung—thirty years old, married, and newly interested in psychoanalysis—and a nineteen-year-old Russian girl named Sabina Spielrein. Admitted to the hospital where Jung worked, Spielrein was the young doctor's first psychoanalytic patient. She had been diagnosed as a "psychotic hysteric"—in other words, as a hysterical young woman whose symptoms were far worse than fainting spells—and was seen as a challenging subject on which to try a new word-association test. Thus as her screaming fits and delirium cleared, largely of their own accord, Fraulein Spielrein began meeting with Dr. Jung every other day at the hospital. There she sat in a chair, her bright peasant's dress falling in folds around her, and her long, dark braids hanging down her back. The doctor sat behind her. While she gave her associations to a list of words and told stories from her troubled childhood in Russia, he wrote down what she said, especially noting any pauses or jumps in her associations.

In a matter of months Jung and Spielrein became friends. For something called "work therapy," he placed her in his own research laboratory. For education, he gave her his dissertation to read. And for general health, the two took walks together or sat in the sun. Both doctor and patient seemed energized by the new association. Jung received three promotions that year, and Spielrein enrolled in the medical school at the University of Zurich two months *before* leaving the asylum. Upon discharge, she assumed the duties of student, out-patient, and laboratory assistant. All three involved long, private talks with her friend, Carl Jung, whom she saw daily.

By 1908, three years after Spielrein had left the asylum, she and Jung had almost certainly become lovers. Returning to her boarding-house from classes, she would look for Jung's calling card, on which was written the time and place of their next secret meeting. Thus in addition to daily meetings at his office on the far side of the *Zurich See* and the occasional exchange of letters, the two would meet on the steep green hillsides outside the city, in her small apartment, or in some other quiet spot. Wherever they met, the now rapidly maturing Russian with her dark hair and eyes and the blond, charismatic doc-tor would throw themselves into discussions that simultaneously re-vealed the similarity of their temperaments and the intensity of their lonely yearning.

"My dear," he wrote, "you cannot imagine how much it means to me to have the hopes of loving a person whom I must not condemn, and who does not condemn herself, to being smothered in the banal-ity of habit."[6] He has, he continued, become much more attached to her than he believed possible. This was doubly astonishing because, "it is only with great difficulty that I can actually muster that belief in man's natural goodness which I so often proclaim."[7]

Initially, the two seemed to have come together cautiously. For a time they had taken turns resisting each other's advances, for Jung did not want a scandal, and Spielrein did not want to ruin her chances of attracting a well-to-do husband. Yet Spielrein kept putting her fingers on precisely those topics dearest to Jung's heart. She claimed she had prophetic dreams: Jung was fascinated. She seemed able to read his thoughts: he had been interested in this very phenomenon as a college student. She explained to him why Wagner was for her the most psychological composer: "Dr. Jung's eyes filled with tears. 'I will show you, I am just writing the very same thing.'"[8] It seemed to both of them that they were soul mates.

Sometime in this period, Jung became Spielrein's "poet," as she termed it, "i.e., my beloved. Eventually he came to me and things went as they usually do with 'poetry.' He preached polygamy; his wife was supposed to have no objection, etc., etc."[9]

In the literature of the time "poetry" was a common metaphor for lovemaking, and although various historians have interpreted Spielrein's and Jung's "poetry" as meaning kissing and fondling or sexual intercourse, it is clear from Spielrein's diary that at the very least there was an intoxicating amount of sighing, gazing, moaning, and holding, and that the effect of all this stimulation on her was riveting. When she played the piano in the evenings, she pretended that Jung was listening, and when she worked on her dissertation, which supported many of his ideas, she thought of the project as "our little son, Siegfried." Spielrein sensed the power of Jung's imagination—its remarkable breadth, its daring—and when the two sat "in speechless ecstasy for hours,"[10] she felt securely enfolded in a private world of great richness. In love with Jung, she was smarter, stronger, and more beautiful. Standing before her mirror and admiring her "lovely and well developed" curves, she had to admit that everything in her life revolved around Jung—her hero, her teacher, her beloved . . . and her former doctor.

Not long after the two began composing "poetry," however, Jung got scared. When his wife gave birth to a longed-for son at the end of 1908, he convinced himself that Spielrein was going to choose this moment to go public with their affair.

"I am looking for a person who can love without punishing, imprisoning and draining the other person . . . ," he wrote to her three days after the birth of Franz and one day after he had met with her and begged her to end the liaison. "Return to me, in this moment of my need, some of the love and guilt and altruism which I was able to give you at the time of your illness. Now," he added, "it is I who am ill."[11]

Shortly thereafter Spielrein's mother received an anonymous note (probably from Jung's wife) warning her that Dr. Jung was setting a match to her daughter's reputation. Confronted with the note, Jung caddishly told Mrs. Spielrein that if she wanted him to treat her daughter properly, then she should pay him for every one of their meetings.

"The doctor knows his limits and will never cross them," he wrote, "for he is *paid* for his troubles. That imposes the necessary restraints on him."[12] At the same time, Jung cut Spielrein's time back from one or more hours each day to a single hour per week. When she objected, he lectured her for being an insatiable, ungrateful woman. Stung by the condescending letters written to her mother (which she read) and enraged by Jung's eagerness to discard their relationship of more than four years, Spielrein flew into one of her famous rages. Showing up at his home, she pushed her way into his office, knife in hand, scuffled with him, cut him—or possibly herself—then went tearing off again with a bloody hand. As she later confided to her diary, she attracted quite a crowd.[13]

Spielrein was devastated. Not only had she been betrayed by her friend, colleague, and lover, but now she doubted her own capabilities as well. Sometimes she thought she wasn't wonderful enough to hold the doctor whom everyone loved, and other times she thought she was incredibly stupid to have tried. Tormented by the fear that the four-year affair had been nothing but a mistake, she made an unusual attempt to reclaim, not Jung's love, but her picture of him as a loving and wonderful healer. If she could do this, the liaison would maintain its ambivalent status as a relationship with a gifted but difficult man. Spielrein explained all this in several letters, which she sent to a stranger whom she believed treasured Jung as much as she did—Sigmund Freud.

"Dear Professor Freud . . . ," she wrote, "I . . . would like to part from Dr. Jung completely and go my own way. But I can do that only to the extent that I am free to love him: if I either forgive him everything or murder him."[14]

It took Spielrein the better part of a month to write out a passionate, disorganized account of her love affair with Jung, but when at last it was mailed off to Freud, she apparently felt better. Turning Jung in to the authorities had lifted a lot of weight from her chest, and she began refocusing her attention on her studies. For his part, Freud passed most of the information Spielrein gave him straight back to Jung, and the two had a couple of condescending chuckles at her expense.

Although Spielrein courageously confronted Jung and made him apologize to her and her family, in writing, the affair was not over.

When she needed someone to read her dissertation, she ran to Jung.

The most important outcome of our discussion was that we both loved each other fervently again, she wrote in her diary. My friend said that we would always have to be careful not to fall in love again; we would always be dangerous to each other. . . . At the beginning he was annoyed that I had not sent my paper to him long before, that I did not trust him, etc. Then he became more and more intense. At the end he pressed my hands to his heart several times and said this should mark the beginning of a new era.[15]

The new era bore a striking resemblance to the old one. Again Spielrein burned for Jung, and again her moods and self-esteem were tightly tied to his words. If one summer afternoon she walked down the warm cobblestone streets of Zurich in private raptures, the next day she asked herself, "So why am I filled with agitation again? Why this pain?"[16] Her nights were particularly dreadful, filled as they were with endless longing and fantasies. Perhaps, she thought to herself, Jung's wealthy wife, Emma, will be seduced by a Frenchman.

In spite of this new round of confusion, Spielrein gradually found a stance she could maintain. Investing most of her energies in an attempt to synthesize a position halfway between Freud's more intellectual and Jung's more emotional theories, she remained attentive to Jung but no longer one of his possessions. In fact, some four months into "the new era" Spielrein left Zurich and moved to Vienna, where she sat in on Freud's Wednesday evening gatherings and referred to herself as his pupil. After a year in the intensely competitive atmosphere of the Viennese psychoanalytic circle, however, Spielrein was convinced that neither Freud nor Jung nor the Wednesday evening analysts took her work seriously. In April of 1912 she stopped trying to impress them or reconcile their growing differences and moved to Berlin. There she met Paul Scheftel, a Jewish physician as handsome as he was difficult, and three months later married him. At the same time, and for reasons both theoretical and personal, Freud and Jung broke what was supposed to have been *the* closest relationship within the select circle of psychoanalysts.

"I propose that we abandon our personal relationship entirely," Freud wrote to Jung after a long period of tension.[17]

"I accede to your wish .. , " Jung responded. ". . . 'The rest is silence.'"[18]

Thus by 1913, when Sabina Spielrein was twenty-eight years old, she and Jung and Freud were going their separate ways—and discovering what each had lost. Freud moved another step away from the open collaboration he had tried to establish with his fellow analysts and increasingly worried about loyalty and allegiance. Later he became deeply depressed. For Jung, the loss of what were arguably the two most important relationships of his life was more painful still. Without Freud insisting on intellectual honesty and daring, and without Spielrein encouraging the intensely emotional and imaginative side of his nature, Jung slipped from the delicately balanced position he had occupied. No longer able to hold himself between mind and emotion, male and female, past and present, Christianity and Judaism, his productive state of ambivalent yearning collapsed, landing him in a cul de sac, "a dead end." Jung suffered through an extended period of nightmares and morbid waking fantasies. At first he distracted himself from sadness and guilt by lecturing in America and building little stone villages at a rural retreat—an old childhood pastime. Later, he suffered periods of barely controllable psychosis. As for Spielrein, when Freud and Jung parted company she was pregnant and already unhappy with her marriage. Although she occasionally wrote to both men, she was never close to either again. The relationships were over, but the reminiscing and the evaluating were not.

With the passage of time, the pattern of a life becomes distinguishable, and certain encounters stand out as inspiration, turning point, or missed opportunity. As Jung looked back, he increasingly saw Spielrein as all three. She was a light or a star that had, in combination with other influences, turned him toward the mystical complexities of the psyche, and then held him on that course. In a paper discussing her case, he had given her the pseudonym Alice Stern, which in German means "star," and in one of his stone carvings he represented her as a bear, which he knew was the constellation containing the polestar—the mariner's guide. In a late letter to her, he claimed that he was her star too. He had lit "a new light that you must safeguard for times of darkness."[19]

"The love of S. for J.," he wrote later still, "made the latter aware of something he had previously only vaguely suspected, that is, of a power in the unconscious that shapes one's destiny, a power which later led him to things of greatest importance. The relationship had to be 'sublimated' because otherwise it would have led him to delusion and madness. . . . Occasionally one must be unworthy, simply in order to be able to continue living."[20]

Here, at last, was a full admission—two, actually—first that Spielrein had accomplished what she had so ardently hoped for. She had been Jung's inspiration and muse. She had been as important to him and his work as he had been to hers. "Whatever the specific contributions of Spielrein or Jung to the Jungian system," wrote Bruno Bettelheim, "Jung asserts . . . that it was in their love affair that the system itself originated."[21]

And second, Jung acknowledged again that he had been a cad—unworthy. It was he—not she-the-former-patient, not she-the-young-or-frivolous woman—who had sacrificed their love in order to go on with his life.

Toward the end of the life that Jung had so often and so ruthlessly preserved, he described the discovery of the unconscious force—the anima—that Spielrein's love had inspired. He said that he became aware of a woman's voice in his head that expressed a point of view that was different from his own male point of view. He called this feminine force his anima, and he recognized the voice as Spielrein's.

"She had become a living figure within my mind," he wrote.[22] She was his "soul mate," as Spielrein had termed this deeply spiritual aspect of their relationship.

At first, the presence of this "ghost," which apparently had a mind of her own and was not merely a way of thinking that Jung could call upon at will, annoyed him. However, late in his life he reported turning to her in times of trouble. Jung turned to stones for comfort too, and as he grew old he spent more and more time at his rural retreat building a stone house and learning to carve stone plaques. These remain as expressions of his last preoccupations, and the three stone carvings that focus on the anima include a Russian bear with the inscription, "Russia gets the ball moving"; a mare, "May the light arise which I have born in my body"; and a plaque that was either broken or destroyed.[23]

Jung and Spielrein never saw or corresponded with each other after 1919. After spending a few years in Geneva, where she briefly became Jean Piaget's training analyst, Spielrein returned to Russia. There she worked as an analyst and teacher until Stalin came to power and psychoanalysis went into hiding. Her three brothers may have been killed under Stalin, and when the Nazis occupied her town in 1941, she, her daughters, and the rest of the city's Jews were reportedly taken into a synagogue and shot.

For nearly forty years, Spielrein's only "headstone" was the thirty papers she had published and the disguised references to her that Jung made in his scientific papers, memoirs, and stone carvings. Then, in 1977, a carton of letters and diaries was discovered in the basement of the Palais Wilson in Geneva. Spielrein had worked there, and left the box behind when she moved to Russia. Miraculously, the papers were not thrown out. Instead, they were sent to a Jungian analyst in Italy who had written on Spielrein and who quickly began a more extensive work. By this improbable series of events, Sabina Spielrein became the subject of *A Secret Symmetry* by Aldo Carotenuto and later, *A Most Dangerous Method* by John Kerr. Through these works she has emerged from the synagogue in Rostov-on-Don to take her place as a psychoanalyst in her own right and as the patient, colleague, and lover of Freud's "crown prince," Carl Jung.

The Jung-Spielrein affair raises two of the most common questions associated with erotic intimacy in therapy. First, how are we to make sense of an experience that seems to combine great affection with mean-spirited abuse? This is a particularly important question for the people involved in the affair to answer—how do they go about turning this kind of confusion into a coherent story? Second, what cultural forces or expectations shape the stories that finally come to rest in their minds and in ours as well?

As is common in many cases, critics of the Jung-Spielrein relationship are divided. Some judge her treatment to have been unorthodox and inspired. Others consider it outrageously unethical. Yet they largely agree that Jung's intense interest in Spielrein drew her out of her psychosis, and that her intense interest in him led him to an unusually deep understanding of the psyche.

"Profound changes took place in both doctor and patient," wrote Ethel Person, a psychoanalyst working today, "and must be largely attributed to the transformational power of love."[24]

Or, in the same vein, "We ought to ask ourselves," the celebrated analyst Bruno Bettelheim wrote, "what convincing evidence do we have that the same result would have been achieved if Jung had behaved toward her in the way we must expect a conscientious therapist to behave toward his patient? However questionable Jung's behavior was from a moral point of view—however unorthodox, even disreputable, it may have been—somehow it met the prime obligation of the therapist toward his patient: to cure her. True, Spielrein paid a very high price."[25]

Subsequent reviewers have angrily called this a transparent excuse. Jung was known to use women all his life—he had a forty-year affair with Antonia Wolff, another former-patient-turned-analyst, and in his sixties he eased her out in favor of Ruth Bailey. In *Against Therapy* Jeffrey Masson comes out strongly against Jung. His behavior toward Spielrein he deems inexcusable, and, in his opinion, Spielrein got better in spite of, not because of, Jung.[26]

From Spielrein's point of view, however, the relationship seems to have organized her life for better as well as for worse. It gave her a purpose. Initially, she became a lovestruck admirer of a charismatic doctor, and later an able psychoanalyst and writer. Although the periods of passionate harmony with Jung that she lived for were interwoven with anger at his cavalier treatment of her, Spielrein seems to say in her diary and letters that Jung was the man she loved most in her life. No other man ever drew from her, or matched, the full range of her powerful emotions and insightful thinking. Spielrein expected great things from herself at a time in history when women often measured their success in terms of collaboration with, or inspiration of, a man. These expectations, personal and cultural, combined with her memories of walks and conversations and embraces to lead her to the belief that there was more love in her relationship with Jung than there was abuse. Other people in other times would come to different conclusions.

Sandor Ferenczi and Gizella Pálos

As Sigmund Freud was receiving letters from Sabina Spielrein complaining that Carl Jung was a faithless lover and cad, he was also receiving letters from his Hungarian disciple Sandor Ferenczi hinting that a married patient was becoming uncommonly important to him.

"My personal well-being (psychic) was good . . . ," he wrote Freud in October 1909, "as long as it was possible to keep frequent company with Frau Isolde. (I will call her that, which was also her name in one of my dreams.)"[27]

A few days later Ferenczi admitted to Professor Freud that the relationship was further advanced than he had intimated: "Evidently I have [found] *too much* in her," wrote the thirty-six- year-old bachelor, "lover, friend, mother, and, in scientific matters, a pupil. . . . So, I have everything that can be distributed by nature between the two sexes combined in a single person."[28]

Freud was not at all pleased. He was hearing about irresistible attraction from far too many colleagues, and he was afraid that psychoanalysis would collapse into a trivial form of immediate gratification. He warned Ferenczi to look elsewhere for a wife, but to no avail. Ferenczi and Gizella Pálos continued to discuss her divorce and their possible marriage. In addition, the doctor took his future stepdaughter into analysis—a common practice in those days, but in this instance a disaster. Ferenczi began treating the young woman for depression, and several months later he fell in love with her. Elma was so deliciously young, he told Freud. She could have babies. For months Ferenczi and his future family were in a state of chaos. He tried to choose between the two women without angering either. Pálos, vehemently objecting to her lover marrying her daughter, wrote to Freud. Freud shook his head in disbelief. Elma prepared to announce her engagement. Finally, Ferenczi chose Elma. However, the day before the announcement was to be printed, Elma wondered aloud if she would break off this engagement as she had broken off a previous one. Abruptly, Ferenczi woke up. Elma was hurried into treatment with Freud, and when that didn't work, into a marriage of convenience that was not a happy one. Eventually, Ferenczi married Pálos.

Although never presented as a glorious chapter in the early practice of psychoanalysis, Ferenczi's personal struggles with love and erotic attraction led him to a series of insights that significantly changed the practice of psychotherapy. Ferenczi had first tried to copy Freud. Using the standard technique of frustration, he had remained totally detached from his patients. He sat behind them during analysis, revealed nothing of himself, and adhered to the "rule of abstinence," which meant he did not touch them, not even to shake their hands. This was supposed to frustrate their desire for a real relationship with the analyst, and force them to create an imaginary or transference relationship. Based as it was on their old way of doing business in the world, the transference gave the analyst a map or picture of their troubles.

Useful as this technique was in Freud's hands—and it was immensely useful—it was abhorrent to Ferenczi. Identifying so easily with his patients' loneliness and dejection, he longed to make up for their unhappy childhoods. He wanted to show them how restorative a good relationship could be. Moreover, as he treated patients over long periods of time, he began to suspect that in successful analyses a realistic connection (as opposed to an imaginary or transference relationship) was established between analyst and analysand *even when the frustration technique was used.* "Patients at some level are actually acutely aware of all our real feelings and thoughts."[29]

"I tried to pursue the Freudian technique of frustration honestly and sincerely . . . ," Ferenczi wrote in a diary that he kept during the last several years of his life. "Following its failure I tried permissiveness and relaxation, again an exaggeration. In the wake of these two defeats, I am working humanely and naturally . . . on the acquisition of knowledge that will allow me to help."[30] Noting that Gizella Pálos, now Mrs. Ferenczi, felt the same, he let her express his deepest sentiments. "Mrs. Ferenczi felt, and rightly so, attracted to the essence of psycho-analysis—trauma and reconstruction—but repelled by all analysts for the way they make use of it. . . . She longs for an analyst who will be analytically as gifted as she is, who will be concerned above all with truth, but who will not only be scientifically true but also truthful regarding people."[31]

How to be truthful regarding people: Ferenczi came at this problem from a dozen different directions and modified his technique with each discovery. Characteristically, he took each of his insights to an extreme—*ad absurdum,* he liked to say—then fell back to a more moderate and more informed position. None of these exaggerations, however, was as dangerous as his experiments with indulgence. During this period his aim was to remain deeply relaxed in the patient's presence and let her do almost anything she wanted. In one case this led to a kind of group analysis conducted in a patient's hotel and including the analysand—a woman the size of an elephant—her female companion, two monkeys, three dogs, and several cats. In another case, it involved holding two- and three-hour-long sessions seven days a week and taking the patient with him on vacation. In the most celebrated case, it involved letting himself be kissed and cuddled by the strangely brilliant American analyst-in-training, Clara Thompson—and this one brought down the wrath of Freud. Unlike the jolly letters the Professor had sent to Jung twenty years earlier over the Spielrein affair, Freud's response to Ferenczi had real anger beneath the surface. Kissing and snuggling was going to destroy psychoanalysis from the inside by attracting silly practitioners as well as from the outside by ruining its reputation.

> You have not made a secret of the fact that you kiss your patients and let them kiss you. . . .
>   Now picture what will be the result of publishing your technique. . . . A number of independent thinkers in matters of technique will say to themselves: Why stop at a kiss? Certainly one gets further if one adopts 'pawing' as well, which after all doesn't make a baby. And then bolder ones will come along who will go further, to peeping and showing—and soon we shall have accepted in the technique of analysis the whole repertoire of demiviergerie and petting parties, resulting in an enormous increase of interest in psychoanalysis among both analysts and patients. The new adherent, however, will easily claim too much of this interest for himself . . . and God the Father Ferenczi, gazing at the lively scene he has created will perhaps say to himself: Maybe after all I should have halted in my technique of motherly affection *before* the kiss.[32]

"And then you are to hear from the brutal fatherly side an admonition . . . ," Freud continued in a more serious tone, "according to my recollection a tendency to sexual play with patients was not completely alien to you in preanalytic times, so that the new technique could well be linked to an old error. That is why I spoke in my last letter of a new puberty.[33]

Ferenczi was stung, not by Freud's objection to kissing, which he expected, but by his mentor's lack of faith in him. As he saw it, being indulgent was not seducing his patients as other analysts had been known to do; it was seriously asking the basic question, "What helps?" It seemed to Ferenczi that Freud increasingly disregarded this question in favor of learning about neuroses and advancing the political fortunes of psychoanalysis.

To Freud he wrote:

> Your fear that I might develop into a second Stekel is, I believe, unfounded. "Sins of youth," mistakes, once they have been overcome and analytically worked through, can even make one wiser and more prudent than people who have never experienced such storms.[34]

And to his diary he confided:

> I tend to think that originally Freud really did believe in analysis; he followed Breuer with enthusiasm and worked passionately, devotedly, on the curing of neurotics (if necessary spending hours lying on the floor next to a person in a hysterical crisis). He must have been first shaken and then disenchanted, however, by certain experiences, rather like Breuer when his patient had a relapse and when the problem of countertransference [the analyst's feelings toward the patient] opened up before him like an abyss.
>   . . . Freud no longer loves his patients. . . . He still remains attached to analysis intellectually, but not emotionally.[35]

Ferenczi was especially worried that such a stance could not be assumed without condescension. It seemed to him that Freud's therapeutic technique was becoming less and less personal until the doctor was left "levitating like some kind of divinity above the poor patient, [who was] reduced to the status of a mere child."[36] Worse, the transference, or imaginary relationship that the patient formed in the absence of feedback and which constituted the map of her problems, "is artificially provoked by this kind of behavior."[37] In other words, in an effort to remain objective and safe from the "unbearable upheaval" of real relationships, Ferenczi believed that Freud may have created an artificial situation that evoked artificial responses from patient as well as doctor. What kind of recovery could that lead to?

Although Ferenczi never broke off his relationship with Freud, he increasingly took the position that young children are hurt by the hypocrisy of their parents, neurotics injured by the hypocrisy of society, and patients further confused by the hypocrisy of analysts. If a patient doesn't fit your way of working, Ferenczi told his students, probably thinking of his own analysis with Freud, change your technique.

Thus in the last several years of his life Ferenczi experimented with "mutual analysis," whereby analyst and analysand literally took turns on the couch. This was not an extension of his indulgence technique, which he now realized mixed real life into analysis too thoroughly. He could not let his patients believe that they could be cured simply by staying with the kind doctor. Recovery required more than tenderness, and being an analyst required not only self-control but the willingness to kill off the fantasy that the patient could rest forever in his love. He had to admit that "the hangman's work is inevitable."[38] So back came the boundaries and discipline. In mutual analysis the doctor retained some authority, but the process worked toward mutual respect, equality, and independence. The technique had some daunting problems, Ferenczi admitted, one being confidentiality and another the anxiety he felt as he put himself "in the care and control of a madman," but it had some surprising advantages as well. The recovery was "no longer based on authority,"[39] and the patient was no longer shocked by the analyst's imperfections. In fact, Ferenczi thought that no matter how hard an analyst tried, he was bound to repeat the same mistakes that parents and lovers had already committed to the detriment of the patient. Unlike these other people, however, the analyst admitted his inability to understand perfectly and to help effectively. He said he was sorry. At the last, Ferenczi wondered if successful analysis did not lie in mutual forgiveness.

Ferenczi's "sins of youth" have a different feel to them than Jung's affairs. The mistakes made by the unconventional Hungarian became grist for his mill—data he used to answer the question, "What helps—and what doesn't?" As he had written to Freud, such mistakes can help a therapist become a wiser, more prudent clinician. As we will see later, learning to be an ethical practitioner by making mistakes is neither ideal nor uncommon.

Otto Rank and Anaïs Nin

A very different kind of doctor-patient relationship was begun by one of Ferenczi's colleagues and sometimes collaborator, Otto Rank.

Known today for the interest he took in the trauma of birth and in artists, Rank was another member of Freud's inner circle who broke with the professor and moved away from Vienna. Settling in Paris with his family, he practiced there for seven years before moving to the United States. When he met Anaïs Nin in Paris in 1933, Rank was discouraged. He was forty-two, unhappily married, and beginning to feel that psychoanalysis was being misused. The treatment was helping people to conform, he thought, rather than to find a resolution to their conflicts through art. An attractive young patient passionately devoted to the artist's life was just what Rank needed to restore his energy. Nin arrived in November.

Anaïs Nin is best known for keeping a 150-volume diary full of sexually explicit descriptions, and having an affair with the author Henry Miller, whom she met about a year before Rank. Initially, she urged Miller to go into therapy, but when he became Rank's friend instead of patient, Nin decided she would try a second analysis. (Her first was with René Allendy, a French analyst whom she said she seduced to get even with Henry Miller, who was frequenting "little whores.") Perhaps, she thought, Rank would advise her on Miller and her husband, or at the very least he would provide new material for her diary. As she noted, she went into analysis "for the sport of it, not to solve, but to aggrandize, dramatize my conflicts."[40]

Nin and Rank spoke the same language. They both had passionate natures, loved art, and enjoyed nothing more than a contest of wills— a battle of wits. Rank started right in on Nin's exhilarating and exhausting preoccupation with sex. Noting that having lots of sex doesn't change a neurotic child into a woman, Rank supposedly told Nin that she was a child, a wife, and a mistress—but not yet a woman. With remarkable sensitivity toward her own inner workings, Nin took in Rank's interpretations but soon realized that it was "the *presence* of Rank the man which imparts the wisdom he gives."[41] Not what he said, not what he prompted her to remember, but primarily, said Nin, it was his enthusiasm, his warmth, his being-in-the-room that "defeats the past."

Rank skillfully led Nin toward an understanding of herself until an unexpected conflict in Nin's life pushed her into changing her analysis back into a diversion—a tactic she had used before, and one that Rank had certainly seen in others. Nin, who had been told she would never conceive, became pregnant by Henry Miller. On the one hand, she was thrilled. Now she would be a real woman, complete. On the other hand, she was appalled, for she believed that if she kept the child it would displace her as the pampered darling in her husband's eyes. Equally distressing, it would be in competition with its own father, Henry Miller, whom Nin thought of as her own project or child.

In the face of this conflict, exacerbated as it was by the unavailability of safe abortions, Nin launched herself into a new affair and distracted herself with a passion so fiery it made her physically ill. On May 19, she told her diary that she wanted Rank as a companion in this time of trouble. Less than a week later, she thought she might be falling in love with him. Two days after that she announced, "I will not be haunted. I will kiss Rank. *Et tout sévanouira—tout fondra*," she added. ("All will evaporate—all melt away.")

"I fussed and fretted to obtain my new hyacinth blue dress from the cleaner. I would go to Rank the next day in my new dress because he was going to kiss me. I went to sleep full of dreams, energies, desires. I got up vibrant, courageous, impulsive. I rushed to Rank."[42]

Slender and beautiful in her slippery silk dress, Nin left her chair in Rank's office, knelt before her doctor, "and offered my mouth." He held her for a moment, then asked her to come back and talk about her work. Nin didn't get the kiss, but she knew from the embrace that she had gotten Rank.

When Nin returned to Rank's office the next day, the two were "mowed down by the same desire." They kissed. They embraced. They reached for each other roughly. And they talked. Emerging from his office, she walked for a long time along the grassy periphery of the Bois de Boulogne, "tasting, retasting, remembering only the emotions. "It was for me you wore this new dress—you never wore it before?'"[43] The new turn of events with Rank was enough to keep her mind occupied until the next day when she thought again of "the unwanted child" she had not yet "ejected." Almost within the hour, "I arrive at Henry's room, and he opens his arms."[44]

Now three months pregnant, Nin was going to a *sage femme* who gave her quinine and other concoctions to abort the child. With each treatment the need to reinforce the image of herself as artist and lover increased. Predictably, she made love desperately to two and then three men. When she caught herself beginning to seduce a fourth, she was brought up short by what she thought of as her diabolical compulsion. "Not love, but revenge, or love and revenge always mixed." She believed that she betrayed men because men were treacherous. Her father had left her and the rest of the family, Henry Miller had left his second wife for Nin, her husband's friends and colleagues had betrayed their wives (and her husband) to have affairs with Nin, her first analyst had betrayed his profession and his wife, and now Rank had broken his vows. She, too, would love and betray them all. Approximately five months pregnant, she finally had an abortion.

Rank and Nin became lovers just as he decided to move to the United States. He was separating from his wife and urged Nin to accompany him to New York, where they would work together as analysts. Nin agreed, but soon tired of both Rank and analysis. After a two-month whirl in New York, she took up again with both her husband and Miller, who had followed her from France.

Nin's affair with Rank raises, but does not perfectly illustrate, the delicate question of responsibility. How are we to know what kinds of power and responsibility a patient has and what kinds he or she does not have? Do we assume that male and female patients have the same responsibilities? Or should rules for the two genders be different? In the case of initiating sex, there is nearly unanimous agreement that a patient, male or female, is never responsible. Nin may have thrown herself at Rank, but this did not release him from his ethical responsibilities. Even when she insisted that she wanted to make love, it is assumed today that this is not true consent but merely a reflection of the analyst's powerful desires and suggestions. It would be argued in court that Nin would not dare say no to Rank, even if she wanted to. She needed his support and consolation too much.

When money, time, and certain commodities other than sex are considered, however, a different situation prevails. Like all patients judged to be mentally competent, Nin was expected to have sufficient power to assume responsibility for keeping appointments, paying her bills, and controlling any urges that might lead to illegal activity such as hurling paint on the doctor's house or assaulting him. In addition, she was expected to use common sense in dealing with *some* of her doctors' requests. If Rank had told Nin to rob a bank rather than to kiss him, she would have borne most or all of the responsibility for the consequences unless she pleaded insanity. In other words, the patient is assumed to be powerless where sex is concerned but not helpless where certain other things are concerned.[45]

Returning to the time of Jung, Ferenczi, and Rank, dozens more stories could be added to make the point that in the first forty years of psychotherapy's history it was recognized that love as well as sexual attraction hovered dangerously near the couch. Whether the analyst followed Freud's "rule of abstinence" and sought to resemble a blank screen or whether he preferred a more natural and egalitarian approach, it was not uncommon for him to be struck by desire. Analysts like Wilhelm Stekel gave in to this desire repeatedly. Others slipped only slightly or only once. But all were familiar with the remarkably powerful longings—the danger that also energized treatment and inspired remarkable insights into the workings of the human mind.

The Problem Comes to America

When the talking cure crossed the Atlantic—in part driven across by the expulsion of Jewish analysts from Europe before World War II—the very concept of "the perils of our trade" began to change as psychoanalysis took on some of the emotional cautiousness characteristic of Americans. Although expatriate analysts like Rank still cavorted in Harlem dance halls or strolled arm in arm with their patients through Greenwich Village, Americans in general were uncomfortable with the adoring dependence that neurotic women seemed to develop on their doctors, especially when the subject under discussion was sexual attraction. James Jackson Putnam, who first put Freudian doctrines to work in the New World, complained that the undercurrent of desire that bore therapy along was simply "an evil which must be accepted." (He also altered the seat of his daughter's bicycle so she would not be unduly stimulated.) Another American psychiatrist burned a book of Freud's because it was "filthy."[46] This prudery, as Freud called it, did not stifle yearning in the New World for long, however, and in the 1940s, 1950s, and 1960s new methods of therapy that encouraged the doctor to take a more active, personal role prompted techniques that variously offered support, insight, drama, wrestling, and sex. No longer cultivating a blank and neutral demeanor, men like Fritz Perls hugged, held, tackled, and made love to their clients. Robert Lindner, author of *The Fifty-Minute Hour,* made emergency house calls, even to a single woman's house at night. Milton Erickson used unusual techniques to shock his clients into fast action. He claimed to have cured one woman of debilitating shyness by having her undress in his office. And Karen Horney, an analyst who challenged Freud's thinking about women and whose books are still in print, seduced so many of her young male analysands that she was expelled from two institutes.[47]

A little later, when self-enhancement movements such as those sponsored by the Esalen Institute in California gathered momentum, sexual intimacy briefly moved from its position as a peril to an active ingredient of treatment—an adjunct. In those hip and flower-powered years when emotional health seemed primarily a matter of letting it all hang out, charismatic encounter-group leaders like Will Schutz offered their followers an extra or additional "genuine encounter" by sleeping with them. These sought-after encounters where people openly expressed and acted on feelings of desire, anger, elation, and despair seemed the best answer to modern men's and women's growing alienation. There was a naive expectation that sex would release and repair the emotional reticence that hobbled modern individuals. Good sex would lead directly to good health. The most notorious of the loose cannons who put this simplistic theory into practice was a Dr. McCartney, who boasted that in forty years of practice he had treated over 1500 women, 30 percent of whom sat on his lap and kissed him, and 10 percent of whom found it "necessary" to undress, fondle, or have intercourse.[48]

In Europe too, the newer, less formal approaches to psychotherapy led to some curious interactions. Frieda Fromm-Reichman, the analyst portrayed in "I Never Promised You a Rose Garden," analyzed and then married Erich Fromm, author of *The Art of Loving.* Melanie Klein, who believed that emotional disturbances could be traced all the way back to infancy, analyzed one of her male patients on her hotel bed while on vacation. And the beloved pediatrician-turned-analyst, Donald Winnicott, held his patients hands, fed them biscuits, and guessed that there were times when a psychotic patient needed physical holding. At the same time, analysts who taught at the C. G. Jung Institute were openly acknowledging the sexual temptations of analysis and helping their students resist.

Both the early laissez-faire attitude imported from Europe and the brief period of permissiveness that flourished—most notably in California—turned a sharp corner in the 1970s, when society's thinking about doctor-patient affairs headed in an altogether different direction. For one thing, sexuality had moved from its central position as *the* underlying cause of most neuroses to being one of several causes of emotional distress. The drive for sexual union and all it represented didn't seem as powerful a motivator anymore, and doctors encouraged their patients to discuss other feelings. For another thing, both love and sex were being reevaluated in light of the women's movement, and Cupid was losing his credibility as the innocent bearer of happiness. Was it possible, some women began to ask, that love was also a chain that shackled them to the roles of mother and housewife? What then of therapy and therapists—that helpful process whereby kindly men calmed rebellious women and enabled them to return to their positions in the home? Could it be, these women wondered, that therapy was sexist and therapists potential enemies?

Reignited by the women's movement, the old turn-of-the-century complaint that some therapies were dangerous and some therapists pigs took on broader meaning and was voiced with greater urgency. This time, professional organizations responded. In hopes of avoiding strict regulation by the state, such groups as the American Psychiatric Association, the American Psychological Association, and the National Association of Social Workers issued codes of ethics that formally banned sexual intimacy between therapist and client and then between therapist and former clients. A few years later state regulations put teeth into these bans. Not surprisingly, the stories told about intimacy in therapy—or at least the accounts discussed in public—changed again. No more stories of celebrated analysts falling in love with patients. No more tales of dumpy little psychiatrists the shape of penguins holding their enormous schizophrenic charges on their laps and feeding them mashed potatoes to calm them down.

And especially no more stories of nude volleyball games and sexual orgies on the therapist's ranch. Instead, the standard account of powerful attraction in therapy became the imbroglio—the horrifying story of a vulnerable young woman coming to a male therapist for help and receiving coercive propositions and sex instead. Within little more than a single decade, all attraction in therapy was subsumed under this category and viewed as abuse. The examples that abound both in popular and scientific writings are part of the new literature of victimization and are emblematic of our day. *Betrayal,* both an exposé and a TV movie, is a good example, as are *The Killing Cure* and *Sex in the Therapy Hour.* In the press it is common to read, "Counselor charged with raping patient," "Psychiatrists and sex abuse: State regulation marked by delay, confusion, loopholes" or "Patients sue Boston psychiatrist, claim she made them her 'slaves.'"[49]

An example from the press that is, unfortunately, not atypical is the story of a young artist, Elise Wylde, who was hospitalized in McLean Hospital in Boston, and cared for there by Dr. Harold Williams. The relationship eventually included sex, which Wylde felt powerless to refuse. Feeling dependent and helpless, and wanting to gain her doctor's attention, love, and approval "at any cost," Wylde agreed to the sex, but felt used. Years later, she successfully sued her doctor.[50]

It is important to realize that public accounts of doctor-patient sex, as opposed to the more numerous private accounts that never go to court, are not like the stories left by Spielrein, Nin, and Ferenczi. For one thing, public accounts are grievances constructed to win an argument, not stories written down day by day to wrestle with conflicting feelings. For another thing, stories in the press and in the scientific literature are told exclusively by patients. Because all forms of sexual entanglement are now considered punishable behavior, therapists can no longer afford to talk or write about their experience as Jung and Ferenczi did. One result of this exclusive reliance on public reports is that doctor-patient entanglements seem simpler, less diverse, and more horrifying than they did fifty years ago. Much of this apparent difference disappears, however, when private accounts are considered—accounts that still retain much of their original complexity and diversity.

Conclusion and Observations

What are we to conclude, then, from this brief sampling of doctors and patients who have become sexually involved with each other over the past hundred years? Bearing in mind that the cases presented here, like any information, may be interpreted in different ways, I will make only a few observations, and very general ones at that. First, it seems clear to me that the talking cure has given rise to strong feelings of lust and affection, which have been handled in five or six different ways. Breuer ran from them, and refused to reenter the field. Men like Freud controlled these feelings rigorously, in part by using a formal technique that kept patients at a distance, and in part by an effort of will. Stop *before* the kiss, said Freud. In contrast, Jung and Rank gave in to the attraction, and although I believe Jung in particular became extremely fond of his patient, Spielrein, both men seem to have embarked upon the affairs primarily to enrich and enliven their own lives. This was true too of Ferenczi, but he also ran experiments on his feelings of attraction and learned a great deal. In the 1960s and 1970s, Perls and Schutz thought the sex they enjoyed was therapeutic—an experiment that was part of the sexual revolution and that has now largely been discredited. Finally, several clinicians, who now must remain anonymous, gave in to the attraction only to learn an ethical lesson. Thus my first observation is that these involvements happen in all kinds of settings and are handled in different ways.

Second, patients too have responded in a variety of ways. Many women such as the artist Elise Wylde have felt utterly wronged. Not only were they misled and betrayed, but they have felt damaged in ways that made normal relationships difficult. Today, some of these patients go to court and seek compensation. At the other extreme, a few patients formed committed relationships and married their doctors. Ferenczi, Sandor Rado, and Frieda Fromm-Reichman married former patients, and the process continues today in secret. For a third group of patients, an involvement with a doctor brought them a mixture of pleasure and pain, help and harm. Women like Spielrein have their counterparts today. They tell stories of troubled love mixed with sadness and abuse.

Third and last, the experiences described here hint at how much our interpretations of doctor-patient relationships rely on cultural expectations for their meaning. When old assumptions held sway—that sex was usually linked to affection, that good patients were grateful patients—then doctor-patient sexual involvements tended to be told as stories of troubled or forbidden love rather than as accounts of cold-hearted abuse. When just plain abuse occurred, as it did, I believe, with Elma and with Wilhelm Stekel's many conquests, there was no readily understandable story for these women to tell that expressed their feelings. No matter what they said, their stories were heard as the plight of a fallen woman or a helpless fool. Today, the culture looks at the relationship between love and sex, man and woman in a different way, and stories of doctor-patient entanglements are tailored to more cynically realistic expectations. Now the Elmas and Elises have a new option. They can tell a story of victimization and abuse that is readily understood by many. At the same time, stories of love between doctor and patient are distrusted and rarely believed.

If history has a lesson for us, it is not merely that doctors and patients become sexually involved. It is also that these relationships occur in every setting, follow different courses, and reach different conclusions. Regardless of this variety, history also suggests that the patient, not the doctor, is usually the one to get hurt. What can be done? Or to pose the question more fully: "No analysis can succeed in which we do not succeed in really loving the patient," wrote Ferenczi, but how does a therapist love hundreds of patients over a lifetime and never take love where it naturally wants to go?[51]

This is a serious question, but we do not know enough to answer it yet. We do not know what combinations of circumstances motivate clinicians to reach for their patients, although we have seen that both personal and professional discouragement often play a part as did the old practice of hiring patients as assistants. But there is much more to be learned. Now is not the time to cut off the discussion of doctor-patient attraction or to limit in any way the stories we are free to tell about these relationships. Let us leave for the next generation as broad and as rich a conversation on this emotional topic as we have inherited from Freud, Jung, Ferenczi, and all the others.

Notes

1. John Kerr, *A Most Dangerous Method: The Story of Jung, Freud and Sabina Spielrein* (New York: Alfred A. Knopf, 1993), 193.

2. Ibid., 128.

3. Ibid., 209.

4. Ibid., 219.

5. Ibid., 379, 189.

6. Ibid., 197.

7. Aldo Carotenuto, *A Secret Symmetry: Sabina Spielrein Between Jung and Freud* (New York: Pantheon Books, 1982), 168.

8. Kerr, *A Most Dangerous Method,* 171.

9. Ibid., 223.

10. Ibid., 226.

11. Ibid., 205.

12. Ibid., 206.

13. Carotenuto, *A Secret Symmetry,* 97.

14. Ibid., 92.

15. Kerr, *A Most Dangerous Method,* 295.

16. Carotenuto, *A Secret Symmetry,* 12.

17. Kerr, *A Most Dangerous Method,* 437.

18. Ibid.

19. Ibid., 491.

20. Carotenuto, *A Secret Symmetry,* 190.

21. Ethel S. Person, *Dreams of Love and Fateful Encounters: The Power of Romantic Passion* (New York: Penguin Books, 1988), 252.

22. Kerr, *A Most Dangerous Method,* 504.

23. Jung's triptych was on the subject of the "anima," a female archetype that Jung believed existed in the subconscious of every man. (Women, he thought, had an "animus," or male counterpart.) "May the light arise which I have borne in my body" appears in Latin on one of the panels.

24. Person, *Dreams of Love,* 253.

25. Ibid., 252–53.

26. Jeffrey Masson, *Against Therapy* (London: Fontana, 1988), 176.

27. Eva Brabant, Ernst Falzeder, and Patricia Giampieri-Deutsch, eds., *The Correspondence of Sigmund Freud and Sandor Ferenczi,* vol. 1, 1908–1914 (Cambridge: Harvard University Press, Belknap Press, 1994), 87.

28. Ibid., 87–88.

29. Masson, *Against Therapy,* 77.

30. Judith DuPont, *The Clinical Diary of Sandor Ferenczi* (Cambridge: Harvard University Press, 1988), 186.

31. Ibid.

32. J. Marmor, "Sexual Acting Out in Psychotherapy," *American Journal of Psychoanalysis* 22 (1972): 4.

33. DuPont, *Clinical Diary of Sandor Ferenczi,* 3.

34. Ibid., 4.

35. Ibid., 92–93.

36. Ibid., 93.

37. Ibid.

38. Ibid., 53.

39. Ibid., 94.

40. Anaïs Nin, *Incest—From a Journal of Love: The Unexpurgated Diary of Anaïs Nin* (New York: Harcourt Brace Jovanovich, 1992), 293.

41. Ibid., 302.

42. Ibid., 334.

43. Ibid., 336.

44. Ibid., 337.

45. This inconsistent view of power and responsibility is thrown into relief by the attention that abusive patients are now receiving. In a national study, 25 percent of female doctors reported that they had been sexually harassed by their patients, and 20 percent reported abuse from patients' families. Some of these doctors were propositioned, others squeezed, some suffered property damage—all illegal activities. This raises an important point. If patients are *sometimes* held accountable for their actions in therapy—i.e., they are assumed to know right from wrong, they are assumed to mean what they say, and they are expected to take responsibility for their actions—then who decides when a patient is responsible and when he or she is not? This confusion is reflected in laws governing sexual misconduct. In some states—Michigan, for example—male therapists can be punished if they have sexual intercourse under pretext of medical treatment, but only with a woman, not a man. Female therapists are not punishable under this statute at all.

Leah Dickstein commented on the abuse that doctors suffer at the hands of their patients in *The Harvard Magazine* (Jan.–Feb. 1995): 19.

46. Kerr, *A Most Dangerous Method*, 233, 241.

47. Diane Middlebrook, "The Analyst and Her Appetites," a review of *Karen Horney: A Psychiatrist's Search for Self-Understanding*, ed. Bernard J. Paris (New Haven, Conn.: Yale University Press, 1995). In *The Washington Post*, 29 Jan. 1995.

48. Marmor, "Sexual Acting Out in Psychotherapy," 5.

49. It is difficult to read a major, or even a minor, newspaper for an entire week without coming across articles on sexual misconduct by professionals. For example, *The Cape Cod Times* ran several on Suzanne King, beginning with an article that appeared on 12 Aug. 1994, p. 29. *The Boston Globe* has carried dozens of such stories, including a review of sexual abuse cases by psychiatrists (4 Oct. 1994, p. 1) and extensive coverage of Bishop David Johnson's alleged sexual misconduct and suicide (27 Jan. 1995, p. 1, and 5 Feb. 1995, p. 20).

50. "Psychiatrists and Sex Abuse," *The Boston Globe*, 4 Oct. 1994, 15.

51. DuPont, *Clinical Diary of Sandor Ferenczi*, 127–30. In June 1932, Ferenczi wrote a series of entries in his diary on the place that love occupies in psychotherapy. He believed that a good analyst possesses an improbable range of talents, namely passion, wisdom, self-control, and self-confidence.

Selected Bibliography

Bates, C., and A. Brodsky. *Sex in the Therapy Hour: A Case of Professional Incest.* New York: The Guilford Press, 1989.

Baur, Susan. *The Intimate Hour: Love and Sex in Psychotherapy.* Boston: Houghton Mifflin, in press.

Bettelheim, Bruno. Review of *A Secret Symmetry: Sabina Spielrein Between Jung and Freud* in *The New York Review of Books* 30 (30 June 1983): 39.

Brabant, Eva, Ernst Falzeder, and Patricia Giampieri-Deutsch, eds. *The Correspondence of Sigmund Freud and Sandor Ferenczi,* vol. 1, 1908–1914. Cambridge: Harvard University Press, Belknap Press, 1994.

Carotenuto, Aldo. *A Secret Symmetry: Sabina Spielrein Between Jung and Freud.* New York: Pantheon Books, 1982.

Dickstein, Leah. *The Harvard Magazine* (Jan.–Feb. 1995): 19.

Dupont, Judith, ed. *The Clinical Diary of Sandor Ferenczi.* Cambridge: Harvard University Press, 1988.

Freeman, Lucy. *Betrayal: Based on the Personal Account of Julie Roy.* Chelsea, Mich.: Scarborough House, 1976.

Haley, Jay. *Uncommon Therapy: The Psychiatric Techniques of Milton Erickson, M.D..* New York: W. W. Norton & Company, 1973.

Kerr, John. *A Most Dangerous Method: The Story of Jung, Freud, and Sabina Spielrein.* New York: Alfred A. Knopf, 1993.

Lindner, Robert. *The Fifty-Minute Hour.* New York: Delacorte, 1986.

Marmor, J. "Sexual Acting Out in Psychotherapy." *American Journal of Psychoanalysis* 22 (1972): 3–8.

Masson, Jeffrey. *Against Therapy: Emotional Tyranny and the Myth of Psychological Healing.* London: Fontana, 1988.

Middlebrook, Diane. "The Analyst and Her Appetites," a review of *Karen Horney: A Psychiatrist's Search for Self-Understanding,* ed. Bernard J. Paris. New Haven, Conn.: Yale University Press. In *The Washington Post,* 29 January 1995.

Nin, Anaïs. *Incest—From a Journal of Love: The Unexpurgated Diary of Anaïs Nin.* New York: Harcourt Brace Jovanovich, 1992.

Person, Ethel S. *Dreams of Love and Fateful Encounters: The Power of Romantic Passion.* New York: Penguin Books, 1988.

Shepard, M. *The Love Treatment: Sexual Intimacy Between Patients and Psychotherapists.* New York: Peter Wyden, 1971.

2 | Walking the Bounds
Historical and Theological Reflections on Ministry, Intimacy, and Power

Fredrica Harris Thompsett

Marking Contextual Boundaries

PAROCHIAL CUSTOMS FROM the Church of England—reformation ancestor of my own denomination, the Episcopal Church—contain many curiosities. Among these is the country custom of "Procession" or walking the "bounds." This involves a perambulation of clergy and people round about the geographical boundaries of the whole parish (not just the church building), inviting God's blessing with psalms and prayers on the harvest, crops, herds, and other living things gathered therein. This manner of marking local boundaries was also intended to encourage neighborliness, charity, reconciliation of differences, and greater understanding among those who lived in close proximity.

The focus of this volume speaks to boundaries that have proved troublesome to those who work today amid the close proximities of ministry. Specifically, our contexts are marked by a new style of "boundary talk," focused on the ethics of sexual misconduct among those who exercise religious leadership.[1] The overall problem is that vulnerable people have been and are being exploited in relationships with those in authority in my own and other churches. From the start I want to be clear that I support the need to address sexual misconduct by clergy and other religious leaders. This work must continue. I know all too well, personally and professionally, the cost of such abuse whether it be physical, psychological, or emotional.

However, in this essay I have a different problem in mind. I worry about ecclesial rule making intended to shape the so-called boundaries of human relationships in today's diverse ministries. What I experience—and what I hear in mandated conversations about ministry, intimacy, and power—is a cacophony of liability-driven assertions about ministry, based primarily on general psychological understandings. The disciplines of church history, theology, and contextually astute ethics are largely missing. My concern, indeed my fear, about much contemporary "boundary talk" is that we will end up living in a theologically flawed, fragmented, tightly contracted, and clericalist landscape devoid of respectful relationships, mutuality, and intimacy with one another and indeed with God!

Let me mark, then, the four overlapping parameters that encompass and inform my reflections on ministerial boundaries. First of all, I regularly work as a church historian. This historical base, for example, informs me that "boundary" is a relatively new word. The word "bound" is not found in the English language until the fourteenth century. The first recorded use of the word "boundary"—according to the *Oxford English Dictionary*—was in 1626, when Francis Bacon sought to describe the vast difference between two terms: "generation" and "corruption." This is a telling example, one that presages current conversations. However, my main point here is that "boundary" is a nonbiblical, post-Reformation, and, in the Anglican tradition, a post–*Book of Common Prayer* word. Of course I know that contemporary concerns about "boundaries" are borrowed from psychology and its therapeutic practitioners. Yet I remain concerned that not very sophisticated psychological warrants are being applied, actually superimposed with at times zealous clarity (in my denomination at least), on top of historical and other foundational understandings of ministry. I will return to this problem.

Secondly, as an Anglican theologian, I write as one devoted to the empowering mutuality modeled in the courageous doctrine of the incarnation. Among other things this means I endeavor to follow the reasoned, experienced capability of my theological forebears to construct theological interpretations while holding together complex realities falsely believed to be opposed, if not outright contradictory, to one another. I have in mind the theological task of overcoming such dangerous, distancing dualisms as between secular and sacred, material and spiritual, humanity and divinity, and sexuality and ministry. Traditionally, for Anglicans and other Christians, the formative doctrine of the incarnation is a case in point.[2] Imagine the boundaries crossed in God's bold, new life as "the Word became flesh and lived among us" (John 1:14)! This is a God in Christ who partakes of the fullness of human life, including the capacity to instill and invite devotion, passion, pathos, affection, and friendship. Such intimate, concrete, and direct relationality is at the heart of Christian formation.

In this essay I will explore the congruence between my own denomination's familiar theological assertions and contemporary perspectives on interpersonal boundaries. I invite readers to review my "Anglican" theological reflections with their own local theologies in mind.

Thirdly, I live and work as a Christian who ministers in a denomination that defines—in print at least—"ministers" of the church alike as "lay persons, bishops, priests, and deacons." This is a wonderfully open definition of church membership and allied leadership, not at all a bounded or rigidly demarcated perspective. Laity and clergy are envisioned as interdependent collaborators who are together responsible for living their shared baptismal covenant in the world. Biblical foundations identify seekers after God's reign in the Greek phrase *laos tou theos*, "members of the people of God," including all God's children—those we would describe today as laity as well as clergy. Holiness in the Anglican and Episcopal pastoral tradition is always communal, rather than owned by one person or class of persons. Thus definitive, absolute, and prescriptive power distinctions between laity and clergy are at base theologically suspect. I will return to this matter as well.

Finally, my scholarship and ministry is informed by the perspectives of feminist liberation theology. In summary, this means I am attentive to the hierarchical, patriarchal molecules in the theological air we breath. A kind of "toxic theology" undergirds incidents of violence, hatred, and sexual misconduct in the life of the church as well as society. Thus Marie Fortune helpfully writes:

At its core the problem is **the exercise of patriarchal privilege.** Those who have held power in helping relationships (in the past usually males) have often presumed to use that power to their own advantage and to the disadvantage of someone who trusted them.[3]

Feminist psychologist Miriam Greenspan continues this line of analysis, reminding us of the unfortunate truth: "sexual and power abuse are *inevitable* in a system so steeped in unquestioned assumptions of hierarchy and power."[4] Marie Fortune believes, all other things being equal, that power can be a shared "neutral reality."[5] However, Fortune and others readily admit that the "playing field" for women and other traditionally oppressed groups is not level. Power dynamics in U.S. churches are seldom, if at all, neutral.

Critically astute feminists know that gender analysis by itself is simplistic. As a privileged, well-educated, middle-class North American, I live in an interrelated social system of dominations. These culturally demonic and demeaning barriers are regularly at work between and among persons of different races, ethnic groups, social classes, sexual identities, ages, and/or physical abilities. Late-twentieth-century popular culture in the United States is also obsessed with sex and violence; meanwhile, its churches are frequently bearers of anti-sexual theologies and sexually phobic attitudes. The unremitting scapegoating of gay men and lesbians is one frightening symptom of contemporary religious fear of sexuality. Clearly we have more to learn about *not* projecting our fears onto others, both ecclesiastically and interpersonally. Given these and other intersecting oppressions, it is pertinent to ask just whose futures, whose reputations do we have in mind as we talk about "boundary" disputes?

I am concerned as well about ecclesial structures that focus on one-to-one individual relationships without constructive awareness of the complex, at times ambiguous or paradoxical societal contexts in which power, human sexuality, and ministry are regularly exercised. Human touch, for example, is governed by cultural rules that vary enormously from one location to another. One researcher, observing the number of times touch was involved in a conversation two people were having in a cafe, found that in Puerto Rico conversational couples touched 180 times per hour, while in London couples did not touch at all.[6] Questions abound: whose cultural rules on boundaries are we legislating, who decides which culture is *the* dominant one, who enforces the rules, and what is the legitimate role of critique by those from nondominant cultures, races, ethnicities, and sexual identities? Do we really understand the subtle and not-so-subtle complexities that need to be unmasked and disentangled if we are to explore, secure, and redeem the intersections of ministry, intimacy, and power? What past, present, and future outlooks can help us stretch, broaden, and reshape as needed contemporary discussions about interpersonal relationships in ministry?

Historical Perspectives on Ministry

Relational "boundaries" come in several forms, some are horizontally between us, others are hierarchically over or under us; then there are the boundaries in time and in thought. Historically, it is helpful to remember that interpersonal "boundary issues" are not brand new to the practice of ministry. They have been there all along. To take just one example, George Herbert in his engaging mid-seventeenth-century pastoral on the cure of souls, *The Country Parson*, has much to say about "The Parson's State of Life." Today we would probably call it "The Parson's Lifestyle"! After familiar invocations that the Parson needs to be "holy, just, prudent, temperate, bold, grave in all his ways," Herbert adds that he should be "not only a Pastor, but a Lawyer also, and Physician." Clearly Herbert expected the "Parson" to be a powerful public "person" in the community.

Herbert (who apparently did not worry about the Parson's relationships with men) then goes on to describes the Parson's preferred relations with women:

> If he be unmarried . . . he never talks with any woman alone, but in the audience of others, and that seldom, and then also in a serious manner, never jestingly or sportfully. He is very circumspect in all companies, both of his behavior, speech, and very looks, knowing himself to be both suspected and envied.[7]

Let me repeat this last phrase: "knowing himself to be both *suspected and envied*." Although Herbert obviously did not name those psychological dynamics which latter-day healers identify as "projection" and "transference," he did know that religious leaders are often powerfully caught in other people's imaginations, suspected on one hand, envied and sought after on the other. Then as now, a minister or other religious leader could become the focal point for another's emotions, both positive and negative.

Herbert's "parsons" were, however, distinctly different from most clergy today; they were broadly, publicly engaged in local society. These clergy were direct descendants of Reformation theologian Richard Hooker's sixteenth-century "presbyters." This classical Anglican theologian was clear that presbyters, like every other Christian searcher, are formed in the "grace dispensed at baptism." Hooker did, however, ascribe to these clergy one particular responsibility. They were charged to convey throughout the geographical bounds of the parish "the power of spiritual procreation." This meant not only affirming life, but assuming responsibility as spiritual midwives for bringing forth new life along the way.[8] Their ministry was to be practiced under public scrutiny in daily, multiple contacts and engaged relationships amid the busy sociopolitical life of the wider parish.

The shift from an assertive, public practice of ministry to more sentimentalized, privatized expressions of clerical leadership has a telling history. In North America this is largely an early nineteenth-century tale, begun during disestablishment. Ann Douglas in *The Feminization of American Culture* points to a long process in which clergy generally lost their public repute and widespread social influence. In part the primary "objects" of clerical attention and their daily collaborators in ministry became women, more often than not. Domestic matters, emphases, and virtues gradually took on more significance in largely white, middle-class parishes; later on, church "parlors" and funeral "homes" were added; and the Protestant clergy eagerly joined "the emerging consumer society . . . [in] its obsession with popularity and its increasing disregard of intellectual issues."[9]

Urban T. Holmes III—whose 1970s books on ministry and imagination bear rereading—concurs with this description. In broad strokes Holmes describes major historical movements in Protestant ministry from the flexible, multiply engaged parson of Herbert's day, to the nineteenth-century "preacher of the Word," and in the 1970s to the spiritual "physician of the soul," whose primary "*raison d'etre* . . . is counseling."[10] Today, we could add that the ministry of the 1980s was characterized by increasing concern for "professionalism" and by proliferating canonical regulation of ministerial practice. Most recently, in the 1990s, focus has been on meeting legal procedures that attest to an individual clergy person's prior reputation. Liability-driven professionalism is an untested latecomer to traditional discernments about ministry.

This overall summary might not be entirely accurate, yet there is enough truth here to note that by the end of the modern period, ministerial leaders were more isolated from the rest of sociopolitical life. The practice of religious leadership was essentially privatized, or at least narrowed considerably from its earlier flexible and multiple public forms. Theologically, I am reminded of Verna Dozier's warning against "reduc[ing] God to the personal, private, 'spiritual' sphere of our lives, and ministry to . . . private, 'spiritual' acts."[11]

Professionalization—with its intended correlation between education, salary, and effectiveness—is a late-nineteenth- and early-twentieth-century newcomer to the history and practice of ministry. Perhaps professionalism was one way to respond to that earlier loss of status and influence. Certainly, images of "the professional" and the "chief executive officer" fit snugly in "corporate" institutional models for the church. As a church historian I find such ecclesiologies suspect, although that of course is another topic. For the purposes of this essay, it is important to remember that institutionally imposed professional standards are *not* gender or power neutral; they too are steeped in the hierarchical system of value, status, privilege, and power in which, to quote Miriam Greenspan's warning, "the professional is somebody. The nonprofessional is nobody."[12] I do not lament the fact of professional standards per se. Rather I am concerned that historical, theological, ethically sensitive perspectives are not directly utilized in deepening, balancing, and shaping today's ministerial accountabilities.

Contemporary Reflections on Intimacy

Two years ago—during the week after Easter, a time when some parish clergy typically "take time off" for rest and renewal—I led a clergy conference. The group was comprised of twenty dedicated, experienced, and, by many accounts, very successful Episcopal clergymen, plus one clergywoman. Together we explored the theological dimensions of topics in my new book, *Courageous Incarnation*: the crisis of children at risk, changing patterns of work, experiences of advancing age, and characteristics of intimacy. I had thought, since the group's median age was 63, reflecting on aging would be the most difficult. Instead the toughest, most revealing conversations we shared were about intimacy. After lifetimes of ministry, men in this group spoke truthfully and poignantly of their personal and professional fear of intimacy, their anxiety about actually touching persons' lives. They shared their belief that they had been taught in this gendered culture—as well as in their church—to fear intimacy. Accordingly a number of them viewed diocesan procedures gathering data on the character of past and present relationships as a logical extension of the message they had learned long ago: there is no room for intimacy in ministry. They noted the incongruent fact that several of them (over half, I believe) had married women who were members of their early parishes, while current guidelines do not sanction such friendships. Some leading experts on professional boundaries expressly forbid clergy socializing among parishioners, bluntly insisting that clergy must meet their needs for intimacy elsewhere.

What, then, is ministry without intimacy? Is there an appropriate role in ministry for mutually *invited* human touch? Are our churches on the way to becoming places in which we "talk" about friendship, comfort, healing, and well-being for one another, while actually living in communities where obvious, good-humored, warm enjoyment of one another is censored away? Will our congregations become locations where religious "practitioners" are distant, intentionally withdrawn, hiding behind credentials, relating to the people of God as their objective "clients"? Miriam Greenspan calls this the "Nobody Home" approach to healing. By significantly overplaying the divisions and power dynamics that separate laity from clergy, will we not avoid intimacy with one another, and eventually intimacy with God?

Is such a prospect possible? Not if we are vigilant. On one hand, I know we must continue to address coercive nonmutual relational behaviors and the sexual abuse of vulnerable people in the life of the church. On the other, I believe we must also face the potential danger of excising touch and other forms of intimacy as a whole from our ministries. In such a world, overzealous journalists, occasionally greedy lawyers, fearful chancellors, and ever cautious insurance companies are more likely to be the truly influential trendsetters for theological formation and ministry.

Future Boundaries and Barriers

Why should we worry? Over time, will we not be able to work out the bumps, the hazards, the irregularities, and even the faulty theology at work in new structural regulations about ministerial boundaries? Yes, perhaps. Yet the larger cultural ethos in which we promulgate these regulations today is worrisome, even critical.

In *Race Matters,* African American theologian Cornel West identifies two intertwined forces undermining human life as we know it: increasing levels of poverty and increasing levels of paranoia.[13] Consider the increase in murderous acts, in outbreaks of anti-Semitism, and in pogroms of many peoples committed in God's several names as formerly united countries in northern Europe, the Balkans, Russia, and now Africa, among others, come apart. In the war in Bosnia-Herzegovina, boundaries defined by hatreds dating from fourteenth-century massacres have emerged as fresh as yesterday's injury. Imagine killing a next-door neighbor of many years to avenge acts committed fifty or hundreds of years earlier, thereby perpetuating another cycle of violence for generations to come. This all-too-real story still lingers before us, as present as the evening news.

The way ahead looks even murkier. We live during a time in which we are seemingly, inch by inch, emotionally and sociologically, walled off from one another by thickening layers of classist, racist, fascist, and other thoroughly xenophobic barriers. Ethicist Larry Rasmussen describes the perils of living in a season of pervasive "moral sprawl and breakdown."[14] In the future, as biblical scholar and theologian Walter Brueggemann warns, it will be increasingly difficult to make moral discernments about human relationships:

> Undoubtedly covenantal discernments will become more dangerous in times to come as resources shrink, as we grow more fearful, as our

public world continues to disintegrate. And therefore it is very important that we do not lose heart. Everything is at stake.[15]

What will the quality of human relationship be in a postmodern world, where folks are increasingly sterile and isolated from one another? How can we expect religious leaders to combat increasing societal paranoia and to remake patterns of shared life if they do not take up the task of building trustworthy communities at home? What responsibilities might churches, synagogues, and other religious organizations aptly take up to foster trust, encourage basic moral formation, and reach out to those "others" who are our societal neighbors? Dare we dream about a future in which the work of the church in society is encouraging the formation of trustworthy communities? In the future will our churches become places of increasing fragmentation, or will they become communities seeking wider connections?

Connecting Boundaries among the *Laos*

So what's to be done? I have in mind initially three suggestions, actually direction markers or pathways for those who live in close proximity.

First of all, I believe our theologies of ministry need to be at least as foundational (if not more so) as psychological warrants. Psychological boundaries can define what is or is not thought to be appropriate relational behavior. So far so good. Therapy, however, most often involves a relationship between two persons; in ministry more than two are regularly involved. Therapeutic language is not designed to describe relationships in ministry. As a lay person I resent boundary talk that calls or describes me as either a "client" or a "congregant" of a given clergy person. I am a baptized Christian, part of the *laos*, the people of God. The Episcopal Church teaches that in baptism we share "a life in Christ." There are principles in the Anglican pastoral tradition that, as the title of the *Book of Common Prayer* suggests, are "strongly and radically communal."[16] Indeed in the current Outline of the Faith, the church is described as "holy" because its members— assumedly all of us—are consecrated and guided by the Holy Spirit "to do God's work."

Yet when it comes to assessing the character of intimate friendships and sexual relationships between clergy and laity, the clergy are (almost without exception) assumed to be the dominant, if not domineering, partner. The moral responsibility and ethical agency of the lay person alarmingly disappears. This is outright clericalism. There is no moral universe that excludes equitable expression by the common people. We must resist seductive attempts to infantilize laity, to put laity "in their place," a safe, "boundaried" distance away. When we are truly ready to consider guidelines for interpersonal relations, we need to articulate theologies of ministry and of human sexuality that for laity and clergy alike stress integrity and accountability, compassion and commitment, initiative and responsibility.

This will also involve cultivating more adequate and nuanced viewpoints on local power dynamics. A host of questions come to mind about power differentiations among the *laos*. Is there, for example, a marked distinction between partying with established adult parishioners as distinct from eighteen- to twenty-five-year-old students? Is it ever acceptable for priests to befriend the local bishop who has authority "over them"? Or, if orders of ministry are unfailingly hierarchical, does this mean bishops can only be intimate and "collegial" with other bishops? What role at all can friendships play in ministerial relationships? When relationships change their primary character—for example, when a college chaplain takes on a therapeutic role with an individual student—why can't relational expectations be renegotiated? Are former "professional" relationships in ministry always determinative for present-day assessments? Each of us know other pertinent questions about power differentiation that suit our local circumstances.

My plea is that we accomplish this unattended theological "homework" with more critical reflection on power and authority in ministry. This will not be easy work. We will no doubt discover that we often say one thing and do another, and that even among friends, prevailing views of institutionally ordained ministries are quite diverse.

Calling Forth Intimacy with God and One Another

In a pointed, poignant sermon on vocation, English bishop Rowan Williams arrestingly observes: "God cannot reach me if I'm not there."[17] Like feminist psychologist Miriam Greenspan, this Anglican bishop worries about a "nobody home" practice of ministry. Williams describes vocation as a process of discovering the truth about oneself:

> God's call is the call to *be*: the *vocation* of creatures is to exist . . . *as*
> *themselves*, to be bearers of their names, answering to the Word that
> gives each its distinct identity. . . . To exist really is to exist as respond-
> ing-to-God. Each of us is called to be a different kind of response to
> God, to mirror God in unique ways . . . from innumerable new and
> different standpoints.[18]

Clearly, responsive, relational engagement is at the heart of theology, calling forth new commitments to God and one another.

A number of years ago I met regularly with a colleague from another institution in a relationship we came to describe as a "spiritual friendship." Essentially we took turns, like co-counselors, focusing on each other's spiritual growth. We met frequently and regularly alone, early in the mornings. He was an ordained head of an institution; at the time I was a professional church bureaucrat. Our working lives were fraught with complex, at times overlapping, power dynamics. Yet it did not occur to me, nor to him as I later learned, that he had more "power" because of his ordination. There was no "Father Knows Best" attitude, no all-knowing sacramental one-upping of the stakes. Rather we were two explorers, ducking in and out the ecclesial underbrush and momentary clearings in our lives to glimpse God's grace at work as we discovered more about who we were called to *be*. Along the way, we laughed, cried, and comforted one another; we were intimate friends.

Was I his "client" or he mine? Neither was true. Frankly, the whole point of our being in this relationship was to know God. God was the real "employer." Like Rowan Williams, we found the Creator God whose ways we endeavored "to mirror . . . in unique ways." Using client-based language to describe institutionally ordained ministry not only demeans laity, it obscures God's role as *the* major player.

Having made this observation, it is important to return for a moment to the matter of calling forth intimacy in ministry and to the primary question of what ministry is about in the first place. I recently asked a colleague who was concluding almost a decade of challenging parish ministry what she had learned most of all. With profoundly succinct clarity she offered three affirmations:

> The purpose of the Gospel is to call forth intimacy and to redeem power.
>
> The work of the people is the formation of a trustworthy community.
>
> Trust is formed when intimacy is genuine and power is shared.[19]

Words to remember! And words about an intimate, risky business. Surely these affirmations are among the risks at the heart of faithful Christian living. Ministry, as Jackie Schmitt observes,

> is not a contract where we deliver X service at Y cost. It is a relationship of mutuality, responsibility and trust, words which make much more sense to ground us in God's love and forgiveness.[20]

While carrying out responsibilities for prohibiting sexual misconduct in the church, we need to take very real care that we do not short-circuit our primary responsibility for calling forth intimacy with God and one another.

Shared Covenants and Public Pathways

Biblical scholar Walter Brueggemann speaks of Christians as a "what if?" people, a people called and inspired to live in the power of God's impassioned promises *now*. Our Hebrew ancestors had a public description for such a living relationship: they spoke of making a covenant with God. Encouraging the formation of covenanting relationships—rather than prescribing narrow contractual roles—has biblical precedent, baptismal affirmation, and theological integrity. I prefer to envision this task as one of building trustworthy relationships. This would involve shifting the emphasis on power away from focusing primarily on people in their "roles," moving it toward supporting people in their "relationships" with one another and with the One who is the real covenant partner. Not because this is easy. Our most familiar friendships are seldom easy. Rather because true, revealing knowledge about humanity involves knowledge about God.

Reviving the traditional biblical concept of covenant—deeply etched in the loyal loving-kindness of God—holds promise for shaping trustworthy communities amid the brokenness and isolation many experience today. Rasmussen's observation, that society currently lives from moral fragment to moral fragment, is born out in conversations I've shared with so-called "ordinary lay persons" who long for wholeness, for lives that are unifying not shattering. Such work is not easy, given the state of defendedness endemic in society today. Yet this is an ancient as well as a postmodern challenge. Martin Smith once described Israel's prophets as tremendous risk takers—those who dared to disrupt "the normalization of estrangement." Brueggemann observes that even in pastoral care the healthy unit of meaning today is not the autonomous individual, rather it is the person bound in deep covenant with others and with "the prior One."[21] Such healing is in God's nature.

Shaping and traversing faithful relational pathways entails open, public conversations with clergy and laity alike involved. We need not privatize what should intentionally be public, ongoing conversations about shared covenants. One helpful educational resource for opening dialogue in a parish or other church group is a pamphlet by Linda Grenz aptly entitled *A Covenant of Trust.*[22] Scriptural conversations could easily precede or flow from this starting place. Tough, risky, even uncomfortable theological questions should be expected and pursued thoughtfully. Such familiar theological concepts as neighborliness, reconciliation of differences, and even forgiveness might be explored. Historical, theological, and local resources would be part of the conversation. Finally, we might also expect and look for positive boundaries, public pathways truly connecting us to one another. Such conversations might even deepen existing friendships, foster trust, and encourage enduring relationships.

Who knows, one day like our ancestors we might end up walking the parish "bounds" together, traversing well-worn common pathways and praising God along the way.

Notes

1. This essay is based on a earlier essay, "Pacing the Boundaries: An Exploration of Ministry, Sexuality and Power," published in *Plumbline: A Journal of Ministry in Higher Education* 22, no. 4 (March 1995): 13–18, 25. I am indebted to *Plumbline* edi-

tor Jacqueline Schmitt, whose additional insight and advice informs this essay.

2. See my *Courageous Incarnation: In Intimacy, Work, Childhood, and Aging* (Cambridge, Mass.: Cowley Publications, 1993).

3. Marie M. Fortune, "Therapy and Intimacy: Confused About Boundaries," *Christian Century* (18–25 May 1994): 524.

4. See her essay "On Professionalism," in Carter Heyward, *When Boundaries Betray Us* (San Francisco: Harper, 1993), 204.

5. Fortune, "Therapy and Intimacy," 525.

6. Research by S. M. Jouard cited in Carolyn Headley, *The Laying On of Hands in the Parish Healing Ministry* (Nottingham: Grove Books Ltd., 1988), 15.

7. See the accessible modern edition by John N. Wall Jr., *George Herbert: The Country Parson, The Temple* (New York: Paulist Press, 1981), 56, 66, 87. Herbert's dates are 1593–1633; *The Country Parson* was published posthumously in 1652.

8. See Richard Hooker, *Lawes of Ecclesiastical Polity*, V.78.3.

9. Douglas, *The Feminization of American Culture* (New York: Alfred A. Knopf, 1978), 7; see also 8–13. I am indebted to Jacqueline Schmitt for reminding me of this critical study.

10. See especially, *The Future Shape of Ministry* (New York: Seabury, 1971), 90–1, 98–9.

11. Verna J. Dozier, *The Dream of God, A Call to Return* (Cambridge, Mass.: Cowley Publications, 1991), 139.

12. Cited in Heyward, *When Boundaries Betray Us*, 201.

13. See *Race Matters* (Boston: Beacon Press, 1993).

14. Larry Rasmussen, *Moral Fragments and Moral Community* (Minneapolis: Fortress Press, 1993), 11.

15. *A Social Reading of the Old Testament: Prophetic Approaches to Israel's Communal Life*, ed. Patrick D. Miller (Minneapolis: Fortress Press, 1994), 53.

16. Roger Lloyd, quoted by O. C. Edwards Jr., "The Anglican Pastoral Tradition," in *The Study of Anglicanism*, ed. Stephen Sykes and John Booty (London and Philadelphia: SPCK/Fortress Press, 1988), 344.

17. Rowan Williams, *A Ray of Darkness* (Cambridge, Mass.: Cowley Publications, 1994), 150.

18. Ibid., 149–50.

19. From a June 1995 conversation with the Rev. Deborah (Dee) Woodward.

20. *Plumbline* 22, no. 4 (March 1995): 2.

21. *Interpretation and Obedience: From Faithful Reading to Faithful Living* (Minneapolis: Fortress Press: 1991), 165.

22. *A Covenant of Trust* (Cincinnati: Forward Movement Publications, 1994); this is a short, accessible and inexpensive pamphlet.

3 | Race and Gender Oppression Can Really Get in the Way

Ethical Concerns in the Counseling of African American Women

Traci C. West

In this essay I explore some of the ethical problems posed by the presence of blurred "boundaries" in professional one-on-one counseling relationships. I challenge the notion that "interpersonal" boundaries in the counseling relationship must necessarily be defined as an individualized, private interaction between two people that is beyond the realm of politics. It is my presupposition that the significant ethical questions about "boundaries" in this relationship are not comprehensively addressed without consideration of sociopolitical realities such as race and race consciousness. When developing ethical guidelines about conflicting or merging "personal needs" (e.g., for friendship or sexual gratification) of the persons involved in the counseling relationship, we must recognize that race constitutes a critical "boundary" issue that exists both prior to the negotiation of these "intimate" issues and in the midst of them. The dynamics of race are always inscribed in the counseling relationship. Even when there are only whites in the room, the privilege of whiteness saturates the interaction. Even when there are only blacks in the room, the subjugated status of blacks infiltrates the discourse. In the intimate, personal, private-sphere dialogue of the counseling setting, race matters—it occludes, distances, bonds, politicizes.

THERE ARE AN array of interwoven, subjugating race and gender barriers that must be negotiated when African American women seek out professional counseling for emotional and spiritual support. In response to a particular crisis such as some form of male violence (e.g., rape, incest, or battering), black women may reach out to clergy or a psychotherapist for help. An ethical analysis of the relationship that forms between a professional counselor and a black woman victim/survivor of male violence requires attention to the distortions of race/gender oppression that infuse and invade the dynamics of that relationship. The potent and relentless presence of sociopolitical realities must be given attention when defining ethical practices for these therapeutic relationships.

We need to identify and unravel boundaries created and maintained by the sociopolitical subjugation of women[1] victim/survivors. Distorting social ideologies about black women's "hardened" femininity, sexual promiscuity, or indefatigable resilience help to nurture violence against them by invalidating their victimization. Deciphering this process of invalidation illumines some of the devaluing moral judgments and assumptions related to black women's social status that can easily influence the interactions between these victim/survivors and their counselors. The distorting ideologies help to diminish black women's social status and attenuate their moral claims about the harmful impact of male violence. Therefore, it is crucial to acknowledge and expose the presence of the "public" (as manifested by distorting social ideologies) in the midst of the "private" dialogues of counseling sessions. Acknowledging these intertwined dynamics helps to more adequately address the reality of the crises that women face and increases the possibility of bringing about meaningful change for them. An exclusively "privatized" approach to the crisis situation that the women face will fail to address the joint personal and political dimensions of it.

My discussion of combined race and gender social cues that help to shape the counseling process is centered on the effects for the victim/survivor (rather than the counselor).[2] The awakening of my consciousness about these issues stems from some of my personal experiences of counseling women about male violence while serving as a parish minister, and later, a campus minister. However, the analysis offered here is primarily based on my research on the psychosocial consequences of violence against black women. This discussion will focus on interrelated aspects of women's victimization by sociopolitical exploitation and male perpetrators of violence that have implications for their therapeutic work with a counselor.

Avoiding Frozen Identity Categories

Now, in this exploration, I, like the black women victim/survivors that I refer to, seek to avoid the constraining, objectifying misinterpretations that frequently prevail when the issue of race is addressed or apparent.[3] For instance, I eschew any assumption that my naming of race/gender issues as intrinsic to the dynamics of counseling with black women constitutes an exhaustive description of all the issues that can arise in this context. The range of concerns that may be present and relevant to the violence a woman has suffered clearly encompasses therapeutic needs and aspects of her identity that cannot be captured solely in terms of race and gender. Also, my inclusion of the salience of racial oppression in this analysis does not indicate my concurrence with the racist supposition that "race is a black woman's problem." On the contrary, although it is not my focus here, it is my strong conviction that race/gender dynamics crucially inform the intimate violence experiences of all women (yes, white women too!).

Moreover, any notion of deriving a "representative" black woman's experience of counseling from the issues raised in this discussion must also be jettisoned. Such categorizing of black women in reified, monolithic terms solidifies social distortions that violate the personhood of women and eliminate possibilities for useful insights into the counseling process. Instead, I maintain that the exchanges between the victim/survivor and her counselor have rich variations and unique complexities that reflect the divergent emotional and spiritual struggles and resources that she brings to that process.

The interwoven nature of individual and cultural mitigating factors within the counseling process is underscored in the work of psychologist Beverly Greene. She outlines several forms that internalized racism and sexism may assume in the psychosocial adjustment of black women. Greene explains the varieties of stress and psychic conflict that may be culturally induced by demeaning race/gender stereotypes and circumscriptions about skin color and body size and shape. Yet, when urging her audience of therapists (who may be engaged in psychotherapeutically treating black women) to be aware of these realities, she also cautions them to be cognizant of black women's individuality. She writes: "Although black persons share many group characteristics, an individual black woman will attempt to cope with racial life stressors with the same characterological and defensive structures used to respond to the other life stressors."[4] In the counseling process, the centrality of destructive psychosocial impacts from heterosexist, sexist, and racist norms of the society upon victim/survivors must be accounted for without assigning a singular group response to these cultural assaults. Mindful of such cautions about overgeneralizing, let us consider specific manifestations of race/gender issues that can impact victim/survivors of male violence in the counseling process.

The Right to Be Perceived as a Victim

The appraisal of a woman's victim status is often a core issue that affects the counseling process in situations of abuse, and it is one with considerable race/gender implications. Usually women have a desperate need for validation of the abuse they have received and the suffering it has caused them. There can be many reasons for this need for confirmation. For example, because of a multitude of sexist social cues, women often struggle with self-blame. They may question their own behavior and wonder if they "asked for it," subliminally "wanted it," or deserved it. In some circumstances of male-perpetrated intimate violence—such as date rape, marital rape, incest, or battering—women may even doubt their perception that an "authentic" assault even occurred. This is particularly true when victim/survivors receive repeated messages from their male abusers, buttressed by depictions in popular culture, to contradict their own perceptions of having been violently victimized. Often, distorted characterizations in popular media label the kind of abusive behavior the women have experienced as "playful," "loving," or "erotic." Whether in the form of encouraging self-blame or denial, women have to contend with insidious and persistent cultural taunts that undermine their own judgments about abuse in their lives. Thus, the pursuit of a counseling relationship usually encompasses a crucial inquiry by the victim/survivor about the legitimacy of her victim status.

A woman's concern about her victimization by a male abuser and its damaging effects on the quality of her life and/or her children's lives can serve as the catalyst for her initiation of contact with a pastor or therapist. In other instances, a woman may initially present an issue such as depression to her counselor and the disclosure or recognition of her victimization from male violence will surface later in the relationship. Within the encounter with the counselor, the extent to which the wrongfulness of the abuse is affirmed or minimized usually becomes a major indicia of the potential for trust in this counseling relationship. Obviously, minimal trust is spawned by counselors who treat the woman's experience of violence with skepticism or as trivial. The extent to which the woman's victimization is validated in the counseling process not only impacts the development of trustful dialogue between them, it also confers or denies the moral worth of her claims, and by implication, of her humanity. When the reality or seriousness of the woman's assault is doubted, the truth of her testimony is impugned and the moral significance of the violent incidents that she has endured is diminished. The counseling process helps to offer a moral gauge for the victim/survivor, giving evidence of whether or not it matters that she was violated.

It is from both the woman's self-perceptions and the counselor's reactions that the characterization of the woman's victimization and the level of trust is generated. The process is analogous to the "call and response" tradition of sermon preaching. When a woman presents an incident of male violence, the counselor responds to her interpretation of the situation. The victim/survivor reacts to the definition of the incident inferred or stated by the counselor. The trust level and the moral assessment are derived from their interaction with one another.

In the dynamics of their encounter, the ability to perceive a black woman's victimization from intimate violence is entangled with how her victim status is culturally defined. The manner in which a woman's race/gender subjugation is assessed or accounted for is a key factor in her encounter with her counselor.[5] We must remember that to some degree the broader society is "in the room" with the two of them. A variety of cultural cues about race and gender that have been internalized by the victim/survivor and the counselor are present in their exchange and may circumvent some of the healing potential in their relationship. Although many powerful resources exist in the varied communal legacies of black women that may enable the counseling process, there are also resilient cultural influences that hinder validation of women's victimization.

For instance, in their study of the consequences of rape, incest, and sexual harassment, Kathryn Quina and Nancy Carlson summarize troubling cultural notions about black women that range from the charge of wanton promiscuity to the enduring label of tough superwoman. The researchers point out that these stereotypes have led to damaging and incorrect assumptions about black sexual abuse victims: that they are not as affected by trauma as whites; that they do not need counseling or emotional help; and that they are more difficult to help.[6] These biases diminish the capacity to envision black women as authentic victims. Cultural messages about women's inherent "toughness" negate their need for help as well as their worthiness to receive it.

Rigid assumptions about a black woman's innate capacity for perseverance and endurance can also erode her self-perceptions of her own victimization and consequent emotional neediness. Incest victim/survivor and battered women's shelter worker Anna Carlson strongly advocated the need for black women victim/survivors to have space to experience vulnerability. She commented: "We're so used to being strong . . . there's just no room for 'I'm sad and I need to cry.'"[7] There is no cultural space for a sad, weak, crying black woman.

Furthermore, when seeking help from a clergy person within the black community, intragroup perceptions of black women as domineering and socially advantaged over black men may inhibit validation of the woman's claims of being victimized by black male abuse. This view of women is reinforced by a wide range of sources from academic to "pop" cultural literature. Afrocentric social scientist William Oliver explains that structural barriers of white racism and institutionalized patterns of discrimination place black males at a greater disadvantage than black females for successfully fulfilling their respective "traditional roles."[8] Black males are displaced from successful fulfillment of manhood because a high rate of unemployment among the men denies them the esteem by which males are valued in our society. Black females are able to fulfill their traditional role expectations because they are able to have a child and care for that child. He posits this social disadvantaging of black men as a contributing factor to domestic violence. Because of their supposed social advantage within a social order that is perceived as disadvantaging the black male, black women are implicated in the violence perpetrated against them. The women are participants in the perpetuation of the violence (even if unwittingly). In addition, the immoral treatment of women is made to seem rational because of men's social disenfranchisement.

Shahrazad Ali offers a similar line of thinking in a more pointed and didactic tone. Ali is a flamboyant and sensationalist black female popular author who directly chides women for their lack of submissive behavior toward their male partners. She approves of limited forms of violent "disciplining" of women by their male partners. Ali further contends that in order to understand the problems that black men face—such as unemployment, lack of political clout, or poor education—black women need to look internally at themselves to discover what "helps keep the Black man down."[9] Here, black women are urged to take responsibility for unjust conditions in the sociopolitical plight of black men and to offer their submissiveness to their men as a helpful response to the inequities that the men endure. Whether in the guise of social scientific fact or "pop" rhetoric, there are strong intragroup cultural biases that preclude the recognition of black women as genuine victims of violent behavior by black men. Instead, this perspective invokes suspicion and blatant castigation of the women as blameworthy and effaces perception of the wrong that they have suffered.

The vicious presence of racism in the lives of black male perpetrators may indeed affect black women victim/survivors and deplete their ability to give primary focus to their own victimization. Evelyn White, an author/advocate for black women's health care, argues that black women's awareness of the systematic oppression of black men through lynchings, imprisonment, unemployment, and the ever prevalent "rape" charge causes women to feel obligated to be understanding and forgiving of black men. Thus, according to White, women are compelled to endure domestic violence in the name of compassion, religion, or "strong, black womanhood."[10] A sacrificial role is demanded of black women because of the racist oppression suffered by black men. Black male subjugation by whites is considered what is most primary, what is most brutalizing.

Anna Carlson, an incest survivor who works as a staff person at a battered women's shelter, summarized the erasure of black women victim/survivors with the comment "One thing that is unfortunate for a lot of black women, like myself, [is that] it's hard to get validation of our experience [of abuse] because we always have to jump to protect the black man, which is not the black man's fault, or our own fault, but has to do with living in racist America."[11] The needs and suffering of black women victim/survivors are thought to be expendable and subordinate to the protection of "our" men. Because we are living under the conditions of white domination, the brutalization of women can be seen as less morally significant. For a woman to fail to acquiesce to this formulation may seem like too egregious a betrayal of her racial group as well as of her intimate relationship with her male abuser.

In the quest for validation of their status as victims of violence, women confront a collection of barriers that may infect the counseling process. Social ideologies that erode black women's right to be blameless, vulnerable, legitimate sufferers must in some way be acknowledged and refuted. For when these subtexts are left intact, they serve as impenetrable barriers that stymie the process of even the naming of the assault and its damaging consequences.

Maintaining the Social Context of Women's Lives as Relevant

The capacity to recognize black women as "authentic" victims of male violence is only an initial step for an effective therapeutic response. Intimate violence by a male perpetrator cannot be adequately understood or addressed when isolated from other forms of social exploitation that buttress male violence in the violation of the minds, bodies, and spirits of women. If the debilitating social dimensions of the violation are neglected and intimate violence is discussed in a counseling setting as a narrowly cordoned off "personal problem," meaningful insight into the dynamics of the trauma that the women face is obstructed.

Devaluations of black women that are embedded in white supremacist ideologies and propagated in the broader culture simultaneously obscure, compound, and participate in the victimization of women. The repeated identification of all poor black women as "lazy welfare cheats" serves as an example of a race/gender stereotype that can have a highly destructive impact on black women victim/survivors of male violence.

Fears about falling into race/gender stereotypes can help to influence women to remain in dangerous situations, subordinating their own safety and well-being. This fear is dramatically illustrated by one survivor of domestic violence who was interviewed by feminist antidomestic-violence author/advocate Ann Jones. This victim/survivor commented on how she tried to avoid falling into "the white folks stereotype" of a black family that she said consists of "mama on welfare and a bunch of delinquent fatherless children," so she "put up with violence all of those years trying not to be the welfare mother white folks hate, and then those same white folks had the nerve to turn around and tell me I should've left my husband and applied for welfare."[12] In this statement, the woman is making an appeal for the appreciation of the social assault upon her worth and dignity that she must confront. The lens of white racist assumptions colludes with the assaults of her male batterer, dominating her self-perceptions and limiting her options for agency. It functions as a sanctioner of her abuse that eclipses attention to her victimization from the male violence.

Another rape victim/survivor makes a similar statement that attests to the multifaceted dilemma that many black women face. She describes her frustration with her therapist, who seemingly failed to understand the primacy of her financial crisis.

> It seemed like all she was concerned about was the fact that I got raped. Hell! I know that was important, but that bastard got my last twentyfive dollars. That was all the money I had, till payday. I can deal with the rape later, but I won't have a job if I can't get back and forth to work.[13]

The crisis of violence that victim/survivors such as this woman face is made up of competing needs. It is not only the intimate violation, but also the injurious assault of socioeconomic deprivation that deserves recognition and demands redress with commitment and action. These women's testimonies pointedly demonstrate that an approach to the crime of intimate violence that attempts to rip it out of the broader social context of women's lives will result in misguided and inadequate responses. Perhaps for these women, the damaging effect of intimate violence is relegated to lesser importance, in part because the link between social and intimate violence is ignored by the responses that they are given.

Claiming Both Women's Victim-Status and Agency

In the current political climate, where conservatives are the dominant voice in almost every sphere of public policy, I realize that my emphasis on the need to clear the way for the recognition and claiming of victim-status by women who have endured male violence can easily be dismissed by liberals and conservatives alike as encouraging black women to "whine about being victims" at a time when no one wants to hear it. (But who can predict a time period when there will be broad-based public receptivity to their claims of victimization?) Besides panderings to mean-spirited and reactionary political expediency, there is too often an uncritical acceptance of the view that victimhood and agency represent diametric opposites. Moreover, even many feminist antiviolence advocates reject the use of the term "victim" as a demeaning label for those who have suffered violent assaults and insist on replacing it with the term "survivor" because it connotes agency and empowerment.

The rigid dichotomizing of victim (or survivor) versus agent is an unfortunate and misleading distinction for women who have experienced intimate violence in their lives. As feminist legal theorist Martha Mahoney points out, the use of such dichotomy rests upon the separation of the act of physical violence from its context of broader patterns of social power and from other issues related to the complexity of needs and struggles in a woman's life.[14] She documents the way that pitting notions of victimization against those of agency nurtures false presuppositions, for this division holds the problematic assumption that it is possible for a woman to isolate the specificity of male violence in her life and then choose to respond to it in one of two ways, depending on the strength of her character or her psychological health.

As Mahoney points out, the ideas of victimization and agency are inaccurately placed in polar opposition to each other, based on their restrictive social constructions.

In our society, agency and victimization are each known by the absence of the other: you are an agent if you are not a victim, and you are a victim if you are in no way an agent. In this concept, agency does not mean acting for oneself under the conditions of oppression; it means *being without oppression*, either having ended oppression or never having experienced it all.[15]

Within this logic, black women's agency is clearly imperceptible. Any acts of resistance by black women victim/survivors to the violence against them will always involve "acting for oneself under the conditions of oppression." Under the existing conditions of white supremacy and male dominance some degree of victim status is constant for African American women.

When the imposition of a strict victim-agency duality is accepted, victim status is conflated with powerlessness, which, of course, effaces resistant acts. Likewise, victimization usually denotes shame because it is understood as the absence of agency. To deter this process of erasure and shaming, and to more adequately capture the intricate fabric of women's realities, African American victim/survivors must be seen as occupying both the stance of victim and agent. In this stance, both aspects should be understood as alternating and overlapping dynamics.

Including Social Change as an Integral Part of Women's Healing

A therapeutic, healing response to black women victim/survivors must include community support and political action. Since the violence that has caused the injury to women is decidedly linked to community norms and sanctions, an appropriate healing response must be also. I am not suggesting that private, individual time for one-on-one dialogue with a pastor or therapist be eliminated. Rather, as I have argued, such a process must acknowledge the ways that the community is "in the room." Further, the one-on-one process needs to be augmented with specific forms of communal healing that help to enact social change to end oppression and violence against women.

Women need to be offered the opportunity to experience forms of communal caring and nurturing that represent alternatives to the devaluing, silencing, and assaultive ones that have violated them in the past and continue to do so in the present. Validation and support that explicitly addresses the race/gender subjugation that is threaded through the totality of a woman's life must be incorporated into this process. Given the political climate confronting black women victim/survivors, male violence can never be adequately addressed when isolated as a personal wound with individualistic origins and consequences. We must remember that male violence is a socially reproduced process that is bonded with other culturally subjugating practices that devalue and discount African American women. Whether this communal experience takes place in a group counseling setting, a church women's group, or some other supportive group context, it must attend to these social/cultural dimensions to effectually oppose the evil of male violence.

Political change is imperative in order to seriously address the race/gender oppression that informs and helps perpetuate the intimate violence that women face. Political resistance that publicly challenges the policies and ideologies that conspire against women's safety and well-being should be part of therapeutic work with victim/survivors. A component of the work ought to include the affirmation and encouragement of participation in concrete political acts of resistance to the interlocking hegemonic constraints that daily threaten the survival and dignity of black women. These acts could include support for women's empowerment and entitlement in the arenas of housing, employment, education, or religion. The participation in social change that I envision here involves not only the victim/survivor's individual acts of defiance, but also the joint activities of her and her counselor, and collective action by her support group(s). The embracing of political involvement helps to honor the capacity for agency in victim/survivors and neutralize the culturally induced shame attached to their victimization. When therapeutic counseling is restructured and broadened in this manner, women's engagement in the shaping of moral discourse in our culture becomes an institutionalized part of their healing process. Women identify systemic perpetrators of the violence, hold institutional resources accountable, and decrease their isolation by developing networks with those in solidarity with them.

The counseling process must affirm the tremendous moral significance of every aspect of the assault on the humanity of black women victim/survivors. As the recognition of women's victimization is fostered alongside other healing responses, the process must not respect false demarcations that divide political from personal origins and impacts of women's violation. The process also has to allow room to incorporate a woman's complex stance as simultaneously victim and resister of the violence. Finally, a compelling and comprehensive healing process creatively nurtures direct engagement in justice struggles to thwart white supremacist and misogynist evils that reproduce violence against black women in our culture.

Notes

1. Since this article is centered on the experiences of African American women, when I refer to "women" it should be assumed that I am referring to African American women. However, I am aware that many of the concerns of victim/survivors of male violence that are discussed here certainly may be relevant to women of other racial/ethnic groups. My alternating usage of the terms "women," "black women," and "African American women" offers the reader an opportunity to understand the experiences of black women as appropriate and significant conveyers of the experiences of all women.

2. For clinical discussions that provide an emphasis on the role of the therapist, *see* Lillian Comas-Diaz and E. E. Griffith, eds., *Clinical Guidelines in Cross-Cultural Mental Health* (New York: Wiley, 1988); Elaine Pinderhughes, *Understanding Race, Ethnicity, and Power: The Key to Efficacy in Clinical Practice* (New York: Free Press, 1989).

3. *See* Alexander Thomas and Samuel Sillen, *Racism and Psychiatry*, (New York: Citadel Press, 1972), especially p. 48 ff. For a discussion of the ways in which race issues are *neglected* and subordinated to gender issues in mental health literature

that refers to women of color, *see* Beverly Greene, "Diversity and Difference: The Issue of Race in Feminist Therapy," in *Women in Context: Toward a Feminist Reconstruction of Psychotherapy*, ed. M. P. Mirkin (New York: Guilford Press, 1994).

4. Beverly Greene, "Still Here: A Perspective on Psychotherapy with African-American Women," in *New Directions in Feminist Psychology: Practice, Theory, and Research*, ed. Joan Chrisler and Doris Howard (New York: Springer Publishing Co., 1992), 22.

5. *See* Jean Lau Chin, "Pychodynamic Approaches," in *Women of Color: Integrating Ethnic and Gender Identities in Psychotherapy*, ed. Lillian Comas-Diaz and Beverly Greene (New York: Guilford Press, 1994); Nancy Boyd-Franklin, *Black Families in Therapy: A Multi-Systems Approach* (New York: Guilford Press, 1989).

6. Quina and Carlson, *Rape, Incest, and Sexual Harassment: A Guide for Helping Survivors* (New York: Greenwood Press, 1989), 208.

7. Anna Carlson [pseud.], Interview by author, April 1994.

8. William Oliver "Sexual Conquest and Patterns of Black-on-Black Violence: A Structural-Cultural Perspective," in *Violence and Victims* 4, no. 4 (1989).

9. Shahrazad Ali, *The Blackman's Guide to Understanding the Blackwoman* (Philadelphia: Civilized Publications, 1989), 47.

10. Evelyn White, *Chain, Chain, Change: For Black Women Dealing with Physical and Emotional Abuse* (Seattle: Seal Press, 1985), 12.

11. Anna Carlson [pseud.], interviewed by the author, Boston, Massachusetts, 22 April 1994.

12. Ann Jones, *Next Time, She'll Be Dead* (Boston: Beacon Press, 1994), 127.

13. A black woman rape victim, 1985, quoted in Julia Boyd, "Ethnic and Cultural Diversity: Keys to Power," in *Diversity and Complexity in Feminist Therapy*, ed. Laura S. Brown and Maria P. P. Root (New York: Harrington Press, 1990), 156.

14. Martha Mahoney, "Victimization or Oppression? Women's Lives, Violence, and Agency," in *The Public Nature of Private Violence: The Discovery of Domestic Abuse*, ed. Martha A. Fieneman and Roxanne Mykitiuk (New York: Routledge, 1994), 60.

15. Ibid., 64.

4 Exploring Embodiment

Leng Leroy Lim

THIS ESSAY IS about how the many embodied dimensions of who we are—race, culture, religious life, sexuality, body, and personal history—are connected to the sacred realm. By "sacred" I do not mean simply what is overtly religious or spiritual, but that source, perceived as either coming from within us or outside us, which brings us inspiration, insight, connection, change, and passions.[1] Thus, we might have a new idea (calling this "inspiration") or find ourselves drawn inexplicably to someone (calling this "love"). The presence of the sacred is overwhelming, and we often either avoid it, pursue it, worship it, hang on to it, or think we are going to die without/with it. We cannot control it, though we hope to, and thus we commonly call this an experience of "God." American teenagers understand that this sacred power is to be found outside overt religious institutions and doctrines when they call someone who is really good at something a "math goddess" or an "athletic god." The exclamation "Oh my God" in moments of sexual ecstasy, circumstantial surprise, or pain, or beauty is accurate: the sacred, profoundly deep and uncontrollable, is being encountered, and we don't know what to do! A sense of helplessness accompanies our encounter with the sacred, and, depending on our cultural tools and personal histories, we may experience anything from joy to rage to fear to comfort. Human beings have always needed to find some way of managing the sacred—if only not to feel so helpless: taboos to govern sexuality, liturgies to regulate religious experiences, even rules of civility to mediate the raw power found in human encounters.[2] What we now call personal boundaries flow from the latter.

This essay seeks to explore the particularly American cultural norms that inform the ethics, politics, and theologies we have formulated to work with interpersonal boundaries and sacred experience. What I am about to say is not provable nor conclusive in any way that benefits from the comforting rigor of Western epistemology. In fact, the comfort and power of Western epistemological rigor are that an insight, once certified as objective truth, can then be generalized, made predictive, and hence useful. Failure to meet such instrumental standards renders the truth-telling of a subjective experience inconsequential, idiosyncratic, and worthless. Admittedly, such an objective method has its place (say in the building of sewage pipes), but is not the project at hand (of helping me/us become more whole.)

Instead, what I am offering is resonance through storytelling. The Confucian scholar Tu Wei Ming says that the human being is a poetic person, and like the separate strings on a musical instrument, which vibrate when one string is struck, we too resonate with each other.[3] This resonance/dissonance is a quality of our intersubjectivity as human beings. Now, to resonate (or dissonate) with a story does not mean a suspension of critical interrogation, but it means that the critical gaze is directed not toward the story itself, but to questioning one's own experience of the dissonance and/or resonance. Why are *you reacting* in your particular way to my story and its conclusions? In the *reaction* itself lies the deeper inquiry.

Boundaries Are Culturally Defined

As an ethnic Chinese boy growing up in Singapore, I shared my sleeping space with my parents until I was six or so. Throughout my teenage years, I shared a room with my maternal uncle and grandmother. It was only when I was 20 years old that I had my own room—after they had passed away. Watching American television as a child in Singapore, I became aware that American kids had a different experience of space than mine. They had their own rooms, and their parents knocked on their bedroom doors before entering. I wanted this same right of privacy, and thought that if I were to get it for myself, I would have to offer it to my grandmother first. I tried knocking on our door before entering. She replied with chagrin that "we are our own people [*gah-gi-eh-lang* in Hokkien, i.e., 'family'], why knock on the door as if we are strangers?" "Well, what if you are changing?" "Then the door will be locked. If it is unlocked, you just come in. Don't knock," she reprimanded me.

I tell this story to illustrate how privacy and other connected issues like private space, interpersonal boundaries, and private property are ultimately culturally informed concepts and practices. "Private" has a virtuous connotation in the West. However, no matter how well one tries to translate "private" into Chinese, it always has a selfish edge to it. (Of course we in the West have also forgotten that in the Latin, "private" is connected to "deprive.") The American request to "leave us in private" is entirely proper, but in East Asia, such an explicit delineation of boundaries is tantamount to hostility and inhospitality.

In the West, we accept the moral validity of *the private*. Certainly our capitalist economic way of life would not exist if we did not have private property. Whatever our feelings about capitalism might be, the development of private property during the advent of the Industrial Revolution in England was emancipatory. An ordinary (i.e., nonaristocratic) individual could own his own land apart from the nobility and village. Into this property were invested all the private energies and initiatives of the *individual* entrepreneur, and from it he accrued all of its products to himself.

Nevertheless, the light of enterprise lit by the industrialist with his private property cast a shadow. In this shadow were hidden all the justifications and rationalizations of greed, labor exploitation, dangerous working conditions, and pollution. There is a saying that every candle casts a shadow, and the brighter the light the stronger the shadow. Cultural artifacts (as concepts, practices, inventions) cast a strong light, and thus a shadow. In discussing interpersonal boundaries as a culturally defined concept, I want to focus on the particularly American cultural meanings and ideas that undergird and motivate this cultural norm, so that we might find out what hides in the shadows cast by this cultural light.

Let me say first that I fully support the light/insight shed by the rhetoric and ethics of boundaries, especially in the area of our sexual and relational lives. For example, it is inappropriate for a clergy person to be in a sexual relationship with someone for whom he or she has pastoral responsibilities. The list establishing boundaries goes on, and it is not my intention to analyze each of them here. My investigation into the shadows cast by the light of boundaries is not meant to undermine the good that has been done, but to focus attention on what is lacking/lurking in the shadows, and why.

The American-ness of Boundaries

What are the historical American cultural assumptions and practices surrounding the use and understanding of boundaries?

First, this great and beautiful land was carved into private pieces by the European immigrants who settled here. Treaties established boundaries between American Indian territory and European settlement territory. These boundaries, however, were consistently violated by the U.S. government, especially when it suited the commercial and political interests of the white majority. To put it differently, white boundaries, meant to keep whites safe from "the savages," had to be constantly expanded, and the expansion was justified on religious, political, and commercial grounds. Later, and extending to the present, boundaries became more rigid around Indian territory (i.e., reservations), but not out of any respect for American Indians. These so-called "good" boundaries preserved and quarantined the poverty and disease present on many reservations. Why spend federal money on Indian reservations when America must after all "honor" their status as separate nations?

Second, America has consistently been well protected: two oceans and two friendly, if not quiescent, countries make up its borders; no foreign army has trampled its shores—Pearl Harbor and the Civil War notwithstanding. Compared to many countries with vulnerable borders or histories of invasion, America has safe borders/boundaries. Yet America has consistently felt itself threatened by faraway places, be they Vietnam, Angola, Iraq, or Nicaragua. This implies that America's ideological boundaries extend far beyond its geographical ones, and thus differences elsewhere on the globe must be perceived as inevitable violations of America's boundaries. The containment policy of the Cold War era drew a line around the globe to check communist expansion, and in the process, America rode roughshod over other people's territories and lives. (To be accurate, the Soviet threat was real, especially when missiles were pointed this way, but the way in which other countries and people from Mozambique to Martin Luther King Jr. were implicated was fantasy.) In the post–Cold War era, when America's ideological boundaries have been most secure, it still perceives threats coming from a variety of quarters, from Muslims to gays. It often seems that there is ultimately no boundary that can be secured for the United States to feel safe. (Although the verdict is not yet out, the Oklahoma bombing, as it now stands, suggests that American dangers are not found primarily in the nightmares of shadowy Muslim figures, but in the blinding light shed by its conservative white sons, of which the Limbaughs and Buchanans of the world are the cultural choreographers.) Prior to the phase of American interventionism, America was isolationist, drawing boundaries that shut out the world. American political culture has thus oscillated between violating other people's boundaries and shutting them out.

What does all this mean for those of us struggling with abusive relationships, erotic boundaries, and a just ethic for our common lives? It means that we must seriously wonder if we in America can trust so wholeheartedly the operative logic and metaphor provided by boundaries. We are now much more conscious of violating and molesting touch, but the response is to promote nontouch. This has its antecedent in the American Indian question, where invasion and isolation are the ways white American culture has deployed boundaries.

Boundaries draw their logic from geopolitics; the setting of boundaries implies a zero-sum game, where the extension of one person's space must necessarily be at someone else's expense. Furthermore, the dominant culture equates American safety with American invincibility.[4] Ronald Reagan's Star Wars is a good example of how the will to be safe also became the fantasy of invincibility. Mimicking the military, psychology and religion obey the same cultural principle that time and appropriate technology/psychotherapy/theology will keep us safe from all attacks.

Healing for those of us who have been victimized or oppressed becomes doubly difficult when our American understanding of boundaries is about isolation, violation, and invincibility. If we confuse safety with invincibility, then we shall often feel victimized. The mere presence of the Other (say a white person who makes a racial—though not necessarily racist—remark), must then feel like an invasion or a guerrilla attack. Consequently, vigilance is always required, consuming precious nervous energy. Politically correct language is another instance, for while it raised the consciousness of people to how words can hurt, it inevitably created an illusion that a person with sanitized language was also trustworthy.

Let me be clear. I am not suggesting that people who have been oppressed should feel guilty about establishing boundaries and demanding that they be respected and honored. The elimination of sexist, racist, or homophobic remarks and practices does not, contrary to current whining, reversely oppress men, whites, or heterosexuals. I am only suggesting that those of us working for liberation—especially those of us who have been hurt—understand the cultural imperatives and blindness of our American-ness.

What then is the underlying American cultural paradigm that rationalizes invasion, promotes isolation, idolizes invincibility, and generally keeps many of us in double binds? It is the American cult of autonomy. Autonomy has allowed white settlers to break treaties with Indians, fathers to do as they would with their children, clergy with their parishioners, men with their wives, rich with the poor, whites with blacks. Even apart from these relationships of power inequality, the American feels invaded if you visit without calling, or have a body space of less than three-feet because you curb his or her freedom/autonomy.

If those of us who have been at the short end of the stick demand and fight for our integrity on the grounds that we similarly have the right to autonomy, then we inherit all the shadows of autonomy. For autonomy masquerading as freedom has created the fantasy that we can happily live isolated, disconnected, uncaring, independent, willful, and unperturbed lives. The task at hand is to find ways to have integrity and personal agency without falling into the trap of autonomy.

The Christian tradition, of which I am a part, says that human liberation and satisfaction come about only when we are in relationship with God, other humans, other creatures, and the many facets of the self. To be in the Body of Christ means that I choose to act and behave in certain ways because I am bound to you in deep and varied ways. This choice to connect implies personal agency, while my very connection to you mitigates against autonomy.

If choosing to connect is the antidote to the paradigm of autonomy, then what are some of the challenges? The making of connections touches on the realm of the sacred and necessarily brings about feelings of tender love and consuming jealousy, bliss and insecurity, ecstacy and pain, generosity and hostility, anger and kindness, and every feeling and impulse in between. Intimate and erotic relationships are particularly fraught with these complicating feelings, *and so are our religious/spiritual relationship because sexuality and religion are touched by the sacred realm.*

One way to chart a course in our intimate relationships is to be found by unpackaging the way we (Americans) have worked with our religious experiences. I am aware there are many religions being practiced in America, and some people are not religious at all. Nevertheless, it is not untrue to say that this country has been shaped, if not in reality then in perception, by Christian cultural myths and images, however positive or negative. I want to address this American-Christian dimension of sacred experience.

Sacred Experience

As a young teenager in Singapore, I converted to Christianity after reading a tract that a teacher had given me. Later, I made what evangelicals call a public witness by going forward during the altar call at a Gospel rally. All of this was very emotional for me. I was a lonely only child from a single-parent family, and Jesus became my best friend. The love of God I heard preached filled me with security. Because my relationship with God was also being shaped by my then limited experience of human relationships, I started to wonder if God truly loved and accepted me. Would a liking for masturbation send me to hell? (I was thirteen, what d'ya expect?) It was at this period of struggle with the validity of my relationship with God that I came into contact with the tracts of the U.S.-based Campus Crusade for Christ. In one of these tracts, faith was depicted as a train, with the engine, labeled "facts," pulling a passenger car, labeled "will," which pulled a caboose, labeled "emotions." The fact in question was the Bible's message of salvation. Emotions and feelings were unimportant to faith, only the will to believe the facts. I was taught that it didn't matter if I felt loved by God, or even if I felt I loved God. God had willed to love me—in fact humans were so unlovable God *had* to will to love—and I was to will to believe in God.

I took this faith-will very seriously, and applied it not only to God, but also to what was a budding teenage sexuality, which in my case was an attraction to boys, thus suppressing all deep and emotional passions. Christian discipleship was about control. Then in my midteens, I came into contact with the Charismatic movement, which was sweeping through the Singapore Anglican Church in the 1970s. For the first time, there was a space to be emotional in church. The singing, clapping, and falling over were a huge orgiastic and joyous release. Very soon, I became addicted to liturgical ecstasy. In the two years following my experience of what Charismatics call the "baptism of the Holy Spirit," I continually tried to re-create my original experience of bliss and power. In effect, I tried to make God give me another zap through more Bible devotion and church services. Praying in tongues and laying-on of hands became ways by which I tried to make God make me un-gay. The attachment to re-creating blissful feelings of closeness with God not only emptied the freedom I had first felt but also opened me to manipulation by the priests and pastors I knew. The next traveling faith healer from California became my drug dealer.

My saving grace in all this, oddly enough, was my gayness. I couldn't make God "heal" me, no matter how many times I used the name of Jesus to command the Holy Spirit to make me straight. (Yes, I was taught this formula.) The Third Person of the Trinity had become my private genie, and the name of Jesus was the rub on the lamp. The genie didn't work, and I stopped going to Charismatic meetings, and almost dropped out of the church. In time, the eucharist alone held me in the Christian life and led me on a different journey of a more embodied/sacramental faith.

Although the story I have told happened in Singapore, much of the Christianity I experienced—in terms of books and evangelists—was American or English. The way in which we in the American cultural milieu have been taught to deal with powerful, deep, and profoundly sacred and life-changing experiences—whether erotic or religious—has been to control (suppress or repress) them, or else to lose control (become addicted to them). The controversies over charismatic gifts and other religious and ecstatic experiences have ostensibly been over truth and validity: Is speaking in tongues from God? Did the Virgin really appear, or could it have been the devil? etc. In fact, the struggle has been more fundamental: power. Members of a noncharismatic church who have had a charismatic experience threaten the authority of their clergy. The poor person who has seen the Virgin presents a threat to Vatican clerical control. The demonization of Jews, blacks, women, pagans, and homosexuals have been ways for the Christian church to stay in control by claiming to be in the truth. Power in America is a double bind: control or be controlled.

Control and Addiction

As I relocate from Cambridge, Massachusetts, to Los Angeles while writing this, I am reminded that the Puritan heritage represented by the former is about suppression and denial (i.e., control) of sexuality, while the latter, as embodied in Hollywood, is about trivialization and attachment (i.e., losing control) to sex. Both the suppression and the attachment/addiction are about the promotion of control. Religious leaders impose an ascetic sexual code, and obedience is rendered to their God (and thus to them). Commercial leaders promote an addictive sex culture and consumption (hence revenue) is channeled to their bank account. Furthermore, it isn't clear anymore that there is a "them" out there doing bad things to "us" so that all we need to do is to get rid of "them"—be they popes, puritans, politicians, or pop culture. American culture makes all of us controlling, controlled and consuming, which is to say we do it to each other. If I cannot directly make you do or be someone cast in my image, then I will make you need me so much you cannot leave, which is to say that I have made you surrender your greatest American asset: personal autonomy. By becoming dependent on me, you may also hope to make me dependent on you. Our worship of the phantasmal fiction of autonomy has made us in America simultaneously abusers and victims of power.

Where then in America can the uncontrollable take place, especially feelings of depth, profundity, pain, sorrow, joy, and ecstasy? Our churches, particularly white noncharismatic ones, do their utmost to ensure that emotions do not run high, not even at funerals. (When I was growing up in Singapore, the wakes at Buddhist-Taoist funerals were times of profound wailing.) In this patriarchal society, deep feelings can be expressed only in the context where power/control is simultaneously asserted: sports events, inebriation, war parades, and rock concerts. Of course one may allow for deep feelings in therapy or twelve-step groups, but then such groups are legitimated only because participants are also culturally perceived to be patients.

A cultural milieu that suppresses and trivializes profoundly deep and sacred experiences must necessarily foster a sense of helplessness and terror when such sacred experiences inevitably arise in our lives. We do not know what to do with sacred experiences. Take the people involved in the Charismatic movement. It is not the validity of their experiences that I question. I know myself that in a traditional Asian cultural milieu like Singapore, which acknowledges destructive chthonic spirits and dissatisfied ancestral ones, the encounter with the omnipotent God of Christianity as manifested in the Charismatic movement has brought healing, miracles, and amendment of life. Divine power has been genuinely experienced in concrete ways. *What has been absent is* knowing *that an ecstatic experience of the transcendent God, however powerful and real, does not by itself enable the recipient to better live and behave* ex post facto. One need only recall Elijah, who after having successfully called forth fire from heaven, proceeded to slay the prophets of Baal. Then after this politico-spiritual victory, he flees (purportedly because one lone woman's threat— Jezebel's—was enough to unnerve him) to the wilderness and becomes suicidal. Then as his paranoid marginalization grips him ("I have been very zealous for the Lord . . . I alone am left"), he experiences another Divine call, this time to another slaughter (1 Kings: 18–

19). Paranoia and feelings of radical isolation can accompany encounters with the Divine, and subsequent behavior can aggressively defend the vulnerable self left behind by a shattered ego. Charismatic Christianity has made some Chinese Christians in my native Singapore more racist and triumphalistic toward other religions and cultures. What we as Christians need to understand is that whether in the bedroom, in church pews, or in nature, powerful experiences come from the heart of a good and loving God. (If we do not admit this, then we are stuck trying to (in)validate another person's experience, thus playing a power game.) However, the sacred does not necessarily tell us what to do with powerful experiences of transcendence, insight, or ecstatic sexual union. There is nothing that says we shall not be incredibly cruel, prejudiced, violent, obsessed, addicted, arrogant, jealous, or sinful in our behavior and beliefs after our experience of power, however holy and divine. Buddhists are therefore right to say that powerful experiences of ecstasy and union should neither be sought after, nor refused, nor clung to. These experiences, though real, are not the heart of the religious and spiritual life. *We must let them go, so they can let us go.*[5] Jesus similarly urged his three disciples not to say anything about what they had witnessed of his transfiguration.[6] These attitudes are in marked contrast to the American church and American society, which are either in denial/repression or addiction/attachment to ecstatic, transcendent, or erotic experiences. The suppression of, as well as the attachment to, sacred experience comes out of a wish to control how, when, and why the Divine gifts us with such experiences. The answer here to the dual bind of the American control-or-be-controlled is to let go as both Jesus and the Buddhists have instructed.

Whether our experiences of the sacred become productive and life-giving to us and to our relationships depends on the degree to which we work with God to be humble, loving, patient, and kind. Hence Paul's caution that without love, all gifts of the Spirit, however valid, can ultimately be vapid. Justice-love,[7] along with the ethic of mutually empowering relationships,[8] becomes the living and growing vessel for working with mystical experiences of knowledge, power, and eros.

But as a Christian, I am not willing to let go of one aspect of mystical ecstatic experience: the experience of the love of God. How then do we work with the experiences of Divine love that threaten to undo us, leaving us unsure as to how to next proceed? Here, Paul's conversion is instructive. Blinded by the light he sees on the road to Damascus, Paul is met by Ananias, who against his own revulsion at Paul (Acts 9:13) answers God's call to receive this previous persecutor of Christians. Paul's mystical experience of Jesus, which is momentarily maiming (he goes blind), is then built upon and reshaped by the miracle of human community, forgiveness, and touch. (No autonomy here.) Ananias receives and lays hands on Paul, restoring Paul's sight. We find here that true conversion is the result of blinding Divine love that is contextualized within the structures of a forgiving and accepting embodied community, represented by Ananias. This means that whatever mystical experiences we have that make us feel powerful and elevated, or undone and diminished, need to be grounded, checked, and moderated by an encounter with embodied human relationships. There is no way to do this other than to know one's own embodiment.

Body as Temple

We are embodied beings, and it is our bodies that feel and know. It is in our material, emotional, mental, and psychological bodies—the totality of our person—that we are on this journey of exploring ourselves and our relationships. In a world where touch often either violates or isolates (as when it is withheld), healing touch becomes rare and necessary. Touch can anchor, grounding us to God's incarnation, bringing us into deep remembrance of the stories and mysteries locked in our bones and genes, helping us see ourselves as God sees us, bringing us holy delight and giving us a vision of what the future can be. The following is a story of healing and sacred touch.

Catskill Mountains, fall 1993. She was a beautiful lesbian-identified woman with soft brown eyes not many years older than I. She and I sat facing each other. Coordinating our breathing, we looked into each other's eyes. Outside, the soft rain fell in rhythmic showers, its grayness punctured by the brilliant red maples of the approaching fall. Our exercise that morning was to talk about our relationship with our genitals. I had no problem with that. What caused anxiety, however, was that at thirty years old, I had never seen a woman's genitals before. She had only once seen a man's. The sharing of stories and the show-and-tell relieved my anxiety and fear, and as I gazed in wonder at this wholly/holy other human being, I felt the fullness and otherness of God's goodness, power, and beauty.

Later, I stood waiting by an empty massage table. At the head, I had placed a flower. The women entered, and in decisions they had taken earlier, they now approached the men they had chosen to be their masseurs. She came to me, smiling; honored, I bowed to her. Then, under the instruction of a woman and man team of instructors, I proceeded to give a full-body massage to this wonderful lesbian sister lying in front of me. I touched where she directed and gave her my undivided attention. *The wonder was that I had never been so present to another human being before, not even to a man.* I realized that because her body—a woman's body—was so unfamiliar, so outside the scope of my erotic map of arousal, I had no prerecorded fantasy tapes to play in my head as I did with men, and I was free to relate to her as another whole and holy erotic being! This was sacramental erotic play. With the mind suddenly empty, I was momentarily incapable of objectification (i.e., maneuvering someone onto my agenda), and so became present to the wonder unfolding before me. We laughed and we cried together throughout the session.

From this workshop (what an American invention!), I realized profoundly the lesson that no growth can come from self-hate. My unfolding connection with women had come about from affirming, rather than denouncing, my connection with men. This new erotic connection with a woman—with a lesbian sister at that!—allowed me to address some troublesome issues brought up by the ex-gay Christian ministry Exodus, which my parents had asked me to see. Exodus argued that homosexuality was caused by an absent father, that gay people doubted their sense of masculinity, wanted emotional contact with men but did not know how, were afraid of women, and were bound to be unhappy because of these very issues.[9] Exodus was right insofar as the issues they raised did describe me; Exodus in fact held up an accurate mirror to my shadows. In fact, ex-gay ministry is more honest (though not accurate) with gay shadow issues than the gay male community is willing to admit.

Gay Shadows

The gay male American community, in its effort at reversing the pathological psychological designation of homosexuals as inherently depressed and sick, had chosen "gay" as a politically liberative self-designation. But once the equation is made that gay = not unhappy, then what kind of space is left for someone experiencing and working with unhappiness or existential pain? Furthermore, if gay male public culture (as opposed to its constitutive sum of diverse people) is recognized as reflective of general white American cultural imperatives, then the pursuit of joy, denial of pain, avoidance of vulnerability, fixation with youth, despair with age, and the privileging of strength and autonomy are the unspoken operatives for "gay." People of color from other cultures whose emotional and relational landscape is not quite so insistently Apollonian are often bewildered by this flattening of culture, thus experiencing the American personality as shallow or superficial. Because the experience of racism is by definition an unhappy feeling, and since white American culture (gay or otherwise) is set up not to notice racism, let alone the pain, nonwhites can feel doubly negated. Granted, white gay males do suffer great anguish from these Apollonian imperatives. Psychotherapy (admittedly helpful to me) becomes that sanctioned place for working through suffering— if he can pay for it! Unfortunately, this healing can take place without any real committed effort toward dismantling the systemic cultural imperatives of white America that have helped produce such pain. White privilege then becomes a shelter rather than a point of departure for working with pain. Ironically, it has been the AIDS crisis— with the attendant pain, burnout, anger, and grief it has produced— that has made sections of the gay (white American) culture more politically, emotionally, and spiritually textured.

Paying attention to our shadows, i.e., those parts of our emotional, spiritual, and erotic lives we would rather not see ourselves, is important to our individual and collective survival as embodied beings. Failure to admit and deal with unhappiness and other shadow issues renders them opportunistic areas for "evangelical Christian" infection. Since ex-gay ministries and any number of pathological religions are willing to at least name—however inaccurately—the pain in people's lives, their offer of a way out of pain becomes powerfully seductive.[10] If, broadly speaking, sex is the drug of choice for escaping pain (and whatever shadow issues like lack of self-esteem, masculinity, vulnerability, etc.) in mainstream gay culture, then Jesus becomes the drug of choice for escaping pain (due to rejection, betrayed love, failing relationships) among ex-gay ministries. The real problem here is America's obsession with light: gays with gaiety, Enlightenment secularists with Reason and Order, evangelical Christians with Gospel Light and Salvation, white people with White, and a large majority with autonomy and control. Light itself is not a problem, unless you become afraid of the shadow that it necessarily casts. Trying to cast out shadows with light is a self-defeating game that leads to paranoia, because the shadows (of loss, mystery, rejection, sadness, imperfection, uncertainty, emotions, sex, body, ecstasy, surrender, vulnerability) are everywhere.[11]

Pain, whether we conceive of it as having a moral quality (i.e., the result of injustice, oppression, or wilful ignorance) or having a nonmoral dimension (i.e., inevitable processes like aging, accidents, mortality—though some will moralize, attributing these to the Fall), is simply part of living. There is no escape from pain. To feel and know pain, as much as to know ecstasy, is to experience ourselves as embodied human beings. We can only *be with* pain. (The story is told of a woman who begged the Buddha to restore her child to life. The Buddha said he would if she could find someone in the world who had not experienced pain. Many years later she returned to the Buddha to thank him: she had not found such a one.) As Christians, to *be with* deep pain, grief, and sorrow is to share in the life of God, even as God is with us in Immanuel.

Exploring Embodiment

Embodied selves therefore need to pay attention to the body as body without divisions, and to explore the varied landscape of embodiment. For me, this exploration has moved me into bisensuality. In connecting with women, I have not finally become straight, as if there is finally anything we are to become except ourselves. To be ourselves (in a Christian rather than an American sense) is to love the self that we once hated; to love the neighbor, whom we once regarded as stranger; and to love God, whose love, generosity, and mysterious workings continuously provide for our security, yet confound our need for certainty.[12] To see love this way has been for me a profound act of repentance, of turning around and around until the pieces come together more and more. In contrast, deformative Christianity, as embodied in the ex-gay movement, and even general American Protestant theology, equates repentance with denunciation/amputation. Cutting off parts of the self, one ends up invariably excluding neighbors and strangers.

The body learns (and therefore heals and grows) by exploration. To explore, however, is not to be promiscuous or abusive. We begin our exploration by being aware of the present American cultural landscape: the logic of hedonism, individualism, consumerism, boredom, competition, insatiability, autonomy, and control. This logic maintains, and is maintained by, the insatiability created by capitalist modes of production which make the poor hungry and the rich insecure; the creation of a bored and overworked people through the subjugation of the bodies of women, people of color, and poor whites; the vulgar democratic promise of individual autonomy masking as freedom; the substitution of pacifying sensations for genuine religious experience. Exploration does not in itself create this unrelenting, dehumanizing logic, though exploration can be risky because of this. Thus, our exploration of our mutual embodiment in worship, ritual, erotic connection, play, and touch needs to be teleological: *we explore in order to know, understand, heal, connect, restore, and share.* We must consciously state these intentions so that they become like a prayer, and eventually an ethic.

For sacred exploration to work there needs to be preparation, intentionality, the setting of limits, and the securing of boundaries *in order that one may then travel into uncharted yet already traveled waters*—already traveled because more often then not, trauma, pain, abuse, neglect, and abandonment are territories our bodies have already traveled. Exploration allows us to chart these traveled waters so that we do not drown in them all over again.

The body is the vessel for experiencing/exploring God. Paul said as much when he proclaimed that our bodies are temples or sanctuaries of the Holy Spirit (1 Cor. 6:19). Following after the language of his time, he talked of the need to keep the temple undefiled. However, we have become so preoccupied with his concerns over sanitation that, scrubbing the floor with a toothbrush, we have let the walls cave in. Instead, we must pay attention to architecture, the fact that temples need to have space framed by walls, roofs, windows, floor, doors, and keys. Religious abuse, sexual violation, body repression, homophobia, racism, sexism, poverty, and all other violations damage the architecture of this body-sanctuary, making it more vulnerable to further damage. Traumatized, we shut the windows to sensuality when we should open them; repressed, we are so barricaded that there is no longer space to even rest; starving, we surrender the keys to someone inappropriate because we do not think we should keep our own keys. If we are uncomfortable with our sexuality, or hate our ethnicity, or are critical of one part of our embodied selves for whatever reason, then we spend the time sealing off windows and setting up partitions. The space becomes so small and our housekeeping schedule so full, we shut the Holy Spirit of God up in the closet with the vacuum cleaner. Preoccupied with sanitation, we end up with sterility. With the latter, no one is allowed to enter, not even God.

The erotic, religious, and ethical task in front of us is to help each other claim, repair, explore, widen, beautify, ventilate, decorate, and secure the container space of our temple-bodies, so that we may *tend the fire of* (i.e., worship) the Spirit of God who seeks to tabernacle with us, just as that homeless God did in the wilderness between Egypt and Canaan.[13] We are also securing our own temple-space so that we may be sanctuaries for each other.

Individuation and Interdependence

Becoming our own individuated selves while being in relation is particularly difficult in American culture, and more so for Asian Americans, or at least Chinese Americans. The autonomy prized by white America devalues the need for human connection. Words like *reliance* and *dependence* come to hold only negative meanings—failure to be autonomous. Where connection is abhorred, the need for connection is acted out in destructive ways, so that, for example, where one ought to end an abusive relationship, one does not. This has come to be called co-dependency. The co-dependent, afraid of losing a relationship, rationalizes that he or she can make the abuser better only by continuing in the relationship. The American predicate here is that "better" (meaning sobriety or greater responsibility) means greater self-control and autonomy.

However, "co-dependency," as used in pathological psychological terms, does not describe Chinese people's difficulties in actuating personal agency. In Chinese culture, individual autonomy as the highest good is considered a destructive fiction. The long historical experience of dynastic upheavals and natural disasters that ruin personal lives means that personal life can only be secured by relationships, mainly familial but also between friends. *If you do not learn to rely, and to be reliable yourself, you perish.* Clearly, such a cultural practice can be a source of great injustice, resulting in the tyranny of the family: parents over children, men over women, mothers-in-law over daughters-in-law, emperors over subjects. Nevertheless, when relationality has become counterproductive, Chinese people have taken steps to find freedom, though this freedom must not be read as the pursuit of autonomy. In the dynastic period, where emigration (leaving the family) was illegal, thousands of Chinese people risked Imperial censure by leaving the motherland for Southeast Asia and elsewhere (because of freedom) only to have their remains returned to the ancestral village (because of relationality). Speaking for myself as a Westernized Chinese, the struggle for personal agency does not come from a situation where the cult of autonomy has ruined relationality (as in the United States), but from a culture where the cult of relationality has stunted agency (as in Asia).

The distinction between co-dependency and restrictive relationality for Asian Americans is important, because the etiology is different. Asian Americans are not becoming more Western when we start developing more personal agency, nor are we automatically co-dependent for viewing reliance and dependency as qualified virtues, We do not have the New York flu, but the Shanghai flu. Now, if we are both sneezing, how important is this distinction? Important with respect to "medication," and to a different sense of self-identity and destination.

Conclusion

Besides pointing out the American cultural imperative of autonomy and the dual bind of control-addiction, I have hoped to expand our discussion of the erotic to include cultural and spiritual elements. Because our internal landscape is as diverse as the external world, I fear there is not going to be any final word about our lives as embodied humans, and thus no final orthodoxy in ethics or politics. This is because our erotic, genetic, and spiritual lives are a flow, drawn from many sources, spreading into many rivulets, but it is deep and strong, with bends and turns. We do not spill over because the earth and the sea hold this flowing. And this holding may be called an experience of God. Finally, we need to remember that the distress with which we greet shifting categories mirrors the anxiety with which the incarnation of Christ as God and human being first produced. God is always doing a new thing, and what is foolishness is salvation. However, we must test every spirit, including the spirit of this essay.

Notes

1. Manfred Halpern, professor emeritus of politics at Princeton University, has called the sacred that source of the new and fundamentally better. I owe some of my thoughts on the unitive nature of the sacred to his course and his yet-to-be-published manuscript, "Personal and Political Transformation."

2. Herbert Fingarette's *Secular as Sacred* gives a good account of how the Confucian understanding of rites (*li*) seeks to sacralize human interactions.

3. Tu Wei Ming, notes from class lectures in *Confucian Ethics,* Harvard University, spring semester, 1995.

4. Carter Heyward first brought to my attention the equation between invincibility and security in the United States.

5. Sogyal Rinpoche writes that "experiences are not realization in themselves; but if we remain free of attachment to them, they become what they really are, that is, materials for realization." Sogyal Rinpoche, *The Tibetan Book of Living and Dying* (San Francisco: Harper, 1992), 76.

6. See Mark 9:9. Throughout Mark's Gospel, Jesus is recorded as imposing silence on those who have witnessed his power—including the demons. This has been called the messianic secret, the intentional withholding in the narrative of Jesus' true identity. Ultimately, the secret is meant to be disclosed and proclaimed. But the secret of Jesus as Messiah is radically ego deflating: the "secret" is that this Messiah *serves* (Mark 9:35), a motif markedly at odds with the proclamation of triumphalism of fundamentalism.

7. This term was coined in the Presbyterian report on homosexuality to its 1990 General Assembly, a report that was subsequently squashed.

8. Carter Heyward, "Undying Erotic Friendships: Foundations for Sexual Ethics," in *Touching Our Strength* (San Francisco: HarperCollins, 1989).

9. The etiology of homosexuality and the tautological logic used to overdetermine the immorality and sickness of homosexuality is found in Joe Dallas, *Desires in Conflict* (Oregon: Harvest House Publishers, 1991). *See also* the video *One Nation Under God*.

10. In *One Nation Under God*, ex-gay leaders make it a point to say they do not do outreach to happy gays, but to unhappy gay people who seek them out. This says to me that the gay community is not paying enough attention to those who hurt.

11. I am indebted to the Jungian Mitch Walker and the pagan Matt Silverstein, two amazing queer brothers, for the Wiccan saying that every candle casts a shadow.

12. Jesus' summary of the Law is that we are to love God with all of our being, and our neighbors as ourselves (Matt. 22:37–40).

13. I owe the phrase to tend the fires to my sister-companion Elizabeth Broyles. Paul in an earlier time asks us not to quench the Holy Spirit.

5 The Joy of Boundaries

Marie M. Fortune

Introduction

IN HER NOVEL *The Robber Bride*, Margaret Atwood describes the experience of a character who is a college professor:

> She unlocks her office door, then locks it behind her to disguise the fact that she's in there. It's not her office hours but the students take advantage. They can smell her out, like sniffer dogs; they'll seize any opportunity to suck up to her or whine, or attempt to impress her, or foist upon her their versions of sulky defiance. *I'm just a human being,* Tony wants to say to them. But of course she isn't. She's a human being with power. There isn't much of it, but it's power all the same.[1]

Whether as teacher, minister, or therapist, we bear the blessing and burden of power in relation to those whom we teach, pastor, or counsel. Many in ministry resonate with "there isn't much of it" but overlook "it's power all the same."

The fact of power and power differentials in a helping relationship prompted Hippocrates to formulate the Hippocratic oath over two thousand years ago and commit himself "to keep [patients] from harm and injustice" with these words: "Whatever houses I may visit, I will come for the benefit of the sick, remaining free of all intentional injustice, of all mischief and in particular of sexual relations with both female and male persons, be they free or slaves."[2] He understood that he was there to address the needs of his patients rather than his own needs. He recognized that the helper could take advantage of the vulnerable. He knew that he had the power to heal or to harm. His formulation reminds us of our responsibility to establish boundaries that ensure that our power is used to heal rather than to harm. Dealing with boundaries is one of the most significant challenges those of us who function in leadership roles in ministry (clergy, religious, or lay) face. This is primarily because the nature of ministry means that boundaries are usually not well defined. We are expected to function in informal, intimate settings (for example pastoral calls to a congregant's home or hospital bedside), and in multiple roles (pastor, teacher, community leader, as well as community member), usually without supervision or oversight. We lack many of the structural supports that our colleagues in secular helping professions have (for example, structured appointment times, fee for service, supervision, etc.). But this is also the genius of ministry. We are able to be with congregants in many different settings: from a sickbed to a committee meeting, from a Bible study to a family dinner, from marriage preparation to the church softball game. And usually we have the privilege of being a part of a congregant's life over time. This gives us the opportunity to be present in moments and ways that other helping professionals lack.

This unstructured, ill-defined role of minister makes the issue of boundaries particularly challenging and all the more important. We are called, hired, and compensated to do ministry with our congregants. It is our responsibility as ministers to understand our roles, stay cognizant of our power and authority, and stay clear on our boundaries in order to fulfill our commitment to maintain the integrity of our ministerial relationships.

Speaking of Boundaries, Power, and Vulnerability

A boundary is "something that indicates a limit," according to Webster. In any relationship, boundaries are the limits that give shape to that relationship. Boundaries are what helps me know where I stop and the other person begins. Boundaries may be determined by role (for example, a judge vis-à-vis a prosecuting attorney), by custom (for example, the appropriate Korean greeting is to bow from the waist without touching), by ethical standards (for example, the Hippocratic oath) or by law (for example, it is illegal for adults to have sex with children). Boundaries are necessarily present in every relationship but differ according to the nature of the relationship. In a mutually intimate sexual relationship between two peers, boundaries may be negotiable and even permeable, but they are nonetheless significant if each person is to remain whole and healthy. In a helping relationship, boundaries are more or less clear and maintained primarily for the benefit of the person who, in this situation, may be vulnerable and in need of assistance.

Boundaries can support a healthy relationship. They can give structure within which a relationship can develop and grow. They can help the two persons in the relationship to develop trust, which creates a safe space for interaction and communication. But boundaries can also become walls and, as such, can be misused to enforce power and control, to manipulate the interaction, or to shut out possibilities for relationship.

Boundaries are the means by which we manage our power and vulnerability in relationship. Power and vulnerability are ways to describe the relative balance of power that is present in every relationship. Power describes the fact of having resources vis-à-vis another being. Vulnerability describes the absence of resources vis-à-vis another being.[3] A child is vulnerable vis-à-vis an adult; a minister with terminal illness is vulnerable vis-à-vis a health care provider; a congregant who has just suffered a loss is vulnerable vis-à-vis a minister; a dog is vulnerable vis-à-vis an adult human. Having power does not equate with misusing that power; being vulnerable does not equate with being harmed. Boundaries are one of the means we have to ensure that we attend to our relative power and vulnerability in any relationship without doing harm.

In a postmodern, late-twentieth-century Western society, some people react negatively to the notion of boundaries of any kind, particularly boundaries in pastoral or other professional relationships. Some people who have patriarchal power argue that their individual freedom takes precedence over all else; in fact, they believe that boundaries interfere with the free exercise of their power and privilege and argue vehemently against any attempt to suggest standards regarding boundaries in professional relationships. From a different perspective, some feminists argue against boundaries, saying that bound-aries are a vestige of patriarchal practice. Their reasoning seems to be that boundaries in helping relationships are ways to establish rigid control and shut out the possibilities of relationship. Still others ro-manticize boundariless relationships as an ideal of mutuality. These feminist concerns often arise from legitimate critiques of hierarchi-cal power structures, which have not only shut women out but have also resulted in serious abuses of power by the most powerful.[4] But few who argue against boundaries are willing to acknowledge the complexities of real power dynamics within most relationships.

Ecclesiology: Some Facts about Our Life Together

Our ecclesiology is the foundation for our understanding of bound-aries in ministerial relationships. Who are we as church? What is our purpose together? How do we organize ourselves?

These are not simple questions and the history of the church is evidence that there has never been agreement on the answers. Rose-mary Radford Ruether observes that "the history of Christianity is a history of continual tension and conflict between two models of church: church as spirit-filled community and church as historical institution."[5] This fundamental tension drives the contemporary efforts to re-form and re-imagine the church. Central to this histori-cal and contemporary struggle is the question of power. Perhaps the issue of power is most clearly lifted up in the efforts within Roman Catholicism to see, name, and dismantle the structures of clerical power that have for so long shaped the church. Ruether summarized the movement to confront hierarchical power in the church:

"If we understand clericalism as the expropriation of ministry, sacra-mental life, and theological education from the people, then women-church—and indeed all base Christian communities—are engaged in a revolutionary act of reappropriating to the people what has been falsely expropriated from us. We are reclaiming sacramental life as the symbol of our own entry into and mutual empowerment within the redemptive life, the authentic human life or original blessing upon which we stand naturally when freed from alienating powers. Theo-logical education and teaching are our own reflections on the mean-ing of reclaiming our authentic life from distortion. *Ministry is the active praxis of our authentic life and the building of alternative bases of expression from which to challenge the systems of evil.*"[6]

Whether we are working in a traditional parish or an alternative faith community or specialized ministry, boundaries are a significant resource because they are the means by which we organize and structure ourselves, enabling us to accomplish our mission. But it is critical that we know what that mission is. After a long, involved discussion of boundaries during a workshop, a participant asked, "But isn't the purpose of the church to increase the intimacy among us?" After seriously considering his question, I concluded no, that is not my understanding of the mission of the church. The mission of the church is to build and sustain a faith community that is able to go forth into the world to bring the Good News of healing and justice where there is brokenness and suffering.

The participant's suggestion that the purpose of the church is to increase the intimacy among its members runs the risk of creating an insular, intimate grouping focusing on itself and the needs of its members. This runs counter to Scripture and the best of Christian tradition. The purpose of the church is to bring people together for learning, nurture, and support so that we can carry the Gospel outward to a hurting world. We need a place to bring our own pain so that, in our healing, we can be empowered to go out into the world with acts of justice, mercy, and compassion where greed, domination, and violence bombard the least powerful. The church should be a setting where we create the space for reflection, growth, challenge, and healing, which make it possible for us to be in ministry together. The intimacy of fellowship can be supportive of this shared ministry, but intimacy should not be the end goal. As part of our mission, the church should be a place of safety for the vulnerable; this means that we do what we can to ensure that children will not be harmed there, that persons struggling with painful memories or current crises will find a setting in which they will not be taken advantage of but can find healing and empowerment. This safety (which can never be absolutely guaranteed) should not be confused with complacency. The mandate to afflict the comfortable and comfort the afflicted still applies.

In the letter to the Ephesians, the author described the mission and the means:

"The gifts [Jesus] gave were that some would be apostles, some prophets, some evangelists, some pastors and teachers, *to equip the saints for the work of ministry,* for building up the body of Christ, until all of us come to the unity of the faith and of knowledge of the Son of God, to maturity, to the measure of the full stature of Christ." (Eph. 4:11–13 NRSV, italics mine)

Ruether's vision is consistent with Scripture:

"Every community that is engaged in a full community life should be engaged to some extent in each of these areas of liturgy, education, and theological reflection, organizing its own material and human resources, committing itself to some social praxis, and deepening its inner life. Communities need to find among their own members, or call into themselves, persons who have particular skills in these various areas. Such persons are designated as enablers or ministers in these various areas, but not in order to do these things for others, who will then simply passively consume their services. Rather, the function of the ministers is to be the helpers and teachers who equip the community itself to engage in these various activities."[7]

If we as ministers are to accomplish our mission and fulfill our leadership responsibilities, we must attend to boundaries. The church should be a place where boundaries are predictable, that is, where there is consistency and continuity. Predictability of boundaries should not be confused with rigidity and control. Clarity does not equal rigidity. Mixed messages promote confusion. Especially for survivors of childhood abuse, for whom appropriate boundaries as children in relation to adults were nonexistent, predictable boundaries in a congregation are a priority for their healing. All persons in roles of leadership should convey clear messages about boundaries; this will enable trust to grow with integrity.

There was a congregation in which a lot of training had been done with church school teachers about appropriate boundaries with children. Parents were appreciative, children felt comfortable, and an environment of safety was created. At the same time, a new associate pastor was called to the staff. He was first introduced by a lay leader at the all-church retreat. "I'd like to introduce Rev. _____. He is a graduate of _____ Seminary, a native of _____. And a 27-

year-old bachelor. Now I'd like to ask all the single women in the congregation to please stand. Rev. _____, this is your new Bible class." The minister was mortified; the women were humiliated. In implying that all the single women in the congregation were available to the new minister, this joke communicated serious confusion about boundaries to the whole congregation. It undermined the efforts to clarify appropriate boundaries for both clergy and laity, and it contradicted this congregation's understanding of its mission.

Finally, the spiritual growth and development of congregants should not be dependent on an individual, personal relationship with the minister. Persons in ministerial roles should exercise leadership and to do so, they bring particular gifts. But an effective minister is always seeking ways to empower the laity, connect members of the community to each other for support, and extend the ministry outward. A faith community that focuses on the charisma of the minister, that promotes individual, intimate relationships with the minister, and that is turned in on itself will not long survive.

Dietrich Bonhoeffer, the German theologian who was martyred by the Nazis during World War II, foresaw the danger of boundariless, minister-focused human communities with a facade of Christian community. In his book, *Life Together*, he warns:

> "Here [in the church] is where the humanly strong person is in his element, securing for himself the admiration, the love, or the fear of the weak. Here human ties, suggestions and bonds are everything, and in the immediate community of souls we have reflected the distorted image of everything that is originally and solely peculiar to community mediated through Christ."[8]

He is describing the distortion of a faith community that is attracted to a false prophet. But he also advocated the fundamentals for a healthy faith community:

> "Therefore, spiritual love proves itself in that everything it says or does commends Christ. It will not seek to move others by all too personal, direct influence, by impure interference in the life of another. It will not take pleasure in pious, human fervor and excitement. It will rather meet the other person with the clear Word of God and be ready to leave him [sic] alone with this Word for a long time, willing to release

him [sic] again in order that Christ may deal with him [sic]. It will respect the line that has been drawn between him [sic] and us by Christ, and it will find full fellowship with him [sic] in the Christ who alone binds us together."[9]

Bonhoeffer pointed to the paradox of ministry in this statement: the line drawn between the minister and congregant by Christ (the boundary that respects and protects the congregant from the power of the minister) in tension with the power of Christ that binds minister and congregants together in fellowship. His observations, although fifty years old, provide important cautions for us today.

In ministry (or teaching or therapy), some important realities should encourage those of us in leadership to consider carefully the importance of boundaries: *The pastoral relationship is intimate* because minister and congregant encounter each other in profoundly significant faith and life experiences; but this does not mean that the intimacy is mutual, nor does it mean that the experience has the same meaning for both parties. Although a physician is present to a patient in circumstances of powerful intimacy (birth, illness, death), the physician does not take her or his clothes off (literally or figuratively). Likewise a pastor is present at many bedsides during dying and presides at many funerals; these are moments of great intimacy but do not carry the same meaning for the pastor as for family members. The pastor may be emotionally involved and may be dealing with his or her own grief at the loss of a congregant, but this is not the time and place that the pastor bares his or her soul in the same way that a family member might. The focus of the attention should be on the congregants' experience in this crisis, not on the pastor's.

Pastoral relationships usually involve multiple roles; that is, the minister is called on to play two or more different roles with the same congregant, which sometimes makes boundaries less clear; for example, when a congregant is also principal of the school attended by the minister's child or is the only car dealer in a small town. In fact the very role of minister in a congregation is a dual role: the minister is fulfilling a pastoral role vis-à-vis congregants at the same time that she or he is an employee of the congregation. Recognition of the possibility of multiple roles can help us manage them more effectively by keeping us cognizant of the particular boundaries appropriate to each role. For example, my colleague who teaches pastoral psychology at a seminary and has a private practice in pastoral counseling will not see his students in his private practice because he does not want to attempt to fulfill the roles of teacher and counselor with the same person. His caution is well founded and indicates his commitment to the best interests of both his students and clients.

The pastoral relationship is one of unequal power between minister and congregant. The minister brings resources (knowledge, expertise, experience, etc.) to a congregation. The resources represent power and authority, which can be used for good or ill. The congregant is not powerless but also brings her or his own resources and may in fact be the employer of the pastor. But the congregant, in matters of spirituality, ethics, and faith gives over some measure of power to the pastor in order to receive some benefit; this is what we call trust.[10] Congregants trust the minister's knowledge, concern for them, and commitment to act in their interests. This often tacit agreement to forego power in order to gain the benefits of a confidential, pastoral relationship creates a difference in power.

In a pastoral context, the fact of unequal power does not necessarily indicate the presence of abuse. Power is not by definition abusive; it is a neutral reality in which we all share to a greater or lesser degree, depending on socially constructed reality and circumstances. Parents have more power than children. They can use that power to protect children in their vulnerability and support them in their development, or they can use that power to neglect, abuse, and exploit a child.

In a pastoral context, the fact of unequal power does require a fiduciary responsibility on the part of the minister. In its fullest sense, "fiduciary" means a responsibility to act in the best interests of the congregant even when such action does not coincide with the minister's personal interests. For example, a congregant may be considering a job offer in another state that would be an excellent move for the congregant. But the minister doesn't want to lose this chairperson of the religious education committee who is so effective. The minister's fiduciary responsibility requires that she or he support the congregant's choice to make the move even though it leaves the minister in the lurch with church school. Or the minister, during a time of loneliness or personal crisis, may feel attracted to a congregant who is seeking counsel regarding her or his intimate relationship. Even if the minister restrains his or her sexual interests, if he or she nonetheless pursues emotional interests (which may be mutual between them) with the congregant at the time when the congregant wants and needs to be focusing her or his energies on the relationship with her or his significant other, the minister will have violated a fiduciary responsibility to act in the congregant's interest rather than the minister's. As Marilyn Peterson observes, "When professionals indulge themselves, their primary relationship is not with [the congregant's] needs but rather with themselves and their own best interests."[11]

A fiduciary responsibility requires care of boundaries in the relationship and protection of the congregant in her or his vulnerability (for example, when dealing with a life crisis or spiritual development).

These realities are present in every interaction we have with those whom we serve. Our awareness of and attention to these realities should be the foundation of our ministerial relationships. The choices we make and actions we take, grounded in our awareness, can become second nature and can serve all of our interests as we live and work in a faith community.

Cultural Legacies

In our struggle to understand and respect boundaries in a helping relationship, we all live with the legacies of our cultural settings. The legacy of patriarchy has given us a painful history of male professionals (because until recently only males played professional roles) who used their professional power with impunity. Many assumed the patriarchal prerogative of sexual access to those most vulnerable (women, children, and some men). Using the power of gender and role (often combined with the power of race and age), they have too often disregarded the appropriate boundaries of helping relationships to take advantage of those whom they served.

The legacy of liberalism (often in reaction to the tyranny of hierarchies) is the denial of real power and power differentials in pastoral relationships. A common response from clergymen to a discussion of power is "I don't have any power as a minister," and from clergywomen it is "I don't *want* to have any power as a minister." The former is not true (denial of power that comes with the role of minister is usually an attempt to avoid responsibility for abusing it) and the latter is not healthy or helpful (denial of the power differential between minister and congregant in order to avoid the often difficult task of using power and authority appropriately). Both rest on the liberal values of autonomy and individual rights with little regard for the fact of power inequities or for one's accountability within a community. Both positions have led to an avoidance of boundaries by some ministers. This denial of power and power differentials has led to an illusion of egalitarian relationships as the solution to the abuses by hierarchical structures. Marilyn Peterson observes:

> "The decision to assume an egalitarian posture is often made in reaction to a hierarchical model. Indeed, the ideology of equality is the underpinning of our democracy, many religious denominations, and some feminist organizations. A former cleric described how he had used this philosophy to blind himself to the impact of his authority:
>
> My own ideology was very much the ideology that is reinforced in the church. I believed in a shared ministry. I believed that people in the church should be friends. I didn't want to set myself apart as superior. Having your primary friends be outside of the congregation didn't fit with this ideal picture of friendship and community. Therefore, my best friends were members of the congregation. Now I know that each person's participation in the church is influenced by the one-to-one relationship with the minister. If the minister is best friends with one or two or three people, that's going to have an influence on the life of the whole congregation. It makes an in-group and an out-group, and things like that are really deadly for a church.
>
> . . . [The professional role] requires that we use our power to take charge of the conditions that keep our clients safe in the professional-client relationship. . . . When we do not act within the framework of our role, our inconsistency makes the boundaries in the relationship ambiguous and our clients [congregants] become confused."[12]

Our best intentions aside, the denial of power and authority by liberals in the ministerial role has created confusion and sometimes rendered us ineffective in the face of injustice and evil. We have on occasion refused to use our power to speak or act forthrightly when that is exactly what was needed. Our passivity has passed for "mutuality." Our priority has been being liked more than being a minister.

The legacy of conservatism has given us rigid boundaries based on wrongheaded criteria with which to address pastoral boundaries.[13] For example, the United Methodist dictum for clergy remains "Fidelity in marriage and celibacy in singleness." This standard is viewed by many denominations as the answer to the question of sexual boundaries in ministry. This expectation that clergy sexual activity take place only in heterosexual marriage is not only unrealistic, it also draws the boundary in the wrong place and does little to protect vulnerable congregants from sexual advances by clergy. The criteria for clergy's (and laity's) sexual activity should focus on one's potential to do harm to another rather than on one's marital status per se. Anything less delivers the facade of righteousness but avoids the harder questions of boundaries within the ministerial relationship.

Finally, the legacy of reaction and defensiveness potentially clouds our abilities to struggle with the complexities of boundaries, power and vulnerability. Currently a common response from clergy to any discussion of boundaries or standards of pastoral conduct is defensive: "Okay. I just won't touch *anyone* anymore." One United Methodist conference implemented a guideline for parish ministers that directed them to always keep the door of their office open when counseling. These are absurd and ineffective reactionary responses, which only avoid the hard work of dealing with appropriate boundaries in the pastoral setting. Peterson makes this observation:

> Rather than holding on to our positive power to heal, nurture, and teach, we transfer and ascribe it negatively to [congregants, clients, etc.]. Since they can hurt us, we feel compelled to defend against them rather than being mutually—though never equally—powerful in the relationship. We look first therefore to secular solutions—our codes of ethics, institutional policies, and professional standards of conduct—to handle the moral injustices between us. Rather than use them as guiding principles to preserve the health of the relationship, we use them as literal *do*'s and *don't*s to "cover our own ass." Being afraid of what our clients [or congregants] might do to us, we draw the boundary of safety around ourselves, become technically compliant, and quietly leave the relationship. In so doing, we shut off what we have to give, which destroys the spiritual bond between us and our clients.[14]

Boundaries are not there to protect the minister from relating to the congregant but rather to support a healthy, pastoral relationship. Fear, defensiveness, or laziness can tempt a minister to misuse boundaries to avoid a meaningful pastoral relationship. We live with these realities and lessons of patriarchy, liberalism, conservatism, and reaction. It is no wonder that we are often confounded when we consider boundaries in ministerial relationships.

The Joy of Boundaries: Benefits for Everyone

Boundaries make it possible *to be in relationship* with another person. Ministry is about relationships between and among those who share a common mission. So boundaries are a gift that gives shape to any relationship, personal or professional. The purpose of clear boundaries in a ministerial relationship is not to preserve some cache of patriarchal power on the part of the minister. Boundaries used appropriately create space where a congregant can reflect on her or his experiences and learn from them without having to deal with the personal needs of the minister.

When we drive down a freeway, we see lines on the pavement, barriers on the side of the road to prevent us from driving off the cliff, signs indicating caution or speed, etc. These are boundaries that enable us to travel at high speed from here to there without hurting anyone or being hurt in the process. Try driving this same freeway at night in a snowstorm. All boundaries are obliterated and we are without any point of reference. So our journey becomes far more perilous. Or consider a tennis teacher in relationship with a tennis student. In order for the game to be meaningful and satisfying, each plays within the boundaries of the tennis court. If they had no net and no court, they couldn't even play tennis. They could sit and have coffee, perhaps, but no tennis. The teacher gives instruction, support, responds to questions, etc. But her goal is to assist the tennis student in learning the game. She works on her own game elsewhere. The context is clear; the goals are clear; the responsibility of the teacher is clear. Even if they play a game for fun at the end of instruction, the teacher remains focused on the student's learning, not on her own game. Boundaries make this relationship workable and meaningful.

A faith community in which leadership (clergy and lay) is strong, boundaries and expectations are clear, and the focus is on mission is a community in which both minister and congregants thrive. Congregants find a safe place to learn, heal, grow, and contribute. Ministers find a place where their gifts are utilized for a common mission and a place where, because of clarity of boundaries, they can have a life as well as a ministry.[15] This means that the minister can and should have friends, activities, and interests outside the ministry setting where he or she can meet personal needs. This means that the minister deserves to have privacy of both time and space, which is very important to support the minister's relationship with his or her partner, family, and/or close friends. Gone are the days when the chairperson of the Deacon Board should have a key to the parsonage or when a lay person thinks nothing of phoning the minister with a nonemergency on his or her day off.

There is no question that the minister can experience profound learning and spiritual growth from pastoral interactions. Certainly there are times when the congregation ministers to the needs of the minister, for example, when he or she experiences the dying and death of a parent or child, a serious illness, etc. Roles may reverse temporarily. But these benefits to us as ministers are not the *purpose* of our being in this role. And the pastoral role is certainly not the place that we should do our primary work on our own healing. Yes, we are all "wounded healers" as Henri Nouwen has observed, but we need to focus on our own healing in another setting or else we will end up using our congregants for our own purposes at the expense of their interests. Ministry provides those of us who responded to its call with the opportunity to use our gifts and contribute to a common mission, which we hope is congruent with our best selves. In the process we may experience the secondary benefits of healing, challenge, and spiritual growth. But we must not let our own journey blind us to the priority of those whom we serve.

Not to be overlooked in the benefits we gain from careful boundaries as a minister is our own sense of trustworthiness. Peterson comments: "Nonindulgence is richly rewarded.... The professional gains ... respect. 'It's a trade-off,' said a cleric. 'In exchange for being responsible for others, showing restraint, making a commitment, and accepting a fiduciary position, you gain respectability. It allows you to feel worthy, to be part of something larger that protects the society. You don't need any more than that.'"[16] Ministry is a public trust. But it is a trust that we earn; it should never be given over to us simply because of our role; nor should we ever expect it. When we strive to be trustworthy, we strengthen our portion of the social fabric, which stretches beyond our immediate circle.

This doesn't mean that we don't make mistakes and cross boundaries on occasion. Everyone does. The real test of our trustworthiness is not our perfection or political correctness but rather what we do about our mistakes and boundary violations. If we acknowledge our responsibility and seek to repair the breech that we created or harm that we caused, we can perhaps rebuild the trust that is placed in us, learn from the experience and move on.

Discerning Our Choices: Caution and Awareness

Those of us who are conscientious about our ministries are constantly faced with temptations and hard choices about boundaries. Of course we are friendly with and care about students, staff members, and congregants with whom we work. We spend social time together on occasion; we attempt to meet mutual needs. But when we *pursue a friendship* with an individual student, staff member, or congregant, someone with whom we have the option to exercise our power and authority, we jeopardize not only our teaching, supervisory, or pastoral role with them but also our relationship to others in this setting and to the common mission that we share. Our judgment is invariably affected; the dynamics of the group are affected; our ability to work together collectively is affected. And none of us is exempt from these dynamics.

The notion that "if I do it, it isn't harmful because I am a good person and mean no harm" is a slippery slope of elitism that can lead any of us to elaborate rationalizations of our own behavior. Is it "better" to relax the boundaries in our professional, pastoral relationships? Probably not. It is certainly more pleasant for me and meets some of my personal association needs. It is not necessarily harmful, but it is definitely risky. And the stakes are likely to be high.

Guidelines and ethics policies from our denominations only paint the broadest strokes of the boundaries we must consider every day. It is clear that good boundaries cannot be legislated by a religious or professional body. Declaring that pastors may not have friendships with congregants is ludicrous and will not create good boundaries and healthy pastoral relationships. A cosmetic quick fix is less than helpful when what is needed is a deeper and fuller understanding of the importance of clear boundaries and a thoughtful, discerning, aware effort to minimize possible harm.

When we find ourselves considering a choice about relaxing the boundaries in a ministerial relationship, we should evaluate the options with these questions in mind:

1. What is the likely impact on or potential harm to the individual congregant? How will he or she be affected by relaxing these boundaries, by increasing the mutual intimacy of our relationship? Am I attempting to meet my needs at his or her expense? What about her or his family? And what about mine?
2. What is the likely impact on or potential harm to the congregation itself? How will others react? Will this appear to be some kind of favoritism? Will it stimulate jealousy or dissension? Will others expect the same degree of mutual intimacy with me?
3. What is the likely impact on or potential harm to the mission of the church? Will my actions undermine the common mission we share? Will others be distracted from their ministries by my actions?

We must consider each of these questions because our choices and actions regarding ministerial boundaries affect much more than just the other person involved. If our mission as a faith community is to sustain ourselves so that we might be able to carry our efforts forth to make justice and bring healing, if we believe that our faith communities should embody the values of justice, protection of the vulnerable, and shared power, and if we affirm the need for persons called forth from among us to sustain, teach, and lead, then we need leaders committed to clear boundaries and a willingness to be accountable for their actions. Good boundaries make effective ministry possible; effective ministry sustains the faith community and carries forth its message and witness.

Are we capable of sustaining clear boundaries in our ministerial relationships? Paul thought so. In his Second Letter to Timothy he said:

> "For this reason I remind you to rekindle the gift of God that is within you through the laying on of my hands; for God did not give us a spirit of cowardice, but rather a spirit of power and of love and of self-discipline." (2 Timothy 1:6 NRSV)

Discipline is not often considered in these discussions because it conjures up associations with punishment and rigid control. Peterson uses the term "self-restraint." "If professionals do not channel and discipline themselves . . . clients [or congregants] lose. In contrast to business, where the profit motive is king, professionals make a covenant with the larger society and with each client [congregant] to give, not take.[17] This constant challenge follows professionals like a shadow."[18] Discomfort with the term "discipline" is unfortunate because we lose the positive meaning of self-discipline as a means to self-control and careful choices about our boundaries. In the Letter to the Hebrews we find:

> "Now, discipline always seems painful rather than pleasant at the time, but later it yields the peaceful fruit of righteousness to those who have been trained by it. Therefore lift your drooping hands and strengthen your weak knees, and make straight paths for your feet, so that what is lame may not be put out of joint, but rather be healed." (Heb. 12:11–12 NRSV)

A paraphrase of this passage makes an appropriate watchword to ministers:

> Now, boundaries always seem painful rather than pleasant at the time, but later they yield the peaceful fruit of righteousness to those who have been trained by them.

At times we may tire of the attention that good boundaries requires of us. It would be so much easier to relax and just be friends. The caution remains:

> Therefore lift your drooping hands and strengthen your weak knees, and make straight paths for your feet, so that what is lame may not be put out of joint, but rather be healed.

If we are to keep faith with our calling, if we are to preserve the integrity of the ministerial relationship, we must heed this mandate to make straight paths for our feet, being careful of the boundaries within our ministerial relationships so that we will bring healing, not further harm.

Notes

1. Margaret Atwood, *The Robber Bride* (New York: Bantam Books, 1993), 24.

2. *The Hippocratic Oath*, no. 1 of the *Supplements to the Bulletin of the History of Medicine*, copyright 1943. Text, translation, and interpretation by Ludwig Edelstein (Baltimore: Johns Hopkins University Press, 1943).

3. "Vulnerability" as it is used here does not refer to the psychological state of being open toward another. It is rather the reality that in some circumstances, any person can find herself or himself with fewer resources (due to age, gender, physical size, life circumstances, etc.) than someone else.

4. I have long shared these critiques. But I have come to realize that to attempt mutuality in a situation where there is necessarily a difference in power between two people is not an effective antidote to the abuse of power by the powerful. Recognizing good, clear boundaries is a more effective means to ensure justice in those relationships. The goal remains the empowerment of persons, which lessens vulnerability but can never eliminate it for any of us. And so boundaries will always be an important aspect of relationships.

5. Rosemary Radford Ruether, *Women-Church* (San Francisco: Harper San Francisco, 1985), 11.

6. Ibid., 87. Italics mine.

7. Ibid., 89–90.

8. Dietrich Bonhoeffer, *Life Together* (New York: Harper and Brothers, 1954), 32–33.

9. Ibid., 36.

10. See also Marilyn Peterson, *At Personal Risk* (New York: W. W. Norton, 1992), 27f.

11. Ibid., 31.

12. Ibid., 64–66.

13. For further discussion, see Fortune, *Love Does No Harm* (New York: Continuum Publishing, 1995).

14. Peterson, 187.

15. In conversation with Wendy Hunt, March 1995.

16. Peterson, *At Personal Risk*, 31.

17. This covenant to give and not take is not to be confused with co-dependent, self-negating behavior. Rather it points up the commitment to regard the needs of the congregant first in contrast to exploitative, selfish conduct, which begins with the needs of the minister/professional as the priority in the ministerial relationship.

18. Peterson, *At Personal Risk*, 30.

6 | Boundaries, Mutuality, and Professional Ethics

Karen Lebacqz and Ronald G. Barton

CAN RIGID ADHERENCE to the rule of not becoming "intimate" with clients actually damage a client? This is what Carter Heyward argues in *When Boundaries Betray Us*.[1] She therefore proposes a new vision of therapy in which intimacy, at least in the form of friendship, is possible between therapist and client. In good feminist style, Heyward uses her own experience as the springboard for her theoretical reflections: she makes her theoretical argument in the context of a description of her therapy process. Her argument raises again important issues on the conversation about boundaries, mutuality, and professional ethics.

Is the maintenance of boundaries always appropriate, or might boundaries be relaxed under some circumstances, or might they even be abusive under some circumstances? In theory, at least, we are confronted with two options: (1) drop boundaries generally; or (2) keep boundaries generally.

Heyward's argument is for option 1—the dropping of boundaries as a rule.[2] We will argue for option 2, the importance of maintaining boundaries as a general rule. While Heyward's use of her personal story invites and has sparked comments on its particulars, we confine ourselves to the general issue rather than the particular case.

Feminist Convictions

A strong feminist conviction is that we are called to justice or "right relationship" and that mutuality is central to right relationship. A concern for mutuality and its links with friendship is widely shared in contemporary feminism. In her recent award-winning book on feminist theology, Elizabeth A. Johnson writes, "The particular pattern of relationship consistently promoted in feminist ethical discourse is mutuality. . . . It is a relation on the analogy of friendship."[3] Many feminists stress mutuality and friendship as primary values of relationship.

Moreover, feminists have begun exploring the possibilities of "friendship" as a model for professional work. For example, in *Co-Creating: A Feminist Vision of Ministry*, Lynn N. Rhodes suggests that friendship is an emerging model for women in ministry: "Friendship suggests both the emotional intimacy we need and the mutuality, nurture, trust, and accountability that we value."[4] Friendship, with its mutual vulnerability, is seen as an antidote to old models of professional power "over" clients. Thus, Heyward's call for mutuality in her own experience of counseling, and as a general principle for professional-client relations, appears to be based on sound feminist principles and to have support from within feminist theology and ethics.

We agree on the importance of mutual sharing and friendship as forms of "right relationship." We agree as well on the need for attention to the power that people have simply because of their professional positions.[5] We further agree that the language and constructs of "co-dependence" fail to offer a critical perspective on such power relations,[6] that we need to link the personal and the political,[7] and that mutual relations have healing power. In short, there is much in the feminist vision of right relationship and in Heyward's articulation of it—including the shortcomings of some contemporary approaches to therapy in light of that vision—with which we agree.

Problems with Intimacy

The question we must confront is this: Should clear boundaries be kept in therapy, even though they seem to fly in the face of these feminist convictions about the importance of mutuality, friendship, and sisterhood? What is the appropriate place of boundaries in professional relationships, including those of ministry and of the counseling professions? Heyward's powerful story and pointed arguments force us to ask whether respect for and advocacy of professional boundaries indicates a "selling out" to a nonfeminist, hierarchical (patriarchal) view of relationships. We think not.

Is mutuality, understood in terms of friendship and personal intimacy, the only form of "right relationship"? Is any professional relationship that, as a matter of principle, rules out friendship, or that sets boundaries and excludes possibilities of mutual intimacy, necessarily abusive?[8] We think not. Indeed, we argue that failure to maintain appropriate boundaries is abusive and unethical.

In *When Boundaries Betray Us*, Heyward does not define with precision the exact meaning of the intimacy sought between therapist and client or of dropping traditional boundaries. While the focus is on friendship, the possibility of sexual intimacy is not explicitly ruled out and may be carried by the language of being "in love."[9] It also is not clear whether the search for intimacy encompasses intimacy only *after* a therapy relationship ends, or whether intimacy *during* the therapy process is envisioned. Heyward initially proposes that she wants to continue a friendship with her therapist after therapy ends.[10] However, at other points, she urges that unless mutual transformation and vulnerability is happening during therapy, the relationship is not a trustworthy resource for the client;[11] this suggests that friendship must be possible during therapy in order for therapy to be trustworthy, and that mutual intimacy is not limited to the post-therapy period.

There are thus several questions: Is the argument one for friendship alone, or does it extend to include sexual intimacy? Is the argument focused only on intimacy following therapy, or does it also encompass intimacy during therapy? An ethical analysis must look carefully at the distinctions between friendship and sexual intimacy as well as distinctions between intimacy during therapy and intimacy after therapy.

In *Sex in the Parish*, we made room for a possible romantic relationship between pastor and parishioner, albeit under carefully controlled circumstances.[12] We did not take the hard line of Peter Rutter, who argues that any kind of intimacy between pastor and client is always and necessarily abusive and wrong.[13] It might seem at first glance, then, that we would be supportive of the argument that mutuality and intimacy between professional and client are not always wrong. Since many people would consider romantic intimacy with its sexual overtones to be the most vulnerable of relationships, it seems that if we were willing to entertain the possibility of romantic or sexual intimacy between a pastor and a congregant, we could hardly object to a request for the intimacy of friendship in professional-client relationships. At first glance, then, it seems that we should be supportive of Heyward's argument. Yet we are not.

Two important qualifications from our earlier work should be noted at the outset. First, in *Sex in the Parish*, we ruled out categorically any sexual or romantic intimacy where the parishioner has gone to the pastor for specific pastoral, psychological, or spiritual counseling involving intimate disclosure of personal life. Thus while it is true that we did not rule out categorically either friendship or sexual intimacy for clergy who relate to parishioners as partners in the building and maintaining of the church and its mission, at no time did we ever countenance such intimacy under the conditions of therapy. Heyward appears to argue for the legitimacy of intimate mutuality under those very conditions. We consider there to be some significant structural differences between the two situations, and we believe those structural differences are morally relevant, as will be discussed below.

Second, we also made clear that when a pastor becomes interested in a parishioner in a romantic way, that pastor ceases to be the parishioner's minister. That is, the professional relationship ends as soon as new forms of intimacy are encompassed. Our support for possible intimate relations could only be construed as support for intimacy following the termination of the professional relationship, not during it. The view we articulated in *Sex in the Parish* is therefore a nuanced and limited one. The view we articulate here is a further extension and elaboration of that one.

Goals of Therapy

Our construction of an appropriate professional ethic for counseling ministries centers on three convictions: (1) that "power over" and "mutuality" are not polar opposites, nor do they define the range of possible professional-client relations;[14] (2) that boundaries are not simply limits to be seen in negative light, but are enablers that create needed space to effectuate therapy; and (3) that "anticipation evokes manipulation": promises of goods to come following therapy mitigate against the healing process of therapy.

Power Over and Mutuality

The old model of professional "power over" clients is problematic. Mutuality and equality are goods in human relational life. Lebacqz argued many years ago that the power of the professional person is ethically problematic and that one of the goals of professional work is the strengthening and liberation of the client.[15] Therapist and client enter their relationship in positions of unequal power, and one of the purposes of the relationship is to redress that power imbalance by empowering the client. Similarly, Alastair V. Campbell argues that professional care is a reaching out to another in the desire to enhance the value that is seen.[16] Thus, we agree that the therapist at root seeks to enhance the value of the client, enabling the client to function in the world as an equal. The goal of therapy should always be for the therapy to end.

Moreover, the means to this goal is not solely the application of rational skills learned in professional training; as Rivera contends,[17] there is an element of personal commitment and relationship that is central to the therapeutic relationship. Empathy is central to professional practice, especially in the counseling ministries. The reaching out of the therapist is *agape,* and requires a peculiar combination of rationality and feeling. Rigid adherence to rules can undermine the achievement of that relationship of empathy or agape. This gives some force to the argument that rules about professional distance can be so rigid that they undermine the goals of therapy.

If equality and mutuality are the goals of therapy, and if the maintenance of boundaries and of rigid rules about professional distance can undermine those goals, then should the boundaries simply be jettisoned? Heyward and several colleagues who appended essays in her book[18] maintain that the acceptance of boundaries and the withholding of the personhood of the therapist constitutes a patriarchal ethic reflecting a dualism of reason and emotion, and that this ethic must be eschewed by feminists.

There is force to this argument. In *Professional Care: Its Meaning and Practice*, Alastair Campbell asserts that "it is in the control of sympathy that the importance of a professional ethos may again be seen."[19] While Campbell cautions against a "case-centered" approach to professional practice in which the professional is insulated from the individuality of the client and the client's pain, he also notes that it is characteristic of professional practice to respond to violent emotions calmly and with understanding. "The ideal professional has learned, in Scheler's phrase, 'to elevate himself heroically above his body.'"[20] This description of the ideal professional as somehow "separated" from natural emotions and "elevated" above the messy stuff of feelings into a state of calm detachment gives force to the feminist argument that professional ethics reflects a hierarchical, dualistic mode of thinking.

Nonetheless, the force of the argument—even the possibilities of dualism or hierarchy—does not settle the question of whether boundaries should be maintained in professional practice.

Relational Power

It is our conviction that we are trapped in an unfortunate limitation of metaphors. The language of "power over," with its hierarchical connotations and implications of force and nonvoluntariness, belies the realities of professional practice. Professional power is never simply a negative "power over." As Stortz notes in her study *PastorPower,* there may be "kinds and conditions under which 'power over' may be appropriately exercised" and the alternatives of "power within" and "power with" (or friendship) are also not without their problems.[21] There is a tendency in contemporary feminist literature to see "power over" in an entirely negative light, ignoring relationships such as parenthood in which power over another is appropriately exercised. There is also a tendency to lift up friendship and "power with" as though such models of power have no problems. Both of these tendencies distort the ethical realities. Power need not be equal to be ethical, and even equal power is not always ethical.

Moreover, there are alternatives to "power over" other than simple mutuality, equal vulnerability, and friendship. In the counseling context, one person remains the helper and the other the help seeker. Yet this does not mean that they are in a hierarchical relationship. There is a kind of mutuality in which one receives support from the other, yet each respects the role and personhood of the other. Picture, for example, a spaceship docking for repairs at a space station. The station has what the ship needs; there is a one-way vector in the relationship; yet it is not a hierarchical, "power over" relationship in the negative sense. It is simply a relationship in which two entities meet for a limited and specified time so that one can get "refueled" and repaired, ready for the next trip. Therapy can be envisioned in a similar manner. One can think of this as a form of mutuality, although it is not simple equality.

Archie Smith Jr. uses the phrase "relational power" to describe the work of pastoral care. By this term, Smith means using the relationship in therapy to empower the client by providing a context of trust in which the client is accepted and can be free to express herself. Two elements are key in this: The first is giving the troubled counselee support and ample room for self expression; the second is communicating the positive value that the counselee does not have to earn acceptance. "Relational power," suggests Smith, is characterized by "the giving and receiving of respect."[22] Writing from the perspective of the African American community, Smith is particularly attentive to issues of misuse of power in professional ethics; yet the relational power he proposes is not a simple form of equality between professional and client.

Similarly, in *Professional Ethics: Power and Paradox*, Lebacqz argued for the empowerment of the client as the form that "justice," or attention to power issues, would take in professional relations. Both Smith and Lebacqz offer a model that recognizes the power of the professional person without adopting a hierarchical, "power over" view. Yet neither suggests that professional power can simply be set aside and simple equality be adopted instead.

Heyward herself recognizes the power that professionals have simply because of being in a professional position. She argues, for example, that even the most empathic priest will inflict harm unless she understands the power she embodies "simply because she is an ordained person."[23] Further, Heyward suggests that a response that eschews such power is pastorally inadequate and professionally irresponsible.[24] She also recognizes explicitly that her own therapist had institutional power.[25] Heyward argues both for an acceptance of professional power and for its transformation; failure to do either, she proposes, is potentially abusive.[26]

We agree with the need for professionals to recognize the power that they have simply because of their role. Lebacqz called attention to this issue many years ago in *Professional Ethics: Power and Paradox,* and Lebacqz and Barton developed the analysis of professional power in *Sex in the Parish.* We further agree that attention to the structures of professional practice and the ways in which those structures secure power to the professionals is always necessary. A professional-client relationship is not a relationship of equality. Precisely because of the ambiguities of professional power, however, a simple adopting of mutuality and friendship as styles of professional work is not adequate.

The Role of Boundaries

Mutuality and equality may be goals of therapy, but goal and method are not necessarily synonymous. We believe that boundaries are important for securing the goals of therapy. Boundaries—of space, time, financial structure, and limits on personal sharing—help to secure the "safe space" within which mutual respect can take place. As Smith notes, clients often come in the midst of "scandal": they are tired, beaten down, discouraged, ashamed, uncertain, weak. In biblical language, we might suggest that they are the "outsider," or at least feel themselves to be. There are ancient roots to the law of hospitality in which there is a power differential between the vulnerable guest who comes asking for refuge and the host who has security to offer. A feminist approach to counseling must attend to the realities of the vulnerability of clients. An "option for the poor" must be exercised in which the vulnerable are not further victimized but are protected from exploitation. It is such protections that professional boundaries are meant to provide. They are a role-specific exercise of the law of hospitality. While rules always run the risk of being unduly rigid, they are necessary to a system that intends to protect the vulnerable from exploitation.

Consider, for example, what would happen if therapists began to develop mutual friendships with their clients, using the therapy hour for their own enhancement as well as for that of the client. Why should the client pay for therapy if it is as beneficial for the therapist as for the client? Is this not exploitive? Or, to put it another way, why would anyone seek out a therapist rather than a friend to talk to, if not because of the professional skills of the therapist? William F. May offers some cautionary words against a too-facile stress on mutuality: "In crisis, the ill person needs not simply presence but skill, not just personal concern but highly disciplined services targeted to specific needs."[27] While relationship may be central to therapy, the therapist is also understood to have acquired particular skills through training. It is for this reason that we choose a therapist rather than a friend for some purposes.[28]

For therapists not to use their skills for the benefit of the client is abusive. The therapist who begins to turn the therapy hour into an occasion for her own therapy and personal growth is exploiting the client for her own benefit. Thus, the very mutuality that Heyward claims she wanted with her therapist could be interpreted as generally abusive. It violates the obligation of the therapist to focus on the client's needs. Therapy is a relationship that exists for a specific purpose: the healing of the care-seeker. In this, it is structurally different from parish ministry, in which pastor and parishioner may work side by side for the general upbuilding of the church and its mission. This structural difference explains why we were willing to countenance certain forms of intimacy in the general practice of ministry, but absolutely forbade those same forms in a counseling relationship.[29]

Because the counseling relationship focuses on the needs of one partner, not of both, we also question whether a genuine friendship can emerge from it. Any "friendship" following therapy may prove disappointing, once the former client discovers that it is no longer a one-way street in which someone else is constantly ready to "be there" for her. Part of the reason that therapy "works" is that someone is there who cares about the client, is focused on the client's needs and issues, and does not make the demands of "normal" relationship on the client. But in genuine mutuality, all of these demands would have to be possibilities. If we seek therapy at the outset because we need a safe space away from all those demands, then the therapy will not be enhanced but will be undermined by the mutuality that Heyward advocates. In spite of our general agreement with the importance of mutuality and its healing power in human relationships, therefore, we remain persuaded that in cases of counseling, boundaries are appropriate, necessary, and should be maintained.[30]

After Therapy

But now we come to the difficult issue of whether a friendship or relationship of mutual vulnerability might be possible "after" therapy. Some have argued strongly and clearly that there is a difference between intimacy during therapy and intimacy afterward. Margo Rivera charges therapists with responsibility for maintaining clear boundaries during therapy, but suggests that having rigid rules about boundaries following therapy is not helpful: "Decisions about what can and can't take place after the professional contract is completed should be left to the discretion [of the people involved]."[31] While Rivera does not call such boundaries "abusive," she does suggest that to assume an everlasting power differential between therapist and client is disrespectful to both parties and implies a static view of relationship.[32]

This is a powerful argument, and gives some support to a client's desire for a friendship with her therapist following the termination of the professional relationship. Yet again, we disagree. In the conviction that "anticipation evokes manipulation," we suggest that holding out the hope of a friendship following therapy reshapes the therapy process itself and mitigates against the healing that should take place in that process.

Suppose the therapist agrees to a friendship "after therapy." There are several problems with this. To begin, it might compromise a good decision about when therapy would end. In her eagerness to explore a new friendship, the client might try to end the therapy relationship prematurely. Many clients are inclined to leave therapy as soon as they begin to feel better, but before significant issues have been addressed. The promise of a "benefit" such as friendship outside therapy only gives inducement to such hasty decisions, and might undermine therapy.

Moreover, we suspect that as soon as the therapist agrees to a friendship "after" therapy, there would be pressure for a friendship "during" therapy. Otherwise, one would have to assume that it is possible to move quickly from a relationship of "no friendship" to one of friendship. How is one to know whether a friendship is possible after therapy if there have not been glimpses of it during therapy? But if there are such glimpses, then holding the line and saying "not now, but it will be all right once therapy ends" seems difficult. An abrupt transition from professional relationship to friendship does not make sense. But if an abrupt transition does not make sense, then boundaries either must be maintained both during and after therapy, or they must go down during therapy, not just afterward. If the maintenance of boundaries is important for the creation of safe space for therapy to occur, then those boundaries must be maintained after therapy as well as during therapy so that there is no inducement to disrupt or modify the therapy process for the sake of the future changed relationship.

Other Problems

We are also not convinced that boundaries between friendship and sexual intimacy could be sustained. If some forms of intimacy are acceptable, why not all forms of intimacy? If mutual sharing is the norm for the therapeutic relationship, then what could be more fully vulnerable and mutual than a sexual relationship? Many clients would seek friendship as a prelude to other forms of intimacy. Numerous authors, including many feminists, have cautioned against the abuses that result from professionals entering sexual relations with their clients.[33]

Conclusions

Finally, there is a kind of bizarre irony in the argument for dropping rigid rules about boundaries. The argument that relationships must be centered on mutuality, sisterhood, and friendship runs the risk of establishing a new, rigid rule! While Heyward does not appear to want to *require* that all relationships be "mutual," but only to hold that no relationship should be precluded from being or becoming mutual,[34] there are problems on both practical and theoretical grounds with the standard of mutuality interpreted as sisterhood and friendship: On the theoretical level, friendship must be genuine friendship, not forced because of one party's desire nor because of some new norm or rule. To set mutuality, sisterhood, and friendship as the sine qua non for any good therapy relationship is to weight that relationship a priori, rather than allowing a genuine relationship to develop. No doubt it is for this reason that Heyward draws back from making mutuality a requirement. But if it is not required of all therapy relations, but only of some, then we have two additional problems.

First, if mutuality is the standard for trustworthy therapy, how is it possible that some therapy relations can fail to be mutual and still be ethical? If not all relationships must be mutual, then it must be possible for some that are not mutual to be ethical; yet the standard seems to preclude this. On a theoretical level, it is not clear how mutuality can function as a standard and be simultaneously not required.

Second, how are we to deal with the practical problems raised by the possibilities for mutuality? For example, what if the client wants friendship, but the therapist does not? If mutuality must be a part of the therapy process, then therapists must be open to friendships with all of their clients. Few people could sustain that many significant relationships! If mutuality is not required for all therapy relationships, but is only a possibility held out for the lucky few who evoke a desire for friendship in their therapists, then therapy runs the risks of exclusivity that Stortz notes as dangers for the "power with" or friendship model. Clients will vie with each other to see who is the therapist's "favorite" and who gets courted for later friendship. This seems destructive of any therapeutic goals.

On both theoretical and practical grounds, therefore, a norm of mutuality, friendship, or sisterhood may be just as problematic for professional practice as is the norm of rigid boundaries.

A Political Critique

Similar issues were raised for us by the case of "Robert"[35] presented in our earlier work. Robert grew up with a "sex only in marriage" view and then got caught conceptually in the "free love" movement of the 1960s. He began to be unclear about what it means to "love" someone, and ended up acting out sexually because his professional training and values were being badly assaulted by an alternative set of values from a contemporary political movement. In our view, Robert chose wrongly in giving up the values associated with his professional training and its restrictions on sexual activity with parishioners.

Any feminist therapist may be in a similar situation, caught between values inculcated in professional training and values of a modern political movement. Feminism is a political movement that asserts strong values. Among those are mutuality, vulnerability, and friendship.

Robert was pulled between two value systems. But just as Robert's case could not be decided a priori by assuming that the contemporary movement was correct and the professional values incorrect, so the therapist's case cannot be decided a priori by assuming that a contemporary political movement is correct and professional values incorrect. If Robert was wrong to give up the values of his professional training, then so might the therapist be wrong to give up the values of her professional training.

A genuine sociopolitical analysis of therapy must include the political implications of feminism as a movement that asserts values that come into conflict with professional values. While Heyward sees the conflict, she appears not to see that this conflict cannot be settled a priori in favor of the values of feminism without consideration of the peculiar nature of the professional-client relationship, its purposes and structures. Only a careful analysis of the nature of professional-client relationships can determine whether the breaking of boundaries is correct in general, and whether it would be correct in any particular case.

In our judgment, keeping boundaries is not simply a reflection of patriarchal hierarchy, but a recognition of the vulnerability and pain of clients. Keeping boundaries serves the purpose of therapy, which focuses on healing that pain, enhancing the value of the client, and restoring power to the client. The maintenance of boundaries does not mean that professional and client are in a hierarchical, abusive relationship. It means that hospitality is being honored. We must broaden our understanding of mutuality to encompass forms of relational power that do not fit the model of friendship or sisterhood. There is work to be done yet in delineating the meaning of mutuality, friendship, sisterhood, and professional ethics. This essay is a small effort toward that end.

Notes

1. Carter Heyward, *When Boundaries Betray Us* (San Francisco: Harper San Francisco, 1994).

2. See, e.g., Heyward, *When Boundaries Betray Us*, 10.

3. Elizabeth A. Johnson, *She Who Is: The Mystery of God in Feminist Discourse* (New York: Crossroad, 1994), 68. Cf. Jan Raymond, *A Passion for Friends: Toward a Philosophy of Female Affection* (Boston: Beacon Press, 1986), 28: "The slogan 'Sisterhood is powerful' signaled a coming together of women formerly separated from each other. Ideals of sisterhood became materialized in feminist literature, theory, and action. Different schools of feminism all stressed the necessity to build a strong solidarity of sisterhood."

4. Lynn N. Rhodes, *Co-Creating: A Feminist Vision of Ministry* (Philadelphia: Westminster, 1987), 123.

5. Heyward, *When Boundaries Betray Us*, 184.

6. Ibid., 126.

7. Ibid., 40.

8. Ibid., 137, 186.

9. See Heyward, *When Boundaries Betray Us*, 33, 47.

10. Ibid., 10: "My desire to build a friendship with Elizabeth following the termination of therapy."

11. Ibid., 11, 64–5, passim.

12. Karen Lebacqz and Ronald G. Barton, *Sex in the Parish* (Louisville, Ky.: Westminster John Knox, 1991).

13. Peter Rutter, *Sex in the Forbidden Zone* (Los Angeles: Jeremy Tarcher, 1989), 25.

14. Cf. Martha Ellen Stortz, *PastorPower* (Nashville: Abingdon Press, 1993), 51–53.

15. Karen Lebacqz, *Professional Ethics: Power and Paradox* (Nashville: Abingdon Press, 1985), chapter 8.

16. Alastair V. Campbell, *Professional Care: Its Meaning and Practice* (Philadelphia: Fortress, 1984), 85.

17. Margo Rivera, "I-Thou: Interpersonal Boundaries in the Therapy Relationship," in Katherine Ragsdale, *Boundary Wars: Intimacy and Distance in Healing Relationships* (Cleveland: The Pilgrim Press, 1996).

18. See, e.g., Miriam Greenspan, "On Professionalism," in Heyward, *When Boundaries Betray Us*, 197, 202.

19. Campbell, *Professional Care*, 82.

20. Ibid.

21. Stortz, *PastorPower*, 10.

22. Archie Smith Jr., "The Power of Scandal and Foolish Transformations," unpublished ms. Dr. Smith is professor of pastoral care at Pacific School of Religion, Berkeley, Calif.

23. Heyward, *When Boundaries Betray Us*, 184.

24. Ibid.

25. Ibid., 178.

26. Ibid., 185.

27. William F. May, "Code, Covenant, Contract, or Philanthropy," Hastings Center Report 5, no. 6 (December 1975), 37.

28. Although Heyward declares, "I did not need to be 'treated.' I needed to be joined by a sister" (*Boundaries*, 153), we suspect that with her wide range of friends and "sisters," she did indeed choose a therapist because she anticipated that the therapist would bring distinctive skills.

29. See Lebacqz and Barton, *Sex in the Parish*, chapters 4 and 5.

30. In our view, the evidence provided by Heyward suggests that her therapist erred not because she maintained boundaries and refused friendship, but precisely because there were a few times that she waffled and appeared to offer the hope of friendship to Heyward. If this ambivalence did happen, we believe it was inappropriate.

31. Rivera, "I-Thou: Interpersonal Boundaries," 192.

32. Ibid., 20–21. It should be emphasized that Rivera's primary purpose is to ensure that therapists look at the issue of countertransference. She argues against rigid rules because they can become blinders that function to avoid confrontation with such issues.

33. See, e.g., Rutter, *Sex in the Forbidden Zone*; Lebacqz and Barton, *Sex in the Parish*; Marie Fortune, *Is Nothing Sacred? When Sex Invades the Pastoral Relationship* (San Francisco: Harper and Row, 1989); Gary Richard Schoener et al., *Psychotherapists' Sexual Involvement with Clients: Intervention and Prevention* (Minneapolis: Walk-In Counseling Center, 1989).

34. Heyward, *When Boundaries Betray Us*, 10.

35. Robert was a pastor who failed repeatedly to keep boundaries with parishioners. See Lebacqz and Barton, *Sex in the Parish*, 84.

7

Boundaries

Protecting the Vulnerable or Perpetrating a Bad Idea

Carter Heyward and Beverly Wildung Harrison

Neither you, Simon, nor the fifty thousand,
nor Judas, nor the twelve,
nor the priests, nor the scribes,
nor doomed Jerusalem itself,
understand what power is.[1]

Sex and violence are two areas where many of us learn to fear ourselves; the more we fear ourselves, the less we try for freedom.[2]

We are white lesbians, seminary professors, and feminist liberation theologians. One of us is a priest, the other proudly laity, and we understand "abuse" as a misuse of power, and "power" as the ability to effect, decide, or act. In real relationships, power is configured around many variables, such as race, gender/sexual identity, age, experience, economic security, physical well-being and strength, intellectual giftedness, professional status and competence, emotional stability, and political clout. We understand "sexual abuse" to be the use of power, in any form, to sexually harass, threaten, intimidate, manipulate, or coerce other people. We know that each of us has considerable power—in bestowed-role authority, personal charisma, and other forms—in relation especially to our students and other spiritually seeking women and men. Like nearly everyone, we sometimes walk a thin line between abusive and creative uses of power.

Therefore, we cannot be smug in assessing ethical issues of abuse. Like most women, we also have been abused, sexually and emotionally, experiences from which we have learned much about power and its misuse.[3]

We agree that change in the sexual basis of our life together is needed. But we realize also that we in this society, and certainly we who are Christians, are not well equipped to envision the needed changes. In order to effect such a radical transformation—and nothing less is called for—we have to dig deeper, to see how we experience power, how we use (and are used by) sex, and how we can act in more morally grounded, spiritually empowering, and socially as well as personally liberating ways.

But do we need "boundaries"? In earlier work, we used boundary language, albeit with caution, while acknowledging its importance in a sexually violent culture.[4] Over time, through ongoing and intense discussion with many sister and brother clergy, therapists, survivors of abuse, ethicists, and theologians, we've changed our minds and come to believe that the constant casting of our perspectives on abuse within the framework of boundaries is a bad idea. We believe there are other, and much better, ways of reflecting on, experiencing, and envisioning the right and wrong dynamics of relation.

So many women and children, boys as well as girls, have been sexually abused. This violence is not abating. In this evil and terrifying social context, many people assume that "good boundaries" are essential to their own healing and to the well-being and safety of others. It is as if "good boundaries" have become synonymous with "right-relation." But we have serious misgivings, politically, ethically, and theologically, about the worldview and spirituality embedded in this equation. "Boundary discourse," with its theoretical ring, is *not* basically about theory (no honest theorizing is) but about the daily lives of real people who are trying to survive and live without terror. We hear, and take seriously, the urgency in the voices of victims and survivors of sexual abuse. It is in the context of such urgency that we also wrestle with how, along with our sisters and brothers, we can help make this world a safer, more just and compassionate home for us all—especially those most violated. In this essay we will discuss why we think that the psychological construct of boundaries will not contribute much that is lasting or systemically transformative toward shaping such a world, safer professional relationships, or healthier women and men. Our reasons for challenging the popular devotion to boundaries are complex.

Most feminists derive their concept of boundaries from ego-psychology, where the notion is suffused with modern Eurocentric, patriarchal, and capitalist assumptions about "self-possession" as healthy and mature. As we will argue, this should be enough to make feminist liberation theologians suspicious. At the psychological level, we do not believe boundaries will keep anyone safe, since safety is not produced by the condition of individual egos. What the psychological concept of boundaries will do *sometimes* is enable us to keep our distance from one another and thereby *feel* safe. We believe this is what boundary discourse does among contemporary feminists: It helps us *feel* safe in a violent and abusive world that is *not* safe at all for those who do not acquiesce to its political, economic, cultural, or erotic rules—and not absolutely safe for anyone. Boundaries secure our *feelings* of safety while doing nothing to generate actual conditions for safety in the society and world. By lulling us into a false sense that all is well between us and the world, "good boundaries" actually may dull our passion for justice and compassion, two foundations of a truly safe social order.

In what follows we attempt to show why the use of boundaries— as concept, language, and feminist politic—actually works against any long-term sustainable effort to create a safer and friendlier world. We will discuss four related themes to make our case: (1) We will look at how notions of boundaries reflect *capitalist social relations* and *patriarchal spirituality*; (2) we will explore the psychological theory that underlies boundary discourse—the "*transference*" dynamic; (3) we will reflect briefly on *vulnerability*, which we believe is theologically the root of much tension about boundaries among feminist theologians; and (4) finally, we will suggest how *professional ethics* might be formulated and ecclesial efforts to curb clergy sexual misconduct might be shaped without resorting to boundary discourse or reinforcing in other ways the patriarchal logic of "self-possession."

Ego Psychology, Capitalist Social Relations, and Patriarchal Spirituality

We are increasingly disturbed by the way feminist religious and theological writers, including some that claim to exemplify feminist liberation theological method, abandon a hermeneutic of suspicion in relation to the psychological categories developed in Western social theory over the last century. Psychology, after all, is the "bourgeois science" par excellence, in which accounts of personal health, growth, and development reflect the ideals of personal and social well-being generated by capitalist political economy. Psychological "normality" dramatically correlates with the ideal "self" of capitalist social relations. Such a "self" is mature and healthy *only* when purposive—rational, productive, and autonomous. This strong, admirable, and normal (white male) person is self-possessed and well-boundaried.[5] But, some feminists protest, women, even white middle-strata women, have never been able to "possess" ourselves in capitalist patriarchy, as if this justifies aspirations by women and people of color for so great a "privilege" as "self-possession" and its requisite, "good boundaries." We do not agree that we, or other women and men of whatever color or culture, should embrace with enthusiasm professional and political practices that daily reproduce capitalist patriarchy's social relations and spiritual ideals of separation, autonomy, and self-ownership.

Whether in its more biologically reductionistic early Freudian versions, its psychodynamic-centered psychoanalytic and neo-Freudian accounts, or its profoundly individuated and spiritualized Jungian versions of maturity as internalized self-appropriation, all ego-psychology presupposes the capitalist ideal of a well-defined "self" or "psyche" that exists primarily for itself and its own. This norm represents and legitimates the existing world of social relations in which right-relation requires boundary-demarcated transactions among the mature, those who "own" themselves and whose badge of strength is the "mature self." Ironically, this bourgeois ideal of self-possession in modern psychology is an extreme parody of what Karl Marx meant by total commoditization or alienation of social life, in which each of us becomes a "commodity" to ourselves. And this is what feminists seek?

Modern ego-psychology reflects capitalist political economy in another important way. The "knowledge" that makes for "salvo" (health), like the so-called "identity" of the "self," also comes to be viewed as a commodity or possession. Doctors, analysts, and therapists "possess" a knowledge about others' psychological situations that these others need. This "gnosis"—or special knowledge—about the emotional and mental condition of other people can be exchanged for money with those who want to know what is happening "in" their psyches, minds, hearts. All theories that image psychological treatment in this self-contained way reproduce capitalist social relations in every relational exchange. The boundaries that doctors, therapists, and other counselors invoke in this model to keep a professional distance from those who seek their help models an invulnerability—set-apartness and dispassion—that patients and clients are invited implicitly to imitate in developing their own healthier ways of living. This psychology, with its adamant defense of "self" and "boundaries," functions to hold existing power relations in place, not to change them.

The "Transference" Dynamic: Psychological Justification for "Professional Boundaries" in Helping-Relationships

The psychological structure undergirding the current enthusiasm for boundaries among feminist therapists, clergy, and other helping professionals is the dynamic of "transference." This refers to the patient, client, counselee, or (in relation to clergy) lay person's intense projection of unresolved relational issues onto the doctor, therapist, pastor, or priest, thereby making the professional relationship, to some degree, *symbolic* rather than an occasion for people to be present to one another as themselves, as authentically as possible. In discussions specifically about transference in relation to clergy, the symbolic power is magnified because traditionally it is held to be, to some degree, "sacred." The connection between "transference" and "boundaries" goes something like this: Because a transferential relationship does not permit emotional mutuality, the person seeking help, because she is assumed to be especially vulnerable in this context, must be protected from the harm that might result if the two people acted as if they were friends. The transference dynamic in professional situations requires that the helper and the one seeking help be kept emotionally separate, hence "boundaries."

Transference dynamics are real dimensions of most important relationships, and all of us should strive throughout our lives to understand more fully how we carry past relationships into present ones. However, for professional healers to theorize their emotional—and economic—power over others as a totally unique and unchanging dynamic that must be protected forever for the other's benefit is outrageous. To use the theory or actual experience of transference for any purpose other than to help people increase their awareness of how power works in their lives, and to help them do so with dignity and perspective, is an *abusive* use of professional, economic, emotional, and, at times, sexual power.

We do not believe it is wise for feminist professionals—doctors, therapists, clergy, and others—to accept, without challenge, the medical model of healing, which requires an allegiance to the doctrine of transference generated by ego psychology. We are astonished and dismayed that some feminist theologians apply this medical model, as practiced in psychiatry, to the pastoral relationship, which should be grounded in religious *community*. Pastoral care should embody ways of healing that continuously challenge highly individualized and crassly elitist professionalism. We are struck by the failure of liberal church leaders, feminists and others, to insist on the significant differences between theological and psychological norms of healing. Instead, the churches today are setting in place policies that not only forbid sex but also discourage close friendship between clergy and those who seek, or have ever sought, their help. This inhibiting of intimacy and peer relating is encouraging the worst forms of patriarchal clericalism.

Consider the policy recently adopted by the Episcopal Diocese of Michigan:

> The authority accompanying a particular position or function ends when the position or function is given up. Ordination, on the other hand, is permanent, and carries with it an authority and a responsibility which remain regardless of the ordained person's position. This

being the case, an ordained person's position in relation to those among whom he or she ministers can never be simply that of one person among peers.

The policy continues,

> As ordained people, clergy are accorded (and take for granted) a certain power in relationship with other Christians—teaching and interpreting authority, credibility in making moral judgments, sacramental authority, authority to be present with people when they are most vulnerable. Whether or not it is acknowledged, whether or not it is intentionally exerted, clergy have this power by sacred trust and its influence colors all the relationships of clergy within the church.[6]

The power here is located unilaterally, explicitly, and mysteriously in the *person* of the religious professional. His or her power is enhanced by an intrinsic "sacredness" that strengthens its erotic buzz. Clergy cannot be peers with their congregants because they possess this "power by sacred trust" which, like the power of God, never ends, even when the clergy person is no longer in the pastoral relationship. Therefore, like psychiatrists and other psychotherapists, clergy cannot be peers with those who seek—or have ever sought—their help, because transference is likely to be operative in the relationship whether or not the persons involved realize it. Whatever happened to those great theologies of mutual ministry and friendship making that excited feminist theologians a decade ago? It seems, sadly, that numbers of feminist theologians as well as many other progressive church leaders are not taking seriously the fact that the increasing professionalization of ministry is an accommodation to the premier values of the dominant culture.

Why have feminists forgotten that Freud's location of transference in the clinical setting was related to his finding "masochism" in women patients? Of course masochism is in women—and it is everywhere else as well. If we could only see that our entire life together is a relational movement through symbolic dynamics of many kinds—such as projecting our desire for a parent's attention onto a partner, or our attachment to a childhood buddy onto a professional colleague, or our hatred toward someone who betrayed us thirty years ago onto our next-door neighbor. Some of the most interesting relational work we do is through the transformation of such symbolic dynamics into authentic embodied connection. The sometimes powerful transference relationship between a priest and someone in her care constitutes no good reason why the relationship cannot over time become increasingly authentic—i.e., mutual. This in fact often happens in the best pastoral work: People move together toward a more fully mutual relationship, and the movement itself, which frequently involves struggling to share power, has a transformative impact on everyone involved.

We have to work at right relation. It doesn't just happen because people like each other, share the same values, or seem to have the same "power" in a particular life situation. Right, or mutual, relation is a dynamic *movement*, never a place to be once and for all. Creative relational and personal power is generated in the struggle for mutuality in professional as in all important relationships. This involves sharing the varied insights and abilities we possess to create situations in which everyone benefits and no one is disregarded or disempowered. Authentic, or honest, presence is essential from all participants. Mutuality, as we understand it, therefore is rooted deeply in a relational ethic, which we seek continuously to embody but which we can never express fully. Like compassion and justice, relational authenticity is a goal and a commitment to do what we can toward creating it together. Those who seek professional help ought to be respected, which means that, insofar as possible, they encounter emotional authenticity in their helpers. American Indian shaman Juana Malek notes that this is why, as a woman trained in psychology, she chooses not to practice therapy but rather to work in different ways as a healer among American Indian and other women who come to her.[7]

As for the astonishing notion that transference exists *in perpetuity,* by virtue of a power-over that does not change, we should remind ourselves that we have heard this before: It is steeped in the same patriarchal logic that has produced an unchanging deity who is not genuinely involved with us and that has convinced us, through generations of forebears, that our souls depend on our accepting this essentially untouchable power over us. This logic also reflects a theology of ministry in which sacredness is mediated only by those set ontically apart from others. Such doctrines, as feminists used to emphasize, are deferential devices constructed by dominant males—who, in the church, have been prelates and senior clergy—to control others by fostering dependency. In order to be "safe" in this system, lay people and junior clergy must accept the power of higher-ranking clergy over them.

Patriarchal thinkers have always found ways to make themselves "experts" in relation to others' lives. The pathologizing and medicalizing of childbirth in the West is a notorious example of such a process, in which dominant-class men have consolidated their professional power over others and, in so doing, have made fortunes and shaped prevailing ethics or norms for action. The pathologizing and medicalizing of psychological trauma and pain similarly reflects a process in which the power to name, define, and to whatever degree possible control, others' psychological health creates a new priestly caste.

It is disconcerting that feminists are colluding in using these teachings to repatriarchalize theologies of ministry. While sexual abuse abounds in the churches and must be effectually addressed, other trends also are at work that prevailing feminist analysis is ignoring: let no one miss the erosion of conditions for creative freedom in patterns of church leadership. This is just one consequence of the increasing bureaucratization and hierarchical control that is occurring. As we see it, some feminists who support new patterns of clergy control have reified and exaggerated the nature of "clergy power" without seeming to notice the social and political shifts taking place that are eroding the strength of local congregations, including their leaders, and undercutting the capacity for clergy and lay leaders to creatively develop conditions for community—and mutuality. Another cultural trend that seems not to worry many concerned about sexual abuse is the growing reinforcement of puritanical sex restrictions that are creating new barriers to deeper personal connection. At this historical moment, simplistic interpretations of "family values" are being touted not only by the Christian Right but also by some feminists and progressive religious leaders.

The most liberating and creative challenge issued by feminist theology to several generations of Christian, Jewish, and other women is that we take back our relational, communal power. Our agency is at stake here: our capacity to live, to make decisions, and to act as fully human persons. Feminists have learned that it is no small thing to wrest our agency—our spiritual and moral power—out of the hands of professionals who often imagine they know us better than we know ourselves. With some difficulty, some gutsy professionals *are* managing to break through these rigid capitalist and patriarchal notions of relational safety: In response to Carter's controversial *Boundaries* book, she has heard from scores of women from across the United States and elsewhere about friendship, love, and relational transformation between healers and those who once were their clients or therapists or were in a pastoral relationship with them. There is nothing "unethical" about these stories. To the contrary, they testify to peoples' capacities to act together responsibly as relationships change.

A Theological Issue in This Debate: Vulnerability

It is our conviction that underlying the boundaries debate among women are some deep-seated theological differences that need ongoing exploration. One of these is the role of "vulnerability" in relation to power. For some in this debate, vulnerability is a weakness, perhaps even an evil. By contrast, we believe that vulnerability is *openness*—to deep engagement with the world, with others, and with oneself. Vulnerability is openness to feeling, to touching and being touched emotionally, and to personal transformation. Vulnerability is, we believe, sacred—a primary dimension of the spirit's own movement in history, the creative and liberating spirit of life that is purposeful and good. Where it is incarnate among us, vulnerability is thus a deeply creative and creaturely capacity to be valued, not treated as if it were a source of pathology or, in the case of a pastor or therapist, a symptom of his or her unprofessional behavior. In fact, the vulnerability of the professional, as well as of those seeking help, can be an important healing resource.

Many women therapists and theologians apparently assume that vulnerable women need protection from their own vulnerability—from having to struggle with emotional pain, complexity, or the processes of learning more effectual moral agency. Sexually vulnerable people need protection from sexually predatory behavior. But this is quite different psychologically, spiritually, politically, and ethically from trying to protect women from feeling their own feelings too deeply, experiencing their own experiences too fully, or struggling with their own pain too much when it may be excruciating and possibly dangerous to them or others. More dangerous, and far more common, is for women to deny their vulnerability, mask their pain, or be shielded from emotionally difficult and ethically complex situations that ought to elicit response.

Vulnerable women need to become agents of our own lives. We do not need protection from the emotional openness that is a psychospiritual root of our agency: our capacity to live our lives fully. This capacity is cultivated only through emotional struggle.[8] One of Carter's students, Atema Eclai from Ghana, helped us see the point clearly in response to someone who was embarrassed to be crying in her presence: "What strength is there in dry eyes?" she asked her friend. By contrast, too many care givers assume that tears and vulnerability, while important in the healing process, are *in themselves* signs of weakness and powerlessness, not courage and strength. Vulnerability is, thus, perceived to be a state of helplessness that people must pass through on the road to wellness, not a place to be grounded and secured—which we believe it is.

Among white Christian feminist liberation theologians, this difficult but potentially creative tension about the place of vulnerability in the struggle for women's liberation seems to us also present, though seldom spoken. On the one hand are theologians who locate women's strength and agency in their resistance to any and all suffering. From this perspective, vulnerability is a problem because it *intrinsically* opens us to suffering.[9] Other theologians, including the two of us, emphasize vulnerability as a condition and source of strength and agency, including our power to heal from abuse and violence and to resist unjust suffering—that which is generated by alienated, abusive power. By opening people to the world as it really is, vulnerability may increase suffering. In no way however does it minimize our rejection of abuse or our capacity for resistance. Vulnerability enables solidarity and compassion.[10] We suspect that there is a connection between the fear of vulnerability and the emphasis on "self-possession" implicit in the celebration of boundaries.

Clergy Professional Ethics and Policies
on Clergy Sexual Misconduct

We detect an easy assumption among feminists that current efforts to correct clergy sexual abuse through tightly drawn regulations are contributing to a positive renewal of professional ethical standards in the churches. The convictions we have sketched here should make clear the skepticism we bring to this presumption.

Many of the new rules and regulations or, as they sometimes are referred to, "clergy codes of conduct," bear little or no resemblance to the normative professional ethics that academic ethicists advocate. And they bear only some vague resemblance to the actual codes endorsed by coteries of professionals themselves. The former emphasize the positive obligations that competent professional performance involves. The latter—that is, codes generated by associations of professional elites—may include constraints but they tend to emphasize the prerogatives and protections needed to sustain the prestige of the profession itself. We need to be clear that the new policies affecting clergy conduct are not set within a competence-based understanding of ministry. And although it seems that church leaders believe the new codes will protect clergy and the institution from litigation and public humiliation, we believe that the actual effect will be to protect institutional interests without extending to individual clergy the protections that more powerful and prestigious guilds carve out for their members. Unlike legal and medical professionals, few clergy are being consulted in determining the shape of policies and regulations that will affect them.

Our sympathies are with the growing number of clergy who begin to suspect that they now have fewer protections and rights in the church than in civil society. The new codes, driven by obsessive fear of litigation and public censure, aim chiefly to formulate limits to clergy-parishioner relationships: They constrict, they name dangers, and they do so with a fixation on sexual conduct that reinforces the reactionary political climate of social control we have discussed already. There is a growing tendency to override all considerations of privacy in relation to clergy lives. Intrusive inquiries that at one time would have been declared unconstitutional and illegal if practiced by the state are becoming routine in the church. In our opinion, these practices more and more will undermine the willingness of self-respecting and mature adults to consider ordained ministries.

Bev's experience in teaching clergy professional ethics in seminary and Carter's in working with candidates for the priesthood suggests that the fear generated by the new regulations makes it more difficult than ever to get students to think creatively about theologies of ministry. Most of even the best students have "safety" *foremost* in mind. Many are scared to seriously discuss components of moral community such as honesty, risk taking, engagement of differences, and skills of conflict resolution. The passivity of seminarians in relation to the new rules is disconcertingly widespread. These rubrics have a chilling effect on the willingness of aspiring ordinands to dream dreams and envision new approaches to ministry.

Ironically, the churches *do* need a renaissance of concern for clergy professional formation and accountability. But what is most urgently called for is a *communal* reconception of professional ethics in the churches. Clergy professional ethics are part of the wider question of the church as a moral community.[11] The responsibilities and accountabilities of clergy and of the wider ecclesial communities must be considered together. The myriads of instances of abusive clergy behavior, sexual and other, must be acknowledged and addressed. So too must the large numbers of instances of church abuse of clergy, and their intimate others and families, however defined. In both types of abuse, the most likely victims are the same: women, whether clergy or lay, especially lesbians; gay men; children; single clergy; and any clergy person who resists traditionalism and theological and political conformity. We must learn to name the total range of abuses and make the connections among them. Inadequate wages and benefits, totally unrealistic psychic and material demands on clergy and lay leaders, even at times the refusal of basic human respect for clergy under the guise of "devotion and admiration," must be included in an understanding of what constitutes church abuse of its leaders, lay and ordained.

As feminists have insisted, the problem of clergy sexual misconduct is rooted in deeply embedded patterns of male sexual socialization in relation to women.[12] The intractable heart of the matter in liberal churches, including most mainline Protestant churches, is that many male clergy have learned to be "successful men" by using seduction at every level of social and professional relationships. It is also a fact that the *most* predatory clergy, frequently those who have victimized many people, are the hardest to bring to accountability precisely because they have so skillfully developed manipulative patterns of gaining people's loyalty and support that are devastatingly effective and so enable them to obscure their sexual behavior and/or its significance. In some congregations, even when multiple occasions of sexual abuse are revealed, the victims are not believed, because the seductive clergyman is so widely admired—and so well protected by his admirers[13]. Only strong communal interventions that publicly confront such clergy predators with their genuinely damaging and morally repugnant use of power hold any hope of effecting accountability and long-term change.

Each occasion of clergy sexual harassment and abuse is serious, but the policies being put in place, if they work, usually do so against clergy who are not so powerful, including in many cases those whose sexual activity is not manipulative or abusive. Those pastors who have developed well-constructed public veneers that cultivate parishioners' adoration and play on their erotic unawareness are far less likely to be called to account than the less prestigious or slick. The net cast by the new policies is far more likely to catch gay men and lesbians, single clergy who are sexually active, and straight clergy whose ministries are theologically or politically controversial. In both of our denominations and elsewhere are numerous cases where powerful perpetrators of multiple offenses, if noticed at all, have been merely reprimanded, because bishops and ecclesiastical superiors have cared more about the prestige of the institution than about ending the abuse. Formalistic and rule-centered ethics, such as the new clergy misconduct codes, have numerous drawbacks. Most particularly, the rules must be applied, and those responsible for their application always have discretionary power about when and where they shall be invoked and what the consequences shall be.

Nothing will address the problem of clergy sexual misconduct except heightened efforts to increase the awareness of clergy and laity alike about power dynamics among us, including awareness of the role played by erotic power in *all* relationships. Greater personal openness and honesty, not less, is called for. We must learn to talk and walk our way through questions of appropriate relationship at every level of church life. Clergy need communities of other clergy and lay counselors to help them assess appropriate options in relationships. Determining when relational dynamics require changes in public and private roles should not take place in isolation. An ability to be honest with ourselves and others about relationships—including those involving intensely erotic dynamics—should be a quality that clergy bring into the ministry and that they need to cultivate with their clergy and lay peers. Of course, the increasing erotophobia and sexual repressiveness in most churches make such prospects dim, to say the least.

The heart of the recovery of the church as an adequate moral community will involve ongoing honest and critical discussion of existing patterns of disordered power. Sexism—and its correlate-structure heterosexism, racism, classism, and cultural elitism—make manipulation and co-optation, sexual and nonsexual, pervasive in the churches. Explicit efforts to name and identify white racism, class privilege, misogyny, and homophobia are central to the recovery of clergy professional ethics and living moral community in the churches. It is time to recognize that formalized rules and regulations are more likely to create mischief than to introduce the sort of moral accountability we so desperately need. The churches that embrace this awareness will pass through these perilous political and moral times with the most institutional integrity.

Notes

1. Jesus speaking to Simon Zealotes, *Jesus Christ Superstar,* lyrics by Tim Rice, copyright 1970 by Leeds Music Ltd., London, England.

2. Melanie Kaye/Kantrowitz, *The Issue Is Power* (San Francisco: Aunt Lute, 1992), 41.

3. In her early twenties, Carter was intimidated into sexually gratifying a clergy leader of an interpersonal relations group sponsored by the Episcopal Church, who told her that if she told anyone, he'd deny it. Like so many who have had this kind of thing happen, she felt shamed and, for more than two decades, didn't speak of it. More recently, she had a different but more devastating experience at the hands of a woman psychiatrist who did not harass, intimidate, or abuse her sexually but used

her own professional understanding of "boundaries" as an emotional bludgeon against Carter's efforts to establish an emotionally honest and trustworthy relationship. For an account and interpretation of this story, see Carter Heyward, *When Boundaries Betray Us: Beyond Illusions of What Is Ethical in Therapy and Life* (San Francisco: HarperCollins, 1993). The outpouring of rage, especially among feminist therapists, against Carter's public critique of this professional situation has indicated to us that "boundaries" are as sacred to most therapists as the doctrine of the Trinity is to most priests. Bev also has experienced sexual harassment in overt forms, including come-ons from men who have begun with, "If only my wife were as understanding as you" and from male clergy who have taken no for an answer only when the no has become very loud and angry. She also had one brief, very hurtful affair with a church leader whose professions of adoring love she believed until she learned of the long line of equally naive women who had preceded her into the bed of this attractive, charismatic, manipulative, emotionally dishonest man.

4. See especially *When Boundaries Betray Us*. Because Bev and several others of Carter's colleagues and friends wrote responses to Carter's experience (their "responses" appear at the end of *Boundaries*), they also have come under fire for their explicit, or implicit, critiques of how boundaries are being used today by large numbers of professional healers. Both Carter and Bev, separately and together, have spoken frequently on this subject over the last few years. For Carter's most recent reflections, prior to this essay, on issues of power in healing situations, see her piece, "Alienation and Pastoral Care: The Social Basis and Ethical Challenge of Psychospiritual Healing," *Staying Power: Reflections on Gender, Justice, and Compassion* (Cleveland: The Pilgrim Press, 1995), 77–98. The theological and ethical foundations of our critiques of professionalism and the use of "boundaries" as constrictive, individualistic relational markers that do nothing to generate justice or promote genuine mutuality or justice are present, implicitly, throughout our work, long before "boundaries" became an issue among feminists. See, for example, the essays in Part III ("Christian History, Community, and Theology as a Context for Feminist Ethics") in Bev's *Making the Connections: Essays in Feminist Social Ethics*, ed. Carol S. Robb (Boston: Beacon, 1985), as well as Carter's earliest theological text, *The Redemption of God: A Theology of Mutual Relation* (Lanham, Md.: University Press of America, 1982).

5. In addition to feminist theological critiques of this capitalist ideology of "selfhood," see John R. Wikse, *The Self as Private Property* (University Park, Pa.: The Pennsylvania University Press, 1977); and John MacMurray, *Persons in Relation* (London: Faber and Faber, 1961), and *The Self as Agent* (Faber and Faber, 1957). This remains a basic problem with most feminist *psychology*—even the widely admired efforts of The Stone Center to move beyond traditional ego psychology's fixation on the individual "self." That is because, on the whole, psychologists have little or no understanding of the *fundamental* role of *capitalism* and its forms of *racism* in shaping theories of human development, personality, pathology, etc. See *Women's Growth in Connection: Writings from the Stone Center* (New York: Guilford, 1991), co-authored by Judith V. Jordan, Alexandra G. Kaplan, Jean Baker-Miller, Irene P. Stiver, and

Janet L. Surrey. Without adequate class, race, or systemic gender analyses, even such promising and courageous feminist efforts do not go far enough toward identifying or transforming the constrictive, oppressive practices of the mental health system. We are aware of a few who *do* address this problem, including psychologist (and Stone Center Associate) Janet L. Surrey and psychiatrist Stephen Bergman in their work together and with others on gender relations, addiction, and multicultural and antiracist commitments; Miriam Greenspan, psychologist and author of the now-classic (and wonderfully constructive) text, *A New Approach to Women and Therapy*, 2d ed. (New York: Tab Books/McGraw-Hill, 1993) (1983); Laura S. Brown, lesbian feminist psychologist and prolific theorist/activist, *Subversive Dialogues: Theory in Feminist Theory* (New York: Basic Books, 1994); and, in England, Celia Kitzinger and Rachel Perkins, lesbian feminist psychologists and teachers, *Changing Our Minds: Lesbian Feminism and Psychology* (New York and London: New York University Press, 1993).

6. As cited in *The Witness* (May 1995), 22.

7. Juana Malek made this point during a panel discussion about boundaries and healing that was sponsored by CLOUT (Christian Lesbians Out Together) at the Metropolitan Community Church in San Francisco, 12 June 1994.

8. In thinking about many of the very negative, in some cases contemptuous and dismissive, reviews of Carter's *Boundaries* book, it seems to us that a common theme running through them is a refusal to believe that a vulnerable person (e.g., a person in counseling) possibly could have as much "power," "agency," or self-awareness in the professional relationship as the person to whom she has turned; and, moreover, that vulnerable people need to be—or can be—protected, in healing relationships, from having to assume too much agency. See, for example, Marie M. Fortune, "Therapy and Intimacy: Confused About Boundaries," *Christian Century* (18–25 May 1994): 524–26; Mary E. Hunt, "Degrees of Separation: Good Boundaries Support Good Relationships," *On the Issues* (summer 1994): 19–21; and Pamela Cooper-White et al., "Desperately Seeking Sophia's Shadow," *Center for Women and Religion Membership Newsletter* (June 1994):

9. See Introduction to Joanne Carlson Brown and Carole A. Bohn, eds., *Christianity, Patriarchy, and Abuse* (Cleveland: The Pilgrim Press, 1989): xiii–30. For implications that lead to a similar conclusion, see Mary E. Hunt's essay "Degrees of Separation: Good Boundaries Make Good Neighbors," and Marie M. Fortune's "Therapy and Intimacy: Confused About Boundaries." Fortune's earlier essay, in the Brown-Bohn volume, would suggest a shift in her views (cf. pp. 148–68).

10. Among white Christian feminist liberation theologians who address the redemptive/liberating role of vulnerability are Dorothee Sölle [see *Suffering* (Philadelphia: Fortress, 1975) among her many works]; Mary Grey, *Feminism, Redemption, and the Christian Tradition* (Mystic, Conn.: Twenty-Third Publications, 1990); and Elizabeth A. Johnson, who writes: "Does love entail suffering in God? In the classical tradition with its apathetic ideal, the answer is obviously no. Love is purely a matter of the will; to love is to will the good of the one loved. . . . The difficulty with this argument, however, is that the notion of love as simply willing the good of

others prescinds from the reciprocity entailed in mature relations. Of course love includes willing the good of the beloved, and the classical ideal is right as far as it goes. But as actually lived, and paradigmatically so in the light of women's experience, love includes an openness to the ones loved, a vulnerability to their experience, a solidarity with their well-being, so that one rejoices with their joys and grieves with their sorrows. This is not a dispensable aspect of love but belongs to love's very essence. In fact, a chief source of the energy that generates "willing the good" and relieving misery lies precisely in this experience of compassionate solidarity with the suffering of those we love. *In the light of the feminist prizing of mutuality as a moral excellence, love does entail suffering in God.*" [*She Who Is: The Mystery of God in Feminist Theological Discourse* (New York: Crossroad, 1993), 265–66; emphasis ours.] Carter also has had instructive and very helpful conversations with sister theologians Sarah Coakley and Denise Ackerman about the critical significance of vulnerability in the theological and political work of liberation.

11. Larry L. Rasmussen's *Moral Fragments and Moral Community: A Proposal for Church in Society* (Minneapolis: Fortress, 1993), is an important ethical study of what is required in shaping the church as moral community.

12. See Karen Lebacqz and Ronald G. Barton, *Sex in the Parish* (Philadelphia: Westminster John Knox, 1991), for a helpful treatment of this problem, which they address critically and clearly without suggesting that all sexual relationships between pastors and parishioners are abusive and therefore should be avoided. Marie M. Fortune's somewhat earlier study, *Is Nothing Sacred?* (San Francisco: Harper and Row, 1989), was the first book-length articulation of clergy sexual misconduct as a major moral issue. In this pioneering effort, Fortune recounts the story of a transparently predatory offender who victimizes many women. Her conviction that it's never okay for the pastoral relationship to become sexual lacks the ethical nuances of the Lebacqz-Barton study. For an excellent analysis of power dynamics in sexually abusive relationships, see Melanie Kaye/Kantrowitz, *The Issue Is Power* (San Francisco: Aunt Lute, 1992).

13. See Fortune, *Is Nothing Sacred?* It is important for the reader to recognize that this narrative is so morally repulsive precisely because it is a classic worst-case scenario, which, unfortunately, still happens too often.

8 Out of Bounds

Miriam Greenspan

A CLIENT IN psychotherapy tells me that her father repeatedly sexually molested her as a young child, explaining that he had a "problem with boundaries." Another woman informs me that both of her children were the result of marital rape; she describes her husband—a violent alcoholic who battered her—as a man who "violated" her "boundaries." A brochure put out by the Massachusetts House of Representatives Committee on Sexual Misconduct is called "Broken Boundaries: Sexual Misconduct by Physicians, Therapists, and Other Health Professionals."

It seems that everywhere you look, the psychotherapy world is buzzing with talk about boundaries. The term is used by patients and therapists alike, by incest survivors and self-diagnosed "co-dependents," by psychoanalysts and radical feminists, by individual and family therapists. In this language, good boundaries make for healthy, safe relationships; in therapy, they keep the relationship ethical by creating a safety zone of distance between patient and therapist. Poor boundaries lead to physical, emotional, sexual, or spiritual abuse.

The phrase "poor boundaries" is used to describe all manner of professional conduct and misconduct—from the social worker who hugs a client at the door to the doctor who rapes a patient he has drugged. Just as smoking marijuana is believed by some to be a step on the road to serious drug addiction, so even the smallest boundary erosion—for example, going over the limits of the sacred 50-minute hour—may be viewed as a temptation that moves the therapist in the direction of overtly abusive boundary violation.

The image of secure boundaries contains an inviolable principle: that of the right to one's own integrity—including the rights to be respected, to defend oneself against exploitation or harm, and to speak out when harm has occurred. But while everyone would agree we need an ethic of nonabuse for professional relationships, the question of whether or not the language of boundaries helps promote such an ethic is debatable. How does the language of boundaries help us understand the complex psychological, ethical, and political dimensions of abuse in psychotherapy? How does it muddle the issues?

To my mind, the language of boundaries is problematic at best. The most serious problem is that it psychologizes the social dimensions of interpersonal violence both in and out of therapy. Both the perpetrators and the victims are viewed as suffering from a psychological impediment that impairs their ability to maintain their border zones. Perpetrators are prone to invading the borders of others; victims have trouble protecting their borders from these onslaughts. By this logic, if only fathers in families would firm up their boundaries, they wouldn't rape or molest their daughters. And if only helping professionals would tighten up their boundaries, they wouldn't sexually abuse their female patients.

The truth is that sexual exploitation and violation in families and in therapy are more than simple lapses in judgment. In the majority of cases, acts of sexual abuse perpetrated by male professionals against female patients exist on a spectrum of male violence against women in general. These acts are particularly likely to occur in relationships with a power hierarchy that replicates the gender hierarchy of our society. Incest in the father-daughter relationship and sex abuse in the therapist-patient relationship are mirrors of each other not because of what therapists call transference and countertransference but because both of these social units—the family and traditional therapy—are patriarchal. That is, they are relationships based on the dominant social power of masculine authority. The language of boundaries, wittingly or unwittingly, camouflages the political dimension of violence against women and dilutes the strong feminist analysis that brought to light the abuses now called "boundary violations."

Personally, I have always chafed at the language of boundaries. The imagery of relationships with hard borders between enclosed individuals does not make me feel safe. On the contrary, it brings up feelings of isolation, exclusion, and disconnection. Perhaps the language of boundaries has little emotional appeal for me because as a child of Holocaust survivors, born and raised for four years in a German camp for "displaced persons" after World War II, I experienced boundaries as the borders that kept my family and thousands of other refugees from entering safer havens. For me, the imagery of interconnection, not separation, feels safe.

Boundaries do not exist in reality; we use the imagery of boundaries to help us understand the relation between self and other. But in the helping professions, the language of boundaries has come to dominate the way we think and practice. In recent years, for instance, the "boundaries police" have been installed in the form of increasingly rigid standards on the part of malpractice insurers, boards of licensure, review boards, and professional organizations. In my own practice, I worry that some of the most feminist and innovative aspects of my work are the most likely to be construed as unethical. For example, I am a great believer in the art of therapist self-disclosure as a way of deconstructing the isolation and shame that people experience in an individualistic and emotion-fearing culture. When strict boundaries are used as the litmus test of professional ethical behavior, this art— and therapist authenticity in general—can appear dangerous.

This situation reflects the hegemony of what I call the "distance model"—the reigning psychodynamic paradigm of psychotherapy. In this model, the less the therapist contaminates the therapeutic process with his presence, the better. Distance is enshrined; connection is seen as inherently tainted and untrustworthy. The danger zone is thought to reside in any manner of person-to-person touching— physical, emotional, or spiritual—that might take place in the therapy relationship. In my training, one expert in marital therapy taught us that the therapist should take notes and inform the patients to behave as though the therapist weren't there—as though his absence, rather than presence, would facilitate their "cure."

But what makes us think that the therapist's absence is more objective than his presence? That emotional withdrawal is more neutral than contact? That distance is more trustworthy than connection? The answer in two words: scientism and patriarchy.

The most appealing quality of the distance model is its appearance of objectivity, which makes it attractive to those who would like therapy to have the absolute authority of hard science. This approach enshrines the cult of the "Expert," whose superior knowledge and power bring cure to the inherently defective, disordered, or sick patient. But the so-called "scientific," value-free objectivity of the Expert is, on inspection, the hidden bias of the dominant culture. The neutrality of the Expert is the silent embodiment of our culture's fundamental and unquestioned assumptions.

One such assumption is the patriarchal bias against relationality and connection. The term "boundaries" itself comes from the psychoanalytic concept of "ego boundaries." In this view, the ego presumably develops its boundaries in the course of separating itself from others, starting with the earliest separation from the mother. The norm of healthy development is the attainment of the masterful, autonomous ego, with "rigid" or "firm" (like a phallus?) boundaries between itself and everyone else. Not surprisingly, male ego boundaries more often exhibit this firmness, while women (the apparently more infirm and watery second sex) tend to have more "fluid" or "permeable" ego boundaries. In keeping with the patriarchal nature of this theory, the masculine ego is posited as the norm. It is just this ego that is embodied in our standards of healthy boundaries for the psychotherapy relationship.

Once we remove ourselves from the spell of this masculine bias, we can see that there can be connection without harm, love without power abuse, touching without sexual abuse in psychotherapy—but the language of boundaries doesn't help us see our way clearly into this arena. Rather, it keeps us steeped in the patriarchal model of self—a model that has been contested not only by feminists but also by social critics, new scientists, deep ecologists, Buddhists, and mystics. For example, the Wellesley Stone Center theorists have posited a theory of women's self-development in the context of relationship and connection, not separation. Social critics such as Robert Bellah have written about the dysfunction and pathology of American individualism. Deep ecologists and ecopsychologists like Joanna Macy and Theodore Roszak have described the bounded self as an inherently embattled and conquering ego that has wrought havoc on the earth and from which we must evolve if we are to avert global ecocide. From the Buddhist point of view, the bounded ego is a profound illusion, and our true nature is, to use Thich Nhat Hanh's term, "interbeing." The imagery of boundaries fits with an entrenched Western world view that sanctifies individualism, private property, and nationalism. The idea that relational safety resides in the defense of one's borders reflects, on a microcosmic level, the social macrocosm.

Why use a language that supports the basic delusion of Western society, that keeps us fixated in the patriarchal ego and stuck in the distance model? Why not let go of this archaic metaphor and use straightforward language to talk about ethical issues in psychotherapy? Abusive therapists don't have problems with boundaries; they have problems behaving ethically, with using their power wisely and well. Boundaries are not violated in therapy; people are. So-called boundary issues in psychotherapy are fundamentally about the misuse of power by professionals.

Ironically, the rigidification of boundaries as a response to abuse by therapists—insofar as it reinforces the distance model—may well produce more, not less, power abuse in therapy. Sexually abusive therapists, for example, in almost all cases manage to convince themselves that their behavior is in the best interests of the patient. It is not that such therapists are not aware of their power; it is that they suffer from the inbred arrogance of the Expert. They have been trained to see their power as curative—and it is just one short skip away from this belief to the belief that their sexual power is curative.

Since publicly challenging the distance model, I have received numerous letters and phone calls from women who have spoken eloquently and often heartbreakingly of the damage they have suffered in the course of a well-bounded professional relationship. In my practice, too, I have seen many survivors of therapy who have not been sexually victimized or exploited, whose therapists have followed the distance model to the letter, but who have experienced a particularly virulent erosion of self-esteem during the course of therapy. For these women, the distance model has been neither safe nor trustworthy; it has been a progressive experience of disempowerment that comes from years of being treated in a system that devalues and pathologizes connection.

Therapists trained in the distance model often view their intuitive inclinations toward connection in therapy as "boundary lapses." Sometimes the client's "manipulations" or "seductiveness" are blamed for these outbreaks of authenticity, leading to a kind of emotional abuse that is not likely to be named as such by professional review boards but that has devastating effects on clients nonetheless.

What we need is a clearly stated ethic of nonabuse for therapy that is not based on the language of boundaries and therefore not beholden to the distance model. The healing potential of psychotherapy has less to do with pseudo-objective distance than it does with safe connection. It is not about detached neutrality; it is about passionate but trustworthy engagement. Compassion rather than distance is the prime mover of what is healing about psychotherapy. And compassion—the willingness to identify and suffer with others—is by definition boundless; it crosses the divide between self and other. This is so for any psychotherapy, whatever the theoretical orientation; it is just that the distance model doesn't name or frame it this way.

But what makes connection safe or trustworthy? And how do we cultivate safe connection? For me, the answers are largely a matter of working within the healing paradoxes of the therapeutic situation—cultivating equality in a hierarchical relationship, mutuality in an inherently nonmutual relationship, empowerment in a power-imbalanced relationship. The therapist who sees himself as an all-knowing Expert and his client as a diagnosis is much more likely to abuse his power than the therapist who sees herself as an accountable coequal in therapy and her client as a person with an inherent wisdom that guides the therapeutic process.

A connection model of therapy requires, for starters, that therapists move away from the conditioned role of the Expert. Safe connection is about trustworthy companionship, not superior or omniscient power. And trustworthy companionship starts with an absolute and unshakable respect for the integrity of the person called patient or client.

This respect includes some very specific skills, including the skill of "active listening." This is not about listening for the preordained categories that fit our theories of the patient but rather listening with an ability to surrender one's theoretical understanding into the living presence and self-knowledge of the other person. The moment that we begin to lose sight of the patient as a person and to rely on our notions of expertise to shield us from the sometimes frightening and often exhilarating experience of human encounter in therapy, we are in the danger zone that is likely to produce abuses of power.

Another aspect of a nonabusive ethic for therapy is the fundamental principle of therapist accountability. Some of the worst emotional harm that comes to patients in traditional therapy comes from this lack of accountability, which is built into the distance model's way of interpreting patients' complaints about the therapy or the therapist as matters of transference, resistance, or pathology. If patients do not have the right to question their therapists' work without the risk of being labeled or pathologized, then therapy comes to resemble the closed and well-bounded systems we call cults.

The sanctity of the client's empowerment in therapy is another fundamental feature of safe connection in a nonabuse ethic. Respect for boundaries is meaningless if the patient's power in the psychotherapy relationship is seen as control, manipulation, or pathology. (I remember one of my supervisors whose motto was "The question in therapy is who controls whom? Make sure it's you who controls the patient.") In an empowerment model, the client is credited not only with her own inherent wisdom but also with the power to control the agenda—insofar as this meshes with the basic ethics of the therapist.

Perhaps one of the most controversial issues of safe connection is the issue of safe touch in therapy. In the distance model, there is no concept of safe touch. But defining all touch as abusive is rather like considering all talk dangerous because it can lead to emotional abuse. There is no one-size-fits-all rule of safety in psychotherapy; what feels safe to one person would feel traumatizing to another. In my practice, I have a client who has asked me to touch her gently on the arm if she is in the midst of intense traumatic memories. Another client has made me swear I will not touch her. In an empowerment model of work, clients get to have the choice about these matters. A good number of people in my practice have been emotionally abused by therapists who have blamed their clients for their own short-comings or confusions. The safe therapist is the self-aware therapist. It is humbling to think how much power we are given in the thera-peutic situation and how much we need to work continually on our-selves to use our power well. Our clients are a population at risk—coming to us when they are most vulnerable and trusting in our help. The patient's trust is not something we ought to assume; it is some-thing we must earn. We must be clear that we are not using clients to gratify unconscious or greedy needs of our own—including needs for power or money.

While it is comforting to think that boundaries keep everyone safe, it is clear that the rigid adherence to boundaries can bring harm as well as help in therapy. Safe connection is more likely than rigid boundaries to protect clients from abuse. It is safer to see the thera-pist as accountable than to see the client as pathological. It is safer to value empathy for the client than to regard it with suspicion as some-thing that makes one lose one's objectivity. The connection model is safer than the distance model. Healing happens when someone feels seen, heard, held, and empowered, not when one is interpreted, held at a distance, and pathologized. Safe connection and healing in therapy are a matter of breaking through old boundaries—including con-ventional divisions between self and other, patient and Expert—and embracing a more open system of interconnectedness that rests on respectful compassion.

9 | Just Boundaries or Mean-Spirited Surveillance?

An Appeal For Neo-Victorianism as Gender Justice

Kasimu

OURS IS A TIME of great confusion in regard to the proper boundaries between females and males, particularly in the workplace. A female lawyer friend[1] who works in New York City recently reported to me that every quarter lawyers in her office are given a "pop quiz" on the "do's and don'ts" of sexual harassment. Invariably the women lawyers "flunk" the male lawyers! In her own language, "They just don't get it!" Such news is not surprising to most of the women with whom I share this story, but men respond with great fear and despair. To a certain degree I share their sense of despair. If men who are *trained* in the legal intricacies of sexual harassment cannot overcome their male socialization enough to satisfy their female colleagues, what hope is there for the rest of us? If those persons whose profession it is to uphold, represent, and defend the law cannot follow that law, then what hope is there of the rest of us learning how to behave toward our female colleagues in such a manner that the women themselves recognize a significant change?

These questions are not academic, they strike at the heart of many men's general sense of distrust and fear, and a growing tide of backlash resentment against women's liberation in general. Quietly, the word passed around in many male professional circles is one of extreme caution, with strong admonishments about the general untrustworthiness of females in reference to the uncertain parameters of professional intimacy, camaraderie, and friendship. Many men seem to believe that the era of the 1980s and 1990s is an erosion of the social revolt against the kind of stiffly mannered behavior typified in previous generations as "Victorian." Thus a kind of "return to Victorianism" would seem to capture the sense of social retreat from the opening up of social boundaries, the relaxing of accepted codes of sexual behavior, and the elimination of rigid mannerisms that characterized the "New Morality" (otherwise known as the "sexual revolution") of the 1960s. If we are not careful we shall slip into a new era of reified Victorianism in which an air of cold formality, icily guarded attitudes, and stiff manners becomes the "safest" male response to the uncertainties of professional boundaries.

This essay is my attempt to wrestle with the question of just boundaries as a positive form of gender justice-in-relation. It is written from the vantage of a male ethicist whose personal and professional life has been surrounded by the kinds of "strong women" Marge Piercy describes in her poem "For Strong Women." Such strong women are "determined to do something others are determined not be done."[2] From these women—of all colors, class backgrounds, and personality types—I have learned to appreciate various feminist/womanist understandings of gender justice. What these strong women are "determined to do" is to place the notion of justice at the heart of how men treat women, both in the public sphere of the workplace and the private sphere of the home.

Although the modern feminist revolution occurred simultaneously with the ferment, travail, and powerful optimism for social change that typified the 1960s era of civil rights, antiwar demonstrations, and student protests, it was only in the 1980s and 1990s that the public attention of males began to be captured by highly publicized "sexual harassment" legal suits. The high-water mark of what one might call the first stage of awareness of sexual harassment occurred in the famous 1991 Anita Hill-Clarence Thomas hearings. Thomas, a controversial former EEOC chairman and conservative African American Republican, was accused of harassing his former EEOC employee, conservative African American Republican Anita Hill. These two ostensibly "credible" witnesses were thrown into the arena of public scrutiny as adversaries upon whose testimony rested the fate of Thomas's Supreme Court nomination. The media spectacle surrounding the event emphasized the ironic drama of two Yale-trained African American Republicans locking horns with each other, but never dealt with the overall issue of gender justice. After Thomas was nominated, there was a public outcry by feminists against the character attack waged against Anita Hill, and Hill, unwittingly, became a national symbol of the need for public education on the issues of sexual harassment. The conscientization of the public, however, has not taken place. Instead there is even greater confusion about the particulars of sexual harassment, mutual consent, and professionalism.

Neo-Victorianism

I believe that it is possible for us to reaffirm a certain level of social formality and to retreat from the overheatedly sensuous era of the New Morality in the name of gender justice-in-relation. Such a "retreat" is not retrenchment, nor is it a call to shut down all forms of intimacy between women and men in the workplace. Rather it can be understood as a new social calling to find ways of preserving and maintaining the dignity of persons that recognizes up-front the ways in which differentials in power and station require the purging of sexually explicit dynamics. I call this toning down of the explicitly informal and sexualized public presence *Neo-Victorianism*. It issues forth as an affirmation of certain general maxims of professional ethical behavior.

Neo-Victorian intimacy insists that social distance can be a kind of respect-filled intimacy. Intimacy involves the sharing of one's self with another. One can share one's thoughts, one's hopes, and one's dreams with another without physical touch or sexual inference. To treat each other with deeply respectful, mutual justice (and here I am assuming a heterosexual orientation) is a worthy goal for male theological/ethical reflection at this juncture in history. While a Neo-Victorian moral agenda is certainly not the sole province of the church, various male followers of Jesus ought to seriously take the risk of exploring the issues of professionalism, intimacy, and touch.

For example, a professor holds too much long-term institutionally confirmed authority over any student for there to ever be anything close to "mutual consent" in a sexual relationship between them. In our era of second-career students such a maxim might seem difficult to affirm because often students and professors are the same age, and attractions can spring up on both sides of the power differential. What does one do when there would appear to be mutual attraction and mutual consent for a relationship beyond the parameters of student and teacher? Wise counsel suggests that while such attractions may be inevitable they ought to be precluded because of the possibly punitive evaluative power of the professor. Such counsel might be difficult for some to imagine but not impossible if we can imagine ourselves into a new form of professional Neo-Victorian intimacy.

Some feminists argue the opposite. Instead these feminists share the controversial ethical maxim that traditional mores of "professionalism," or "professional ethics" subvert and undermine in a patriarchal fashion the possibilities of mutual relation between parties, no matter what their station, office, or function. They tie the controlling urges of patriarchal nonrelationality to accepted notions of "professionalism" that every educated person (including myself) has received in the various educational contexts and institutions of the United States. Carter Heyward even goes so far as to call it "unethical" to subvert mutual relationality in any relationship: "I am, however, challenging as *unethical* any so-called ethic that rules out the cultivation of genuinely mutual relation anywhere in our lives."[3]

The ruling ethical norm underlying this maxim is mutuality in relation. This norm is one that Heyward has spent an entire career elaborating theologically in a series of excellent books, from her dissertation[4] through *Our Passion for Justice*,[5] to *Touching Our Strength*.[6] Throughout these former texts Heyward has placed the norm of mutuality against oppressive norms of domination, manipulation, and coercion, insisting that mutuality subverts the one-sided imbalance and inherent injustice of nonmutuality. Thus the elaboration of her life's ethical contribution into a universal norm ought not to be understood as a thoughtless moral fancy, but must be interpreted as the inherent expansion of a theological insight into an ethical imperative. My task here is to examine this norm in light of the concrete realities of power differentials in professional station and office.

To insist that every relationship between persons (and one assumes with the natural world as well) ought to be one of mutuality has much to commend it. If human beings were to consider the natural world surrounding us as intrinsically deserving of our mutual regard and treatment—that is, insisting that we not impose our development schemes, waste products, and objectifying attitudes upon nature—we might be able to find more ways to clean up the wasteful ecological poisoning of the environment. If mutuality were the ground of relations between the rich and the poor, poverty would be diminished and wealth would be radically redistributed in accordance with the ethical demand for greater equality of financial resources that would inhere to a norm of mutual relation. If mutuality were the primary factor in relations between the darker-skinned South and the lighter-skinned North, cultural imperialism and racism would be lessened and the historical devaluation of native peoples throughout the world would not find a reasonable place to promote itself within the public sphere. Mutuality in relation would undermine the dominating facticity of gender discrimination most assuredly.

So, why, one may ask, is mutuality in relation problematic in regard to the issue of professional ethics in general, and the specific relation of therapist and client in particular? Within the professional arena the buyer, or client, is remunerating the professional for her or his intellectual and technical skills. To be a professional within an advanced capitalist society is to provide a rationalized technical skill to buyers within the prevailing institutionalized economic framework. The buyer, or client, is not paying the professional to be a friend or lover. To do so would relegate the kind of rational social agreement of professional relations/transactions to that of a prostitution arrangement. Although it is true that many professionals may market their services in such a fashion that they perceive themselves to be "prostituting," such an occasional self-perception is generally not recognized as positive. Are we willing to generalize all professional transactions as subliminalized or rationalized prostitution? Unless we are willing to make such a generalization, then we need to find ways of sorting out the continuum of the power differential between the professional and the one paying for professional services. Problematizing the analogy of paying for intimacy even further, the concrete dilemma surrounding the lives of the majority of prostitutes involves resorting to the selling of one's body for sexual favors as an economic means of survival. The prostitute is not seeking mutual relation with a "john," and the "john" is certainly not looking for mutuality. Prostitution is one of the most pointed examples of the instrumentalizing of relation. While prostitution is popularly referred to as the "oldest profession," it is not a "profession" in the modern sense of the term, but is the oldest means of economic survival in a patriarchal system of nonmutuality and the instrumentalizing of women's bodies. Even male prostitution relies on nonmutual instrumental relationality.

Heyward's final note in *When Boundaries Betray Us* is a call for displacing dominant Western political ideological constructions of power with more empowering relational movement.[7] She further notes that healing involves envisioning and embracing *"an ethic of courage and often of risk."*[8] As long as the paradigm for healing in our Western context involves many years of specialized training, the honing and polishing of both technical skills and appropriate interpersonal dynamics, there will be an implicit recognition of power-over social office even if relationality and mutuality inform the actual face-to-face encounters of professionals and clients. It takes a good deal more courage for relations to hold to the bounds of justice than the risky embrace of intimacy. Justice ought to be a more preferable norm of relation than intimacy.

So what does all this have to do with a Neo-Victorian revival of formality in the social sphere? Formality traditionally was a way of negotiating vast chasms of social difference and privilege. It was based on what we now take to be archaic notions of "dignity" as based on the rank and station one was born into, be it that of elite nobility or of the peasant class. While the United States of America does not officially require the kinds of formal deference and gestures of humility required in traditional hierarchical cultures, hierarchy of power still exists. This hierarchy of power is rationalized in the ranking order within every institutional structure, be it in the difference between a senior professor, junior professor, and student; or between the corporate executive officer, vice presidents, levels of mid-management, and support staff personnel. The reigning power-over order has been transmuted by the business mentality of advanced Western capitalism. Even without the traditional titles of nobility, those who rank "above" us have "power over . . ." us. This power-over involves evaluative capacities and institutional authority to promote or discipline, hire or fire, and mentor or ignore. A thoroughgoing debunking of power-over relations would involve a complete recasting of the teacher-student, mentor-disciple, boss-employee, professional-client relationship. Such radical revision is beyond the intent and scope of this author's present concern. Rather, I want to present a few theological-ethical norms of relationship that would inform a Neo-Victorian public persona.

Guidelines for Gender Justice

The Neo-Victorian persona ought to be:

- *Intent on promoting just relationships between those who rank "above" and those who rank "below."* Such just relations would involve a continual uplifting of the Kantian categorical imperative, which states that persons ought never to be treated as means only but always as ends in themselves. Promoting the dignity of another person means that one never uses that person only as a means to one's own private end. It means remembering the sacred spark of Divinity within every person, which deserves an I-thou, subject-subject relationship. Such moral philosophical abstractions become concrete in the interpersonal factoring of tone of voice, attitude, and demeanor we take with those who rank above and below us.

- *Upholding the dignity of persons requires limited physical gestures of affection or intimacy.* In the public sphere a warm handshake ought to be sufficient to demonstrate one's delight or joy, formal recognition, or polite fulfillment of social etiquette. Handshaking is a very complex social cipher, passing on, by its length of time, firmness of grasp, and accompanying words, a myriad of overt and covert inferences about the feelings of one person for another. Yet because it is a traditionally accepted social formality, it has the potential to free face-to-face encounters of possible implicitly inappropriate sexuality.

- *Public hugging or a "Christian kiss" (on the cheek!) encouraged in many worship settings ought not to be the norm in other settings.* Within many religious circles physical gestures of intimacy are frequently exchanged. At a certain level such gestures imply that the coming dominion of God is already breaking in at the present time, and that formerly sexual (inappropriate) gestures such as hugging or even cheek-kisses represent a familial bond of spiritual kinship. For many males it was a powerful experience to warmly hug another male in such contexts as a gesture of brotherly affection without feeling the twinge of embarrassment ingrained in men about so-called "sissy" behavior. Hugging, as a gesture freeing us from societal homophobia, has been liberating, and probably will remain so for quite some time. On the other hand, hugging between heterosexual men and women, even in Christian settings, is rife with the possibility for exploitation and/or misunderstanding. Hugging is such a difficult physical gesture to interpret because it involves such massive bodily embrace. All sensory contact has the possibility for being sexual in some vague sense, and a hug involves a large part of one's body coming into contact with another's. It is therefore inescapably sexual to us. I do not condemn or devalue hugging by naming it sexual, but posit the claim that because it is sexual, even when we try to use it as an expression of social greeting (in other places than the ritualized hug in worship), it connotes "more than . . . " feelings. Such "more than . . ." feelings can become unjust in the public arena not because of a lack of mutuality, but because of the very real possibility that the one possessing more social power will use that power abusively against the one less powerful. Therefore, restricting hugging and other more intimate gestures to worship ritual and the private sphere frees all parties from fears of misunderstanding and legal entanglement.

- *Such formality is vibrant and powerful.* This is not a call to a frozen exchange of hollow pleasantries, or rigidly defined parameters of "rightness." Rather it is a hard-headed, common-sense approach to the current confusion rampant in the workplace, in particular, and the public sphere generally. Freeing those in both higher rank and lower from the possibility of misunderstanding and the threat of legal recourse will free interpersonal relations to move toward mutuality at a different, more just level. Neo-Victorian relationality posits that just relationship creates a social "space" where persons can become, remember, heal, and celebrate just relationship in powerful ways that do not threaten personal boundaries.
- *Interpersonal relationships become vibrant and powerful in Neo-Vic-*

torian formality because it celebrates the infinite variety of personal boundaries. I have found that boundaries protect, preserve, and comfort us. My individual sense of space and emotional comfort may be far closer than that of a colleague or student, but when formal relations are adhered to, no one's sense of personal space is violated.

Fears of being set up for sexual harassment lawsuits will diminish as our patterns of social interchange become more vividly formal. We need to grow comfortable in such formalities not as a defense mechanism against legal retribution, but as a way of affirming gender justice. Beyond current confusion about which words, phrases, and gestures are harassing lies the far greater undiscovered country of Neo-Victorian formality. It is time for us to embrace kind words, understanding gestures, and empathy, not with confusing physical patterns of intimacy that imply sexual interest, but with formal, easily recognized modes of behavior. Such a turn to customary mores of behavior is not a cop-out to conservative forces of retrenchment, but is a recognition that the boundaries of justice may call for restraint, and that liberation into freedom requires recognition of the multiplicity of personal psychic/physical boundaries. Safety, security, dignity, justice, and compassion are more valuable in the workplace than risky ventures into mutual intimacy.

Notes

1. Attorney Dawn Scott works for Legal Aid in New York City.
2. Marge Piercy, "For Strong Women," as quoted in Rebecca Chopp's *The Power to Speak* (New York: Crossroad, 1991).
3. Carter Heyward, *When Boundaries Betray Us: Beyond Illusions of What Is Ethical in Therapy and Life* (San Francisco: Harper San Francisco, 1993), 10.
4. Carter Heyward, *The Redemption of God: A Theology of Mutual Relation* (Lanham, Md.: University Press of America, 1982).
5. Carter Heyward, *Our Passion for Justice: Images of Power, Sexuality, and Liberation* (New York: The Pilgrim Press, 1984).
6. Carter Heyward, *Touching Our Strength: The Erotic as Power and the Love of God* (San Francisco: Harper and Row, 1989).
7. Carter Heyward, *When Boundaries Betray Us* (San Francisco: Harper San Francisco, 1993), 244–45.
8. Ibid., 246.

10 | Legal Issues in Clergy Sexual Boundary Violation Matters

Sally A. Johnson

DURING THE PAST decade, there has been a virtual explosion of legal developments[1] relating to "boundary" violations by clergy,[2] principally sexual[3] boundary violations. One of the central issues, although it is not discussed much outside legal circles, is whether the government or religious communities[4] should regulate clergy sexual behavior. As a lawyer and active church member I find myself torn between the competing values involved. There is no doubt that the profusion of judicial and legislative actions regulating and punishing clergy sexual misconduct has resulted, at least in part, from the failure of most religious institutions and leaders either to protect vulnerable persons from predatory clergy or to respond to victims[5] with justice and compassion.[6] Having failed to live out their own values and beliefs, religious institutions have seen regulations, rules, and huge damage awards imposed on them by secular[7] society's legal institutions. In this essay I will summarize the legal developments, discuss the implications for religious institutions, and make some suggestions for dealing with them.[8] My reflections focus on the selection of clergy, supervision of their ministries and activities, the discipline of offenders, and management of complaints of sexual boundary violations by clergy. Some of the issues include:

- Who is responsible for setting appropriate sexual boundaries between clergy and those to whom they minister?
- Who should provide redress, response, and justice to the victims of sexual boundary violations by clergy?

- Should victims have access to secular legal remedies?
- How can the victims' needs for protection and redress be balanced against the need (and right) of religious institutions to be free from governmental regulation and control?
- How does government regulation affect the freedom of each denomination to determine for itself how to select, train, supervise, and discipline clergy and to define how clergy are to exercise their ministry?

Prior to the mid-1980s, little was written about sexual boundary violations by clergy, either generally or specifically about the legal issues and their implications. There were a few criminal prosecutions for such outrageous acts as sexual abuse of children or forcible rape. However, in most instances, inappropriate sexual conduct by clergy toward those they ministered to generally has not been talked about, or if it has, it was handled very quietly, if at all, by denominational leaders. As often as not, an offending clergy person quietly resigned or was moved to another congregation. Frustrated by the church hierarchy's general reluctance or refusal to deal effectively with what they perceived as a serious problem, victims increasingly sought redress, justice, or preventive measures from the secular courts or state legislatures. Clergy were not the sole focus of these efforts. Rather, clergy were included in a broader trend to hold helping professionals and their employers responsible for the devastating effects of sexual boundary violations.

Victims have been and are asking state legislatures and courts to determine what is and what is not appropriate sexual behavior between helping professionals and their patients, clients, and parishioners,[9] what the employers of helping professionals should be required to do when selecting and supervising their employees, and how employers of helping professionals should respond when allegations or claims of sexual boundary violations are made. Many courts and state legislatures have responded.

While courts and state legislatures clearly have the power to regulate the conduct of helping professionals such as doctors, lawyers, therapists (psychotherapists), social workers, teachers, college professors, and the like,[10] there is a serious question whether they have the constitutional authority to regulate the behavior of clergy; to set standards for the selection, placement, supervision, discipline, and deployment of clergy; or to determine what responses religious institutions must make to complaints of clergy sexual behavior.

Historical Relationship between Religious Institutions and the Secular Legal System

Many of the original colonial settlers were fleeing religious persecution perpetrated or sanctioned by government. The limit of the new government's power to control and regulate religious life was of utmost concern to our founders. The religion clauses of the First Amendment to the United States Constitution are the foundation for protection of our religious liberty, particularly protection of religious minorities from the tyranny of the majority. The First Amendment provides that:

> Congress shall make no law respecting the establishment of religion or prohibiting the free exercise thereof.[11]

Thomas Jefferson intended the free-exercise and nonestablishment clause to create "a wall of separation between church and state."[12] However, the wall has never been impermeable. While it is outside the scope of this essay to analyze 200 years of First Amendment jurisprudence, an overview is necessary to understand the significance of the recent legal developments related to sexual boundary violations by clergy.

The U.S. Supreme Court has interpreted the First Amendment to absolutely prohibit governmental regulation or control of religious *belief*. Religiously motivated *conduct or action* can be regulated or restricted only when it poses a substantial threat to public safety, peace, or order, and then the means used must be necessary and effective to accomplish the government's compelling interest and must not be more coercive than necessary.[13] The religiously motivated conduct of polygamy and religious snake-handling have been banned or regulated under this analysis.[14] The practice of treating seriously ill children with prayer rather than conventional medical procedures has sometimes been regulated and sometimes been determined to be protected by the First Amendment.[15] The First Amendment forbids courts

from determining the truth or validity of religious doctrines or tenets; they may only inquire whether the religious beliefs are sincerely
held by the parties in question.[16]

If conduct is not religiously motivated, the government is free to
regulate it to the same extent it regulates other similar secular conduct. For example, if a church negligently fails to remove snow and
ice from its church steps, it will most likely be liable for money damages to a person injured in a fall on the steps, because the failure to
remove the snow probably was not motivated by religious belief.

As will be seen later, the questions of whether conduct is secular or
religiously motivated and what religiously motivated conduct threatens the public safety, peace, and order sufficiently to justify governmental regulation are at the heart of many of the legal issues related
to sexual boundary violations by clergy.

Regulation of Helping Professionals

The regulation of clergy sexual behavior by courts and legislatures
must be viewed within the context of the regulation of the sexual
behavior of other helping professionals. Whether a person has the
ability to give meaningful consent to sexual activity is key to regulating sexual activity between helping professionals and those they serve.
The legal theory involved (as opposed to the theories of power dynamics and psychological underpinnings) is "consent." Over the past
200 years, the government has moved slowly from heavily regulating
sexual behavior, including behavior between consenting adults,[17] toward a consensus that government regulation of private sexual activity between consenting adults is not appropriate.

Sex between adults and children is a crime because a child is viewed
as incapable of giving informed consent to sexual activity. Having sexual
contact with a mentally impaired person is a crime in many states because they are viewed (rightly or wrongly) as incapable of giving meaningful consent. In some states the same is true of a person incapaci-
tated by alcohol or drugs. Similarly, a person threatened with force is
viewed as legally incapable of giving meaningful consent.

Over the past decade, the question of whether a helping professional's
client or patient can give meaningful consent to sexual contact with

the helping professional has been hotly debated. Those favoring government regulation of such behavior argue that sexual contact between helping professionals and their patients or clients is as fundamentally wrong as sexual contact with children or using force to obtain sexual contact, because the client's dependency on the helping professional makes meaningful consent impossible. A patient lying naked in a physician's office is not viewed as being capable of consenting to sexual activity with the physician because she may be dependent on him for restoring her health.[18] Similarly, a therapist's client is viewed, in some states, as being incapable of giving meaningful consent to sexual activity with the therapist because she may be dependent on him for her emotional well-being and stability. Many people believe adults are not capable of giving meaningful consent to sexual activity with a clergy person because they may be under the influence of the clergy person's power and authority or be dependent on him or her for their spiritual well-being. Thus, the presumption of, or risk of, the client's dependency and resulting vulnerability has led many people, and a significant number of state legislatures, to conclude that clients cannot give meaningful consent to sexual contact with helping professionals. Those opposing such regulation argue that each relationship must be judged on its own merits and that to presume all clients are dependent and vulnerable robs them of their own power and authority and destroys the possibility of healing through a mutual, rather than hierarchical, relationship.

While the Hippocratic oath has prohibited the seduction of patients by physicians for thousands of years,[19] it is only in the past decade that a handful of states have specifically criminalized sexual contact between physicians and patients.[20] Physicians have also been held liable for money damages for their sexual contact with patients.[21] In many states, sexual contact between physicians and patients is regulated by state medical boards and professional codes of conduct.

In the past few years, sexual contact between therapists (counselors, psychotherapists, etc.) and their clients has been debated and written about extensively. Fourteen states have specifically criminalized sexual contact between therapists and their clients and sometimes their former clients. Wisconsin enacted such a law in 1983, with Minnesota following in 1986.[22] Five states have passed laws imposing civil liability on the therapist and, in three of those states, on the therapist's employer.[23] And, as with physicians, the contact may also be regulated by state boards or professional associations.

Regulation of sexual contact between lawyers and their clients has been limited to a few cases holding lawyers liable for money damages to their victims and prohibition of such contact in ethical codes in several states, although the debate on the appropriateness of such "relationships" is expanding.[24]

Whether sexual relationships are appropriate between college and university professors and their students continues to be considered and debated.[25]

Recent Regulation of Clergy Sexual Contact with Parishioners

In the past decade, clergy have also been the subject of laws enacted by state legislatures to protect those they minister to from inappropriate sexual contact. In most instances clergy have been included in laws governing other helping professionals, while in a few instances laws specifically regulating clergy sexual behavior have been passed. In three states, while the laws prohibiting sexual contact between therapists and patients do not specifically refer to clergy, it is likely clergy would be deemed to be therapists under those laws. In four other states, sexual contact between clergy and those they counsel is specifically criminalized. And in Minnesota, it is a crime for a clergy person to have sexual contact with anyone to whom they provide religious counsel or guidance.[26]

In 1986, Minnesota adopted a law allowing a person damaged by a sexual relationship with a clergy[27] person who provided "psychotherapy"[28] services to recover money damages from the clergy person and his employer.[29] The employer is liable if, prior to hiring the clergy person they failed to perform a required background check in which the clergy person's prior employers are contacted and asked if the clergy person ever engaged in sexual contact with a "patient."[30] The employer may also be liable if it had reason to know of sexual misconduct[31] by the clergy person and failed to take reasonable action. "Reasonable action" is not defined in the statute; it is determined by the courts on a case-by-case basis after a claim is brought to court. Similar laws exist in four other states.[32]

To determine whether government regulation of clergy sexual behavior is constitutionally permissible, the first question that must be answered is whether the prohibited sexual behavior is "religiously motivated." The answer is, "it depends." It depends on the particular behavior, the roles or status of the persons involved, and the beliefs of the clergy person and/or his or her denomination. Few would argue that sexual intercourse with a child is "religiously motivated conduct." However, there are varying beliefs and practices about the role of touch in ministry, pastoral counseling, and pastoral care in particular. Is hugging ever "religiously motivated"? Holding a person's hand? Massaging a person's neck and back (clothed or unclothed)? Can genital contact between a clergy person and a parishioner ever be "religiously motivated"? Many people emphatically say no. Others think it can be. The answer may well depend on assumptions about the nature of ministry, which in turn reflect values regarding sexuality, professionalism, clericalism, the nature of faith communities, and other issues. While a clergy person, denomination, or religious community may not be able to point to a specific tenet or belief regarding the "religious motivation" for a particular touch that may or may not be sexual, the structuring of the religious institution and the practice of ministry that makes the sexual contact an option may well be "religiously motivated," and, in fact, integral to a person's faith commitment. Thus, it is not at all clear that secular legal institutions may constitutionally regulate clergy sexual behavior on the grounds that the conduct is, per se, not "religiously motivated."

When it comes to the selection, training, and supervision of clergy, and the management of misconduct complaints, such conduct is clearly "religiously motivated," and subject to government regulation only if it threatens the public safety, peace, or order. While sexual boundary violations by clergy are certainly serious and potentially devastating to the victim, it is not clear that they threaten the public safety, peace, or order. Requiring religious organizations to conduct background checks on their clergy regulates the religiously motivated conduct of clergy selection in a manner that may not be necessary or effective to prevent the harm. Similarly, holding church bodies liable for failing to take "reasonable action" if they had reason to know of sexual contact between a clergy person and a parishioner is regulation of the church's religiously motivated supervision, deployment, and discipline of its clergy.

Regulation of Clergy Sexual Behavior through Case Law

In addition to statutes enacted by state legislatures, the law on clergy sexual boundary violations has developed over the past decade on a case-by-case basis in civil lawsuits brought by victims against offending clergy, their employers, and denominational bodies. The claims against the clergy person (as opposed to his or her employer or denominational body) may include assault, battery, intentional infliction of emotional distress, or negligence in counseling (such as the mishandling of the transference phenomenon, failure to properly diagnose, and failure to refer appropriately). The clergy person will be ordered to pay money damages to the victim if one of these claims is established. However, clergy often lack adequate resources to pay damages, and insurance generally does not provide coverage for the claims made directly against the clergy person.

As a result, the victim (and his or her attorney) look for an entity with a "deep pocket" to pay a large damage award. That usually is the offender's congregation or other employer and various denominational bodies further up the hierarchy such as a synod, diocese, association, conference, or other regional or national body. Victims may claim that the clergy person's employer or denominational body is in some way responsible for the harm they have suffered. There are two basic legal theories used to try to hold the employer or denomination body responsible. One is known as "vicarious liability" or "respondeat superior" liability. The other is the breach of duty, either the duty to use reasonable care (negligence) or fiduciary duty of the employer or denominational body itself.

Vicarious liability. Victims often claim that the clergy person's employer or denominational body is liable for the clergy person's sexual boundary violation because the wrongful conduct occurred while the clergy person was functioning in the role of a clergy person (as opposed to committing the wrongful act in the role as a neighbor or volunteer baseball coach). The legal theory of vicarious liability or respondeat superior holds an employer liable for the wrongful acts of its employee if the acts were committed as part of the employee's job duties, even if the employer itself did nothing wrong and had no reason to know the employee would do anything wrong. In many states, victims have lost on this theory because courts have decided sexual misconduct is clearly outside the offender's job duties.

Breach of duty by the employer/denominational body. The second legal theory used to hold the clergy person's employer or denominational body liable is breach of a duty owed by the employer or denominational body to the victim. The most common claim is that the employer or denominational body was "negligent" because it failed to use "reasonable care" to prevent the harm to the victim. "Reasonable care" is the care a similarly situated person (or institution) would use under similar circumstances. The claims may include negligent training, selection, placement, supervision, retention, or discipline of the offending clergy person by the employer or denominational body. Boiled down to its essence, the claim is, "You, the church, put the offending clergy person in a position where he could hurt me. You knew *or should have known* he might hurt me, so you are responsible for the harm he did to me."

To determine whether the employer or denominational body was negligent, the court must decide what duty was owed to the victim, whether the duty was breached, and whether the breach caused the victim's damages. That, in turn, means courts are deciding what standards religious organizations have to follow in training, selecting, placing, supervising, retaining, and disciplining clergy in order for their conduct to be "reasonable." This is a profound development. Historically it has been left up to each religious organization to make these kinds of decisions about its clergy. Now courts (and sometimes state legislatures) are doing it. Will all denominations be held to the same standards? Should religious institutions have to use the same standards secular corporations use? Many people argue they should because clergy have a lot of power over people and, therefore, the potential for abusing that power and causing harm. Others think such regulation by the courts and legislatures violates the religious freedom of religious institutions and unduly restricts their ability to operate out of different values and norms than secular society.

In some cases, victims have not only claimed that the offender's employer or denominational body was negligent because it breached its duty to use reasonable care, but have also claimed it breached a "fiduciary" duty owed to the victim.[33] This is a significant development for several reasons. A "fiduciary" is held to the highest standard of care, much higher than the ordinary "reasonable care" negligence standard. A "fiduciary" is bound to act *only* for the best interests of the person to whom they owe the duty, subordinating the interests of the fiduciary. The most common fiduciary relationship is that between a trustee and a beneficiary of a trust. The trustee is obligated to manage the property in the trust solely in the best interests of the beneficiary of the trust. The trustee cannot do anything to further his or her own interests at the expense of the interests of the beneficiary.

On the surface, it appears fair to regard clergy and religious institutions as fiduciaries toward those they minister to. However, there are serious problems with courts imposing such a standard on clergy and religious institutions. In other contexts, it is usually clear when a person or institution undertakes a fiduciary duty (i.e., trustee of a trust, manager of a pension fund, etc.). Generally, the fiduciary explicitly consents to undertake the heavy burden of fiduciary responsibility. In the church context, it is not always clear when a clergy person or denominational body takes on the role of a fiduciary. Are clergy persons fiduciaries toward every person they encounter while performing professional duties? To a person they work with on a committee? To all persons to whom they provide pastoral care? To everyone who attends a worship service? Similarly, it is not clear what is in the "best interests" of such persons. Is it their emotional well-being, spiritual well-being, family harmony, financial security, or physical well-being the clergy person must guard? What if those are in conflict? For example, if a woman tells a clergy person that her husband is physically abusive toward her, is it the clergy person's responsibility to help the woman leave the relationship to ensure her physical safety or to try to get help for the husband so that the family can be preserved?

And, most importantly, should the state be allowed to decide what duties clergy persons owe those to whom they minister? How can a legislature or court decide what is in a church member's best interests? In terms of a denominational body's duties, the problems are even more complex. When a victim reports a clergy person's sexual boundary violation to a denominational body, is the body's responsibility to do everything it can to help the victim, or to provide "due process" for the clergy person, or to punish the offender, or to make sure the offender gets help, or to protect the denominational body from civil liability, or to make sure any criminal activity is punished? If the denominational body has a "fiduciary" duty to the victim, it must act only out of concern for her best interests and may not take into consideration the needs of the accused clergy person, the congregation, the wider church membership, or the institution's own interests. It would be prohibited from balancing these often competing interests.

Discussion of Specific Issues

Having discussed generally the legal theories and issues raised by government regulation of clergy sexual boundaries, let us turn now to some specific issues in light of recent legal developments.

Definition of appropriate boundaries. Under any of these legal theories, the essence of a victim's claim is that sexual contact between a clergy person and a parishioner is inappropriate and wrong. The result of legislatures passing laws and courts hearing civil damage cases by victims is that secular legal institutions, rather than religious institutions, are deciding what the appropriate sexual boundaries should be between clergy and those to whom they minister. While most people can agree that clergy should not have sexual intercourse with children, we don't all agree on where other sexual boundaries should be drawn for clergy. For example, should a single clergy person be permitted to have sexual contact with a single adult parishioner he is dating? Should a clergy person be able to have a sexual relationship with a person to whom she provided pastoral care five years ago? Two years ago? Is currently providing pastoral care to? Does it matter if either or both of the parties are married? Are parishioners ever capable of consenting to sexual contact with their clergy person, or are they always under the influence of the clergy person's power and authority? If not, should clergy ever be allowed to marry or even to date a parishioner? Should the answer vary from denomination to denomination, based on their understanding and beliefs about the role of the clergy?

In the author's opinion, it is not appropriate for the government to set sexual boundaries for clergy; each denomination should be free to define for itself what is and what is not appropriate sexual behavior for its clergy.

Selection of Clergy

Prior to the recent proliferation of clergy sexual misconduct cases, it was clear that the First Amendment prohibited judicial review of decisions made by religious bodies about their religious employees, particularly their clergy. Resolving such issues entangled courts in church doctrine and belief. The cases that established this interpretation of the First Amendment typically involved a clergy person who had been disciplined or fired and who brought suit against the employer or denominational body for reinstatement or money damages. The following language is typical of courts' reasoning in those cases:

> Personnel decisions by church-affiliated institutions affecting clergy are *per se* religious matters and cannot be reviewed by civil courts, for to review such decisions would require the courts to determine the meaning of religious doctrine and canonical law and to impose a secular court's view of whether in the context of the particular case religious doctrine and canonical law support the decisions the church authorities have made. This is precisely the kind of judicial second-guessing of decision-making by religious organizations that the Free Exercise Clause forbids.[34]

Despite this long-standing interpretation of the First Amendment, the Colorado Supreme Court did not hesitate to uphold a jury's finding that a denominational body was negligent and therefore liable to a victim for the sexual misconduct of a clergy person because it knew before he was ordained that his psychological records showed he had problems with depression, low self-esteem, and sexual identification ambiguity. There was no claim that he had engaged in inappropriate sexual behavior before he was ordained. The jury apparently concluded the denominational body should have been able to foresee his later sexual misconduct or should not have ordained him lest such conduct occur.[35]

The danger of allowing courts to decide such claims was well illustrated by many aspects of that case. For instance, a clinical psychologist was allowed to testify for the victim on the structure and polity of the denomination. His testimony led to a finding that the regional denominational body was responsible for the clergy person's misconduct. Not only did the court become embroiled in reviewing the church's doctrine and polity, it allowed a lay psychologist to testify as an "expert" witness as to the denomination's beliefs and structure and the limits of authority and control of various denominational officials.[36]

A recent Alaska case illustrates the potential control, albeit indirect, courts have on the way churches choose their personnel. In a case involving a lay nursery worker, not a clergy person, the Alaska Supreme Court said a church could be liable for the nursery worker's sexual abuse of a child because the church failed to perform a background check on the worker despite the fact that the *only* thing they would have found out is that the worker was herself the victim of childhood sexual abuse; she had no prior history of abusing anyone.[37] As a result of that decision, an attorney who lectures and writes extensively about legal issues for religious institutions has concluded that all churches should ask all church workers who work with children (whether paid or volunteer, clergy or lay) whether they have been the victims of childhood sexual abuse before the church allows them to work with children.[38]

Setting aside the question of whether there is sufficient clinical support for such a standard, the court established a requirement that churches perform background checks on personnel who work with children or risk being held liable if they do not. Unfortunately, the posture of the case makes it impossible to know under what circumstances, if any, it would be appropriate for a church to allow a childhood sexual abuse victim to work with children.[39] Would it be acceptable if the person had been in therapy, or had a certificate from a psychologist saying they were stable? What if they had undergone a religious conversion experience that put Christ at the center of their life? Again, the issue is the appropriateness of the secular legal system making these decisions for religious institutions rather than the institution deciding for themselves.

In another Colorado case, the jury held the denominational body liable for a clergy person's sexual boundary violation because, while it did not know of any prior sexual misconduct on his part, it knew he had a drinking problem, and if it had investigated his twenty-year-old divorce, it might have discovered his ex-wife suspected him of cheating.[40] The denominational body was found liable for more than $46,000 of compensatory and $46,000 of punitive damages for its negligence in selecting the clergy person. Again, by holding the denominational body liable for money damages for failure to foresee future sexual misconduct based on knowledge of arguably unrelated circumstances, the court set down standards other churches must follow or risk large damage awards if they do not.

Some people argue religious institutions are still free to make decisions about their religious personnel, particularly their clergy, in whatever way and according to whatever processes and standards they choose, but that they must expect to be held accountable for money damage if they do it incorrectly. What this argument ignores is the inevitable "chilling effect" this has on religious practice and decision making.[41] For example, in light of the Alaska case discussed above, will a denominational body risk choosing a victim of childhood sexual abuse to be a clergy person, regardless of their current emotional health? In light of the Colorado case, should a denomination risk choosing someone as a clergy person who admits to having issues about their sexual identity? Some would argue these are just the kind of people who should be chosen because they are more likely to have empathy for others who are struggling with similar issues and experiences. Or in light of the other Colorado case, should a denomination ever risk allowing a clergy person with a drinking problem to continue functioning as a clergy person?

There is no doubt that new state statutes and court decisions have affected how clergy are selected in many denominations. While the results may be positive, there is danger to religious freedom and the autonomy of religious organizations from unchecked government regulation.

Pastoral counseling. A case filed in 1980 in California sparked intense legal debate on pastoral or religious counseling and clergy malpractice.[42] The family of a young man who committed suicide claimed that the pastor who was counseling him for his problems negligently failed to refer him to a secular psychologist or psychiatrist for treatment. The court considered whether pastoral or religious counselors should be held to the same standard of care as secular counselors, whether pastoral counseling is "religiously motivated" conduct or secular activity, the limits of judicial inquiry into religious beliefs, and the scope of constitutional protection for religious counseling.[43] These are the same issues involved in clergy sexual boundary violation matters.

Management of complaints. Several recent cases have the potential for profoundly affecting how, or whether, denominational bodies respond to victims who come to them to report sexual boundary violations by clergy. The author is not aware of any state laws or cases imposing a duty on denominational bodies to respond to complaints made by victims. However, the two Colorado cases referred to above suggest that *if* a denominational body undertakes to handle a complaint, it must do so well or it may be liable for compensatory and punitive damages for "revictimizing" the victim. In these cases, the denominational body was held liable not only for the actual sexual misconduct of the offending clergy person, but also for their own conduct in responding to the victim's complaints. The Colorado Supreme Court upheld the jury's finding in the *Moses* case that the diocese and bishop had a fiduciary duty to the victim because she trusted the bishop, the bishop knew or should have known she was relying on the bishop to look out for her interests, and the bishop invited, accepted, or acquiesced in her trust. The Court also upheld the jury's finding that the bishop and diocese breached this fiduciary duty because the bishop took no action to help her, failed to help her understand she was not the only person responsible for her sexual relationship with the priest, and did not recommend counseling for her, but did tell her to talk to no one about the situation except her husband and her therapist.[44] The jury awarded damages of $1,216,500 for the diocese's negligent hiring and supervision of the priest and its breach of fiduciary duty in handling her complaint.[45]

In the *Klein* case, the denominational body responded to the victim by removing the offending clergy person from active ministry, providing pastoral care to the victim, and making a referral for her for professional counseling. In the lawsuit, she claimed the denominational body failed to make sufficient pastoral care available because it had inadequately prepared the interim pastor to provide that care. For its negligence in responding to her complaint, it was found liable for $350,000 of compensatory and almost $250,000 of punitive damages.[46]

In light of these cases, some denominational leaders may decide they cannot risk making a mistake in responding to a victim and will opt not to respond at all. What stronger chilling effect could there be? Even if they risk responding, it is difficult, if not impossible, for them to respond based on their religious beliefs (in the case of Christians, out of Christian love, charity, and pastoral concern) when they know that every move they make may be scrutinized by the court and could subject the institution to liability for large damage awards.

The disciplinary process itself. When allegations of sexual misconduct are made to a clergy person's congregation, supervisor, or denominational body, they have a choice. They can respond in some way, or they can do nothing. Of course, most of us expect them to do something. And what most of us expect them to do is to investigate, use "due process" to protect the rights of the clergy person and the victim, to decide the truth or falsity of the allegations, and to take appropriate actions in response to their findings. We may expect that, for the accused clergy person, "due process" requires he or she be presumed innocent until proven guilty; that proof of guilt be established "beyond a reasonable doubt," during a trial by a jury of peers; that the accused be protected from self-incrimination; and that the accused have a right to a lawyer. Similarly, for the victim we may expect that "due process" requires that he or she have a right to testify, to call witnesses, to participate in the proceeding, to have a lawyer, to be kept informed of the progress of the investigation and proceedings, and to be treated with respect and dignity.

Despite our expectations and notions of fundamental fairness, each denomination should be free to develop its own processes and procedures consistent with its beliefs and values, even if they do not incorporate our secular notions of due process. Some denominations may choose to require clergy to answer questions about their sexual conduct even if that means they incriminate themselves. Or, they may decide lawyers have no role to play in a church process and only get in the way of finding the truth and helping the parties deal with the spiritual dimensions of the situation such as repentance, forgiveness, and reconciliation. Others may decide to use a lesser burden of proof, such as "preponderance or greater weight of the evidence," or even "reasonable basis to believe the alleged wrongful conduct occurred." Some may choose to treat the matter as one of clergy wellness (or lack thereof) and focus on restoring the offender to health and function rather than focusing on discipline and punishment. Similarly, some may decide to take disciplinary action against victims who make false allegations against a clergy person based on the Ninth Commandment, "Neither shall you bear false witness against your neighbor."[47] While religious leaders may hesitate to implement such actions in light of the secular laws prohibiting retaliation against a person who makes a complaint of sexual harassment, each denomination should be able to decide for itself what actions will subject a clergy person or lay member to ecclesiastical discipline. Whatever our personal beliefs about the appropriateness of any of these choices about church discipline, religious institutions should be free to struggle with and decide how they will handle such situations for themselves based on their own beliefs.

Effect on intra-organization communications. One of the areas that has been greatly affected by secular legal developments is how denominational leaders communicate within their denomination about allegations of clergy sexual boundary violations. As part of the investigatory, discipline, and healing processes, denominational leaders have to decide what information about the allegations, victim, clergy person, and the like will be shared and with whom. What should the victim be told about the clergy person? What should the clergy person be told about the victim or the allegations? What should denominational leaders be told about the clergy person's medical or psychological history or treatment? What should the congregation or wider denominational membership be told?

Each of these decisions may expose church organizations to claims from either the victim or the clergy person. The victim may sue for invasion of privacy if personal information about her or her identity is revealed without her consent. The clergy person may sue for defamation if information about him is revealed.[48] Denominational leaders feel as if they are walking through a legal minefield as they try to decide what information to share, with whom and when. Those decisions should be made based on the denomination's religious beliefs and processes, not on what might or might not subject the denomination to secular liability for money damages.

Should victims be able to go to court? If courts will not review a clergy person's claim that their church wrongfully fired or disciplined them, why should they hear claims by victims of clergy sexual boundary violations that the religious organization should not have selected the offenders to be clergy persons, should have supervised them more closely, or should have removed them from their position so that they could not harm the victim? The underlying issues are the same: how a denomination chooses, trains, selects, supervises, and disciplines its clergy. The only thing that is different is who is harmed by the denomination's decision. In one instance it is a clergy person. In the other it is, usually, a lay member of the denomination.[49] Some argue the government has the right to be involved because it has a compelling interest in protecting people from what they view as essentially secular behavior, that is, sexual conduct by clergy.[50] However, holding denominational bodies liable for the wrongful acts of their clergy is not the only way to provide the needed protection. *If* the conduct itself, sexual contact with parishioners, is not religiously motivated and thus subject to government regulation, victims can obtain redress by bringing claims for money damages against the offending clergy person directly or pursuing criminal charges against the offender. And, if the denominational body does not respond to a victim's requests for action (removal or other ecclesiastical discipline of the clergy person, payment for therapy, evaluation and treatment of the offender, etc.), the victim can publicize the denomination's failure to act. These options avoid the First Amendment issues and the profoundly chilling effect of legislative and court decisions regulating not only clergy behavior but denominational decision-making and behavior.

Effect of Insurance on Clergy Sexual Boundary Violation Issues

Insurance has played a significant role in clergy sexual misconduct matters. If offending clergy had enough money to pay damage awards to victims, it is unlikely courts and legislatures would have felt it necessary to find ways to hold employers and other denominational bodies liable for the offender's misconduct. Insurance coverage often provides the money to pay damage awards. The existence of such coverage, or lack thereof, has influenced the outcome in clergy misconduct cases. Most insurance policies do not provide coverage for "intentional acts," acts a person intended to commit that cause harm. Deliberately hitting someone over the head with a two-by-four would be an example of an intentional act not covered by insurance. Generally, clergy do not have insurance coverage for their acts of sexual misconduct because those acts are "intentional," that is, the clergy person intended to have sexual contact with the victim even if he or she didn't think it was wrong or didn't intend to cause any harm. In the past, a clergy person's professional liability policy (if there was one) might have provided coverage for sexual misconduct, but most policies have now been revised to exclude such coverage or limit the coverage to a small amount such as $25,000.

In contrast, the negligent acts or breaches of fiduciary duty by denominational bodies are often covered by insurance if insurance was purchased. A congregation's policy limits (the limit of the amount of money the insurance company has to pay) are often much lower than the regional denomination's policy limits. For that reason, victims' lawyers developed legal theories that allowed them to go after the entities with the most insurance. In the past few years, many insurance companies have revised their policies so that they clearly exclude coverage for all claims arising out of the sexual misconduct of clergy, regardless of the legal theories used. This can leave a denominational body with substantial exposure for damages that are not covered by insurance. And laws in many states prohibit punitive damages from being covered by insurance since the purpose of "punitive" damages is to punish the wrongdoer. Endowment funds, operating budgets, and church buildings could have to be sacrificed to pay damage awards.

Rather than eliminating all coverage for clergy sexual misconduct, at least one company provides coverage only if the insured entity promises to comply with conditions imposed by the insurance company, conditions that are intended to reduce the likelihood of misconduct or claims by victims related to the management of complaints. The conditions include adoption of sexual behavior standards, some of which are set by the insurance company, limitation on the number of counseling sessions a clergy person can provide to a parishioner; rules about how complaints have to be managed; and conditions on when an offender can be restored to his or her position (or any position).[51] While this approach has the advantage of providing some protection to the denominational body's assets, it does subject it to regulation of its decision making by a third party. However, subjection to this regulation is *theoretically* voluntary because the denominational body can choose to purchase insurance from a different insurance carrier or can choose not to have insurance.[52]

Suggestions for Religious Institutions

In light of the secular legal developments, religious institutions might wonder whether there is any room left for them to live out their own beliefs and values regarding clergy sexual boundaries. There is. Since it was the general failure or refusal of religious institutions to deal with claims of clergy sexual boundary violations internally that led victims to seek justice and redress from the secular legal system, it is the author's opinion that religious institutions must develop and implement their own processes and procedures, consistent with their theology and belief structure. If they do, victims will be less likely to turn to the secular legal system to address their concerns.

First, the denomination or religious institution must define appropriate clergy sexual boundaries. Those boundaries should be effectively communicated to all clergy and religious organization members.

Consideration should then be given to how clergy are selected. What are the denomination's beliefs? Is a clergy person "called" to their position by God? If so, how is the call discerned? What education, training, or experience, if any, are required? Is there a certain level of physical, psychiatric, psychological, emotional, or spiritual health required? If so, how is it determined? Are there behaviors, conduct, or conditions that disqualify a person from being a clergy person? What are they? The reason for such disqualification should be articulated and should be consistent with the denomination's beliefs about fitness for ordination and ministry.

Denominations also should consider providing education or other resources to clergy and religious organization members on what causes or contributes to sexual boundary violations by clergy.

Processes for dealing with violation of sexual boundaries by clergy should be developed and disseminated. Church institutions must decide who, if anyone, is responsible for pursuing and resolving complaints about clergy behavior. Is it up to the victim to find and present evidence against the clergy person? Does someone in the denominational hierarchy take on the role of "prosecutor?" Whose responsibility is it to watch out for the interests of the accused clergy person? The clergy person himself? The denominational hierarchy? Churches should attempt to balance the interests of the accused clergy person with those of the victim. The needs of the faith community also have to be considered, as do the effects on the religious institution itself. What compensation, if any, the denomination is willing to provide to victims also should be addressed. And whether or under what conditions an offender can be permitted to function as a clergy person must be decided.

These suggestions are not meant to be exhaustive. Fortunately, there are now a variety of resources written by religious leaders or others familiar with the religious issues involved to help religious institutions deal with these questions and issues.[53] The institutional soul-searching involved in this process may yield some interesting and potentially disturbing information. It may show that the institution professes one set of beliefs but acts out of other beliefs. It may find that it acts as if it valued the institution's reputation more than the healing of victims, congregations, and offending clergy persons. It may find that it values clergy persons, regardless of their transgressions, more than it values making sure the church is a safe place for those in need. The review will give the institution the opportunity to examine its values and beliefs and bring its actions in line with them.

The legal developments of the past decade relating to clergy sexual boundary violations have raised more issues than they've answered, but the issues that have been raised cannot be ignored. Religious organizations are in danger of losing, or have already lost or abdicated, much of their right and ability, legally speaking, to stand apart from secular society and live by their own rules and values regarding clergy sexual boundaries. But the pendulum may have swung far enough. Perhaps the imposition of large damage awards and government regulation has shaken religious institutions out of their complacency. If religious institutions act with integrity, consistent with their well-developed and theologically sound beliefs, the secular legal system may be less likely to think the heavy hand of the law is needed to regulate the decisions of religious institutions. Clergy and other religious leaders should take steps to make sure this happens.

Notes

1. A decade in the timeline of legal developments is not much more than the blink of an eye.

2. In this essay, when I refer to "clergy" I intend to encompass the ordained, called, or recognized pastoral or spiritual leadership of a faith community. The author is most familiar with Judeo-Christian religious traditions, but the concepts and observations discussed should be applicable to most, if not all, religious traditions.

3. One of the often overlooked issues inherent in this subject is the difficulty of defining what is meant by "sexual" behavior or conduct. As with pornography, "we know it when we see it," but trying to define it clearly, particularly for legal purposes, is nearly impossible. A glance, eye contact, a spoken word, or a gesture can all be highly sexual, while touch, including touching of the genitals or other intimate body parts, can be completely nonsexual.

What is sexual depends, in part, on the intention of the actor and the perception of the receiver. One person can intend something to be sexual that is not perceived as such and vice versa. It is beyond the scope of this essay to discuss this issue fully, but it is an important one for anyone concerned with clergy sexual behavior.

4. There is no single term that adequately encompasses the myriad forms of religious groups. I have used a variety of terms throughout the essay, including "religious community," "religious institution," "denomination," "congregation," and "church." None of them should be construed as being limited or exclusionary unless the context clearly so indicates.

5. There is no one term that adequately names or identifies persons who have been or claim to have been harmed by clergy sexual boundary violations. Some criticize the use of "victim" because it may imply that all allegations of misconduct are true rather than presuming the accused clergy person is innocent until proven guilty. Others suggest that "survivor" is more empowering. Others use "complainant," arguing that it is more neutral. I have chosen to use "victim."

6. Other reasons may include the changing role of women in society, increased willingness of victims to discuss their experiences, and recognition that it is unacceptable for women and children to be subjected to physical and sexual abuse (rape, domestic violence, child sexual abuse, sexual exploitation, etc.).

7. "Secular" refers to nonreligious institutions, particularly institutions of the government such as the courts (criminal and civil) and legislatures, as distinguished from ecclesiastical or denominational courts.

8. Material in this essay has been abridged from statutes, court decisions, and other sources and should not be relied on for legal advice. The law on the topics discussed varies from state to state and is subject to change at any time. Questions about individual problems or specific situations should be addressed with your legal counsel.

9. Just as there is no one term that adequately encompasses the variety of religious groups, there is no one term that describes the individual participants in religious groups. I have referred throughout primarily to "parishioners" and "members" but intend those terms to include all persons who participate in religious groups, or who receive pastoral or spiritual care from a clergy person.

10. While it is within the power of courts and legislatures to regulate the conduct of helping professionals, there is a serious debate as to the appropriateness and effectiveness of various aspects of that regulation, including regulation of sexual boundaries. For example, some argue that regulations that medicalize, professionalize, or make hierarchical the relationship between therapist and client are harmful.

11. U.S. Const. Amendment I.

12. Thomas Jefferson, *Life and Selected Writings,* ed. Adrienne Koch (New York: Random House, 1993), 332.

13. *Cantwell* v. *Connecticut,* 310 U.S. 296, 303 (1939). The status of the "compelling interest" test is uncertain. In 1990 the United States Supreme Court held in *Employment Div. Dept. of Human Resources* v. *Smith,* 494 U.S. 872 (1990) that a general statute could be applied to prohibit religiously motivated conduct without any assessment of the extent of the burden on the free exercise of religion or of the substantiality of the governmental justification for imposing that burden. 494 U.S. at 882–90. In response, Congress passed the Religious Freedom Restoration Act of 1993 (RFRA), which prohibits any government from imposing a burden on the free exercise of religion, including through the application of a rule of general applicability, absent a showing that the rule is the least restrictive means of furthering a compelling state interest. 42 U.S.C. 2000bb. Legal scholars are now debating whether RFRA is constitutional.

14. *Reynolds* v. *United States,* 98 U.S. 145 (1877) and *Hill* v. *State,* 88 So. 2d 880 (Ala. App. 1956).

15. Ann MacLean Massie, "The Religion Clauses and Parental Health Care Decisionmaking for Children: Suggestions for a New Approach," *Hastings Constitutional Law Quarterly* 21 (spring 1994): 725–75.

16. *United States* v. *Seeger,* 380 U.S. 163, 185 (1965).

17. Various permutations of human sexual behavior now either accepted or overlooked have been regulated or criminalized throughout American history. Legislatures of the past chose to target such activities as adultery, birth control, cohabitation, dancing (with and without clothes on), fornication, "immoral" activities in hotels, mixed-race marriages or sexual relations, seduction, and the wearing of bathing costumes on public highways. For discussions of these topics, see the following entries in Am. Jur. 2d (1976 & Supp. 1995): Adultery and Fornication; Annulment §11; Birth Control; Divorce and Separation §8; Hotels §§ 21, 40, 65; Lewdness, Indecency and Obscenity; Marriage §§ 78, 102; and Seduction.

18. Nanette K. Gartrell et al. "Physician-Patient Sexual Contact: Prevalence and Problems," in *Breach of Trust,* edited by John C. Gonsiorek (Thousand Oaks, CA: SAGE Publications, 1995), 21; Linda Mabus Jorgenson et al., "The Furor Over Psychotherapist-Patient Sexual Contact: New Solutions to an Old Problem," *William and Mary Law Review* 32 (Spring 1991): 661.

19. *Steadman's Medical Dictionary,* 25th ed., s.v. "Hippocratic Oath."

20. Colorado, Michigan, New Hampshire, Rhode Island, and Wyoming. Linda Mabus Jorgenson, "Sexual Contact in Fiduciary Relationships," *Breach of Trust,* 252.

21. Id. 263–64.

22. Wisconsin, Minnesota, California, Colorado, Connecticut, Florida, Georgia, Iowa, Maine, North Dakota, New Hampshire, New Mexico, South Dakota, and Texas. Id. at 252.

23. The states are Minnesota (includes employer), Illinois (includes employer), Texas (includes employer), California and Wisconsin. Minn. Stat. §148A.03 (1994);

Ill. Ann. Stat. ch. 740, para. 140 (Smith-Hurd 1989); Tex. Civ. Prac. & Rem. §81.002; Cal. Civ. Code §43.93 (West 1993); Wis. Stat. Ann. §895.70(2) (West 1992).

24. Linda Mabus Jorgenson and Pamela K. Sutherland, "Fiduciary Theory Applied to Personal Dealings: Attorney-Client Sexual Contact," *Arkansas Law Review* 45 (1992): 459.

25. The Statement on Professional Ethics (1987) of the American Association of University Professors says that professors must "avoid any exploitation, harassment, or discriminatory treatment of students" but "exploitation" is not further defined.

26. Minnesota specifically criminalizes sexual contact between a clergy person (or someone who purports to be a clergy person) and anyone to whom they are giving religious counsel or guidance. Minn. State. §609.344(1) 1994. Iowa, New Mexico, North Dakota, and Wisconsin have statutes that specifically criminalize sexual contact between clergy persons and persons to whom they offer counseling. Iowa Code Ann. §709.15(1)(a) and (f) (West 1994); N.M. State. Ann. §30-9-10 (Michie 1993); N.D. Cent. Code §12.1-20-06.1 (1993); Wisc. Stat. Ann. §940.22 (West 1992). California, Florida, and Georgia laws criminalizing sexual contact between therapists and patients are worded in such a way that they could be construed to apply to clergy who offer counseling. Cal. Bus. & Prof. §729 (West 1995); Fla. Stat. Ann. §491.0112 (West 1995); Ga. Code Ann. §16-6-5.1 (1992).

27. The statute pertains to all "psychotherapists," which are defined as physicians, psychologists, nurses, chemical dependency counselors, social workers, members of the clergy, marriage and family therapists, mental health service providers, or other persons, whether or not licensed by the state, who perform or purport to perform psychotherapy. Minn. Stat. §148A.01, subd. 5.

28. "Psychotherapy" means the professional treatment, assessment, or counseling of a mental or emotional illness, symptom, or condition. Minn. Stat. §148A.01, subd. 6 (1994).

29. Minn. Stat. §148A.02 and 148A.03 (1994).

30. "Patient" means a person who seeks or obtains psychotherapy. Minn. Stat. §148A.01, subd. 4.

31. The statute prohibits "sexual contact" between a psychotherapist (which includes clergy) and a patient. "Sexual contact" means any of the following whether or not occurring with the consent of a patient or former patient:

(1) sexual intercourse, cunnilingus, fellatio, anal intercourse or any intrusion, however slight, into the genital or anal openings of the patient's or former patient's body by any part of the psychotherapist's body or by any object used by the psychotherapist for this purpose, or any intrusion, however slight, into the genital or anal openings of the psychotherapist's body by any part of the patient's or former patient's body or by any object used by the patient or former patient for this purpose, if agreed to by the psychotherapist;

(2) kissing of, or the intentional touching by the psychotherapist of the patient's or former patient's genital area, groin, inner thigh, buttocks, or breast or of the clothing covering any of these body parts;

(3) kissing of, or the intentional touching by the patient or former patient of the psychotherapist's genital area, groin, inner thigh, buttocks, or breast or of the clothing covering any of these body parts if the psychotherapist agrees to the kissing or intentional touching.

(4) requests by the psychotherapist for conduct described in (1)–(3). Minn. Stat. §148A.01, subd. 7.

32. See note 24.

33. A fiduciary is a person holding the character of a trustee, having duties involving good faith, trust, special confidence, and candor toward another. Trustees, executors of estates, attorneys at law, guardians, conservators, and public officials are fiduciaries. *Black's Law Dictionary*, 6th ed., s.v. "fiduciary," and "fiduciary capacity."

34. *Scharon v. St. Luke's Episcopal Presbyterian Hospitals*, 929 F.2d 360 (8th Cir. 1991).

35. *Moses v. Diocese of Colorado*, 863 P. 2d 310, 315 (Colo. 1993).

36. Id. at 325–327.

37. *Broderick v. King's Way Assembly of God*, 808 P.2d 1211 (Alaska 1991).

38. Richard R. Hammer, *Church Law and Tax Report* 6 (May/June 1992): 11–14; Hammer, Steven W. Klipowicz, and James F. Cobble Jr., *Reducing the Risk of Child Abuse in Your Church* (Matthews, N.C.: Christian Ministry Resources, 1993), 38, 77, 80–81.

39. The Broderick case was before the Alaska Supreme Court on the church's summary judgment motion to have the case dismissed before it went to trial. The case was settled without trial after the Alaska Supreme Court's decision.

40. *Klein v. The Rocky Mountain Conference of the United Methodist Church*, Civ. Action No. 94CV0521 (Colo. Dist. Ct., J. entered Nov. 4, 1994).

41. The coercive and chilling effect resulting from the imposition of tort liability (liability for civil damages) or governmental regulation has been recognized by a number of courts and legal scholars. Jay A. Quinn, "Court Involvement in Church Discipline," *Bibliotheca Sacra* 149, no. 594 (April–June 1992): 223; Ira C. Lupu, "Where Rights Begin: The Problem of Burdens on the Free Exercise of Religion," *Harvard Law Review* 102 (1989): 961–66; James K. Lehman, Note, "Clergy Malpractice: A Constitutional Approach," *South Carolina Law Review* 459 (1990): 474–79.

42. Lawrence M. Burek, Note, "Clergy Malpractice: Making Clergy Accountable to a Lower Power," *Pepperdine Law Review* 15 (1986): 137; Samuel K. Ericsson, "Clergy Malpractice: Ramifications of a New Theory," *Valparaiso Law Review* 16 (1981): 164; Ben Zion Bergman, "Is the Cloth Unraveling? A First Look at Clergy Malpractice," *San Fernando Valley Law Review* 9 (1981): 47; C. Eric Funston, Note, "Made Out of Whole Cloth? A Constitutional Analysis of the Clergy Malpractice Concept," *California Western Law Review* 19 (1983): 507; Robert J. Basil, Note, "Clergy Malpractice: Taking Spiritual Counseling Conflicts Beyond Intentional Tort Analysis," *Rutgers Law Journal* 19 (1988): 419; Thomas F. Taylor, "Clergy Malpractice: Avoiding Earthly Judgment," *Brigham Young University Journal of Public Law* 5 (1990): 119; Note, "Clergy

Malpractice: A Constitutional Approach," *South Carolina Law Review* 41 (1990): 459.

43. *Nally v. Grace Community Church of the Valley*, 230 Cal. Rptr. 215 (Cal. Ct. App. 1987) (opinion deleted from official report after reversal), *rev'd*, 47 Cal. 3d 278, 763 P.2d 948, 253 Cal Rptr. 97 (1988), *cert. denied*, 490 U.S. 1007, 109 S. Ct. 1644 (1989).

44. *Moses* at 322–23.

45. The damages were reduced by $118,000 by the judge to comply with a statutory limitation on noneconomic damages. Id. at 314.

46. *Klein.* Judgment was entered by the Court on November 4, 1994. As of June 1, 1995, the case is on appeal in Colorado.

47. Deuteronomy 5:20.

48. Defamation is causing harm to someone's reputation by making false statements, particularly to someone who doesn't have a legitimate reason for hearing the statement. Truth is a defense to defamation, but "truth" may be more difficult to prove in court than the speaker believes at the time of the statement.

49. While most victims of clergy sexual misconduct are lay women, some of the victims are clergy themselves or seminary students who have been sexually exploited by seminary professors, denominational leaders, field work supervisors, or senior clergy where they are serving as assistants.

50. Of course, many people would argue that the sexual behavior of clergy is anything but "secular," that matters of sexuality in general and the sexual behavior of clergy in particular are profoundly religious and theological issues.

51. The Church Insurance Company Pinnacle Policy.

52. The voluntary nature of the regulation may only be theoretical because all insurers may impose similar restrictions, or because the risk of going without insurance may mean there is no real choice.

53. Margo E. Maris and Nancy Myer Hopkins, "The Victim/Survivor," available from the Alban Institute, Inc., Bethesda, Md.; Margo E. Maris and Kevin M. McDonough, "How Churches Respond to Victims and Offenders of Clergy Sexual Misconduct," *Breach of Trust*, 348–67.

11 I-Thou

Interpersonal Boundaries in the Therapy Relationship

Margo Rivera

La theorie, c'est bon, mais ca n'empeche pas d'exister. —Jean Charcot

I FIND IT DISQUIETING that so many therapists at this time in history are focused on the issue of therapeutic boundaries as rules. There seems to be a great deal of energy that is going into creating protocols about the rules of therapy. It seems to me to be a particularly 1990s response. We have indeed come a long way in the past decade or so in understanding the importance of clean and clear therapeutic boundaries in creating an effective healing process. We are well aware of the problems that derive from ignoring the issue of power differential in the therapeutic relationship. But the solutions we have come up with are still pretty primitive, by and large. In many situations we have tried to place simple and not very workable guidelines over the complicated process of in-depth interpersonal therapy and then mislabeled this inadequate solution to a very real issue as "boundaries."

I do a lot of teaching, assessment, and consultation about the practice of therapy—particularly therapy with survivors of severe trauma—and one of the most common questions is, "What should I do?" Sometimes this relates to very basic instrumental issues, and there are often obvious answers to these questions. (For example, "My client told me in detail how she witnessed her child being abused by her boyfriend. What should I do?" Answer: "You have an obligation to ensure that either your client reports the abuse to the authorities or that you do.") Most of the time, however, I find myself saying that the question *"What should I do?"* is the wrong question. The question that is usually more helpful when talking about therapeutic practice is, "What is going on?"

This is particularly true when discussing issues of boundaries in the therapeutic relationship. As in any other relationship between two people, what are respectful, appropriate, and useful boundaries depends on all of the circumstances of the relationship. Boundaries are not context-free rules; in fact, they do not exist outside their context.

In this case, the context is the therapeutic relationship. Consequently, an adequate exploration of the issue of boundaries will require an understanding of the nature of the therapeutic relationship as it has evolved historically; an examination of the concept of "boundaries" as it relates to the therapeutic relationship; and, finally, some reflection on the perils of designing simple rules to address complicated processes (of asking always, "What should I do?" rather than "What is going on?").

The Historical Evolution of the Therapeutic Relationship

The therapeutic relationship, the central vehicle through which therapy takes place, is a relationship like others in some ways and unique in others. It is a business relationship in that it involves a contract. The therapist provides services and usually gets paid for doing so, either by the client directly or by a third party. It is a nurturing relationship of unequal power like the parent/child relationship. It is usually a relationship of positive affect in which the participants appreciate each other, like friendship. Yet it is not strictly business; nor is it friendship. It is also very different from a parent/child relationship.

It is not new, this idea that the relationship between psychotherapist and client has some special elements. Freud introduced the term *transference* to describe the phenomenon in which feelings from the client's formative relationships are felt with intensity toward the therapist, whether or not these feelings have much to do with the reality of the present-day therapy situation at all. It was Freud's belief that it was the ability to reexperience these emotions in the analytic context that was one of the key features that made therapy instrumental in creating deep psychological change. The analytic concept of the therapist being a "blank screen" upon which the client can project his or her own conflicts/feelings/distortions is the basis upon which some strict analysts will not even answer questions like, "Are you married?" "How long have you been in practice?" etc., except with the traditional, "Why do you ask?"

The discipline involved in maintaining this posture of distance is immeasurably difficult. Freud not only did not consistently enact a strict psychoanalytic stance in his own practice, he helped patients financially, gave them gifts, and talked to them about the details of his family life. However, though it is difficult for even the most convinced and fully trained classical analyst to maintain the strict relational limits that early psychoanalysis demanded, the therapeutic model proposed by Freud, in which the analyst uncovers the secrets of the mind and cures the patient through rational interpretations, places the therapist in the position of the person who learns by virtue of her or his objectivity, a scientist uncovering facts. From this vantage point, these limits make theoretical sense. Relational closeness equals contamination of the field in which this authoritative and curative rational understanding is sown. The analytic relationship as defined by Freud is characterized by abstinence and emotional distance on the part of the analyst.

Over the course of the growth and development of the psychoanalytic model, which is the prototype of Western psychotherapeutic practice, there has been a shift from the notion of the insight of the analyst as curative to an emphasis on the active engagement of two people in the project of a collaborative therapeutic relationship as the source of the healing, and many different types of psychotherapy have evolved in the second half of the twentieth century, often in reaction to the classical psychoanalytic model. By the 1960s in North America, the challenge to traditional therapy as represented by psychoanalysis was in full swing, and the classical psychoanalytic framework for structuring the therapy relationship, and all of the hierarchical structure that went with it, was challenged in almost every new therapy that grew up at this time.

Psychotherapies, including Rogerian, Gestalt, Transactional Analysis, Primal, and many others, were rooted in the social contexts of the North American 1960s and 1970s. The intense idealism of these times, and the sloughing off of old ways to make room for what was widely hoped and often assumed to be revolutionary change, was incorporated into these models of psychotherapy. Powerful, short-term therapeutic interventions, like T-groups and encounter groups, in which people emersed themselves in intensely emotional interpersonal communication for hours, days, and even weeks on end, reflected this belief that radical change was not only possible but a fairly simple matter, if only enough well-disposed individuals wanted it enough to work together in trust and with a high level of energy and commitment.

The culture of North America in the 1960s and 1970s had some striking similarities to the eighteenth-century Enlightenment in Europe, especially France. Underlying most of the different forms of therapy practice was a philosophical premise that was congenial and widely held during both these historical periods. Human beings were understood to be basically good, striving for self-actualization in the most pro-social way, and only the limitations of a repressive personal socialization, in combination with political structures that fostered the consolidation of the wealth and power of the few and disempowered the many, engendered the range of individual and social problems that therapists encountered in the treatment room.

The women's liberation movement was some of the most fertile ground for the growth of new models of therapy. Leaderless consciousness-raising groups, settings in which women gathered to talk about their personal experience and to help each other understand these experiences politically, were the first structures within the most recent wave of feminism created to implement that basic feminist principle *the personal is political*.

Consciousness-raising groups never replaced professional therapy as a resource for the many troubled women looking for psychological help, and gradually, throughout the 1980s, much of the energy and insights generated in these settings were channeled into the development of models of professional psychotherapy based on feminist principles. Some of the earliest[1] challenged all the existing structures and practices of the medical model as it relates to women's mental health, and they operated outside the boundaries of mainstream mental health settings. Group therapy was the main and often only treatment modality offered, and an egalitarian therapeutic relationship between group facilitator and participants, with frequent self-disclosure on the part of the therapist, was prescribed. Based on the assumption that women's personal difficulties are a function, not of individual intrapsychic dynamics, but of cultural expectations within a social context in which women hold a subordinate economic and social position, radical political activism on the part of the therapist was usually her key qualification and political activity on the part of the group members was encouraged as an important part of the solution to individual problems.

At the same time as the "radical psychiatry" movement[2] was promoting groups led by women whose training was in the area of feminist activism rather than clinical psychotherapy, there was also an emerging critical voice from within the mental health professions, decrying the sexist nature of most therapy processes and relationships. Psychological frameworks for understanding women were developed that took into consideration women's socialization within a patriarchal culture and focused on women's differences, strengths, and capacity for evolutionary change rather than defining problems as pathology and promoting an adaptation to male standards of achievement and behavior.[3] Skepticism about diagnostic categories was pervasive, and women were encouraged to name their own experience. A self-defined feminist therapy literature tried to integrate some of the challenges of radical feminist therapy, the principles of liberal feminism with its emphasis on sex roles and their discriminatory ascription, and the new psychologies of women to offer an alternative model of therapy practice to feminists.[4]

When the limits of the therapy process were considered at all within these frameworks, the emphasis tended to be on posing a radical challenge to the hierarchal model of traditional psychotherapy. Therapists were encouraged to create equal relationships between themselves and their clients, and notions like transference were frequently debunked as an unnecessary outgrowth of a patriarchal therapeutic structure. There were many practitioners who continued to create strict boundaries between patient and therapist and practice a traditional form of psychological treatment throughout these times of change, including classical psychoanalysts and psychiatrists who embraced a strict medical model of treatment. However, the challenge to these frameworks was deep and widely felt.

There has been a lot of movement in the thinking about the issue of limits and boundaries in therapy in the past ten years. Therapists have been increasingly aware that some of the rebellion against traditional hierarchal therapy structures in the name of egalitarian principles, though salutory in its challenge to a rigid model of treatment, involved ignoring many of the complexities of power that are inherent to the therapy relationship. It has become clear that a cavalier abandonment of concepts such as transference and therapeutic boundaries does not do away with the power differential in the therapeutic relationship. It simply places it out of sight, where it is less likely to be monitored and just as easily exploited.

The struggles among different racial, class, and cultural groups in the women's movement to gain recognition both for the specificity of their experience and the frequent erasure of that experience by white middle-class feminism have informed the contemporary feminist therapy movement, and the woman's liberation movement has been widely influential in the development of cultural constructs, such as models of psychotherapy. Power issues are less likely to be ignored by therapists today than they were in the therapy movements of the 1960s, 1970s, and even early 1980s.

In fact, there has been something of a 180-degree turnabout from the ideology of some of the earlier practitioners. Hogie Wycoff's guidelines for leader self-disclosure in facilitating group therapy—"I struggle with the members of my groups the same way in which I struggle with friends or lovers"[5]—would be endorsed by only a small minority of contemporary therapists. On the contrary, it is now common for therapists to create very strict guidelines differentiating the relationship between client and therapist from any other relationship and proscribing any contact between therapist and client that is not strictly therapy.

"Boundaries" in the Therapeutic Relationship

It is interesting that the word *boundary* as it relates to the therapeutic relationship has come to have one particular connotation—it almost always refers to a limit, a delineation of appropriate barriers or walls between the therapist and client that enable the therapist to fulfill her fiduciary duty to the client without milking the therapeutic relationship to meet her needs at the client's expense. In fact, the concept of boundaries in the clinical context is much broader and more subtle than we would be led to believe by this common conflation of the word *boundaries* with "appropriate limits" (or, as in "boundary violation" or "boundary crossing," clinical and/or ethical misconduct relating to inappropriately tearing down limits in a way that is harmful to the client).

The therapeutic relationship is as much about walls that are let down in ways that are idiosyncratic to the clinical context as it is about walls created around the treatment relationship, defining its framework. Empathy, or vicarious introspection, is basic to both the process of data collection—how we know what we know—in the depth therapy encounter and to its healing effect. We are capable of creating an empathic connection with another person only to the degree that we can allow ourselves to loosen the boundaries that distinguish one individual from another.

Frequently, people tell me things in my first meeting with them that they have not only not told anyone else but that they never consciously made a decision to tell me. I often ask people questions in a therapy session that I would never think of broaching in a social or other type of business setting. This does not occur because I am more brash in a therapeutic communication than I usually am; on the contrary, I am much more aware of and respectful of people's sensitivities when I am relating to them as therapist than I tend to be in other social, professional, or personal situations. This erosion of the limits on what people consider appropriate or safe to talk about takes place because the empathic connection that develops—sometimes slowly, other times almost immediately—between client and therapist is constructed by the process of the dissolution of certain of the interpersonal barriers that are widely experienced as appropriate and necessary in other social settings.

The process of projective identification is an example of a therapeutically useful experience that involves the dropping of the barrier between two individuals such that, as therapist, I sometimes feel my client's feelings transiently as if they were my own and thus am able to understand what my client is feeling, even when she has little awareness of those feelings herself. This temporary release of my affective field for use by the client makes it possible for me to take a stance of sustained empathic enquiry in a fashion that is experienced more as nurturing than as threatening.

I consciously (and also not so consciously) allow myself to be open to my clients in a way that I do not do regularly in other social or business relationships. This is not the kind of openness that results in self-disclosure for the satisfaction of my own needs; it is an openness that I deliberately structure for use as a vehicle for therapeutic intervention. It is the vulnerability of the therapeutic relationship in this particular way—in which the usual barriers to interpersonal communication are regularly dissolved—that makes it so important that proper therapeutic boundaries (in the current use of the word) be responsibly constructed as a basic part of creating a safe healing space for the client.

I do not see myself as a scientist who has to stay out of the affective field of my relationship with my clients in order to maintain some kind of pure objectivity. I do, however, see myself as needing a type of clarity with my clients that I do not pretend to be able to maintain consistently with other people in my life, to whom I look to get my personal needs met—friends, colleagues, and intimates. If I am going to allow a significant degree of openness in myself to my client's feelings, then I must, to be professionally responsible, create a clear enough relationship with that client so that I can not only allow the walls that separate us to come down, so that her feelings resonate deeply within me, but also ensure that, almost simultaneously, I can step out of that place of profound connection and observe each of us and our interaction from a position outside her affective field.

This is not something that can be consistently accomplished in a relationship in which the meeting of the needs of both participants is the agenda. Though this dynamic sometimes occurs in other interpersonal interaction as well as in therapy, it is not the central mandate of personal relationships that one party hold the responsibility for maintaining the basic groundedness (or objectivity, if you will) in the relationship. What is one-sided and often unhealthy in a friendship or intimate relationship—one party taking on the bulk of the responsibility for keeping the relationship on track—is a proper aspect of the structure of the therapeutic relationship.

This does not mean that it is not a relationship, that is, that the therapist does not engage with personal feeling or that some of the therapist's needs are not met. It does mean that the expression of the therapist's feelings and the meeting of the therapist's needs are not the purpose of the relationship. When the expression of feeling on the part of the therapist enhances the client's participation in her own healing process, then that communication is appropriate and constructive within the context of the therapy project.

Another way to look at the purpose of boundaries in the psychotherapy relationship is to consider the issue of what psychotherapy actually is. There are many relationships in which a couple of people talk to each other—personal relationships and professional relationships. What is it that defines the therapeutic relationship and distinguishes it from other personal and professional relationships? Is it the fiduciary aspect of the interpersonal contract, the fact that it is the therapist's job to help the client? This is one aspect of the therapy relationship, but it does not distinguish it from many other personal and professional relationships—for example, that of lawyer and client, that of priest and parishioner, or that of parent and child. Is it the subject matter of the conversations? I do not think so. Important personal issues are often discussed between friends, intimates, and as part of many professional relationships, and there may be a great deal of emotional expression in any of these relationships.

A long-term dynamic therapy isn't about being given helpful advice or discussing issues or even expressing feelings. Although those things happen sometimes in therapy, you can probably get a more complete discussion of an issue in a book that specializes in a particular topic, and friends, relatives and self-help manuals all give a lot more advice than therapists tend to do. Hopefully, the expression of feeling is part of many aspects of an individual's life, and when it is not, that individual usually has a hard time expressing strong feelings in the context of therapy as well.

From a self-psychology point of view, therapy is about restoring bonds that were ruptured sometime earlier in the client's life, bonds with significant people in the person's life and connections within the client herself. An in-depth therapy process promotes the unfolding of the client's patterns of experience within the context of a transference bond in which preempted developmental processes are revitalized and derailed psychological growth can resume.[6] In other words, therapy is, at heart, about the therapeutic relationship. This is not just for people whose basic needs were clearly barely met at all or who were severely abused as children. It is how an in-depth therapy process works for all of us if we allow it to.

By definition, therefore, for in-depth dynamic therapy of the sort I am referring to in this essay to work, a therapeutic relationship is one of significantly unequal power. Because of this, there are certain obligations that accrue to the professional in the relationship to create a structure in which the client can be assured that she will not be exploited. Basically, this means that it is up to the therapist to see to it that she does not use the power dynamic that has been constructed to be healing for the client to get her own needs met at the client's expense.

The rule about "no dual relationships" derives from this responsibility. The basic obligation of the therapist is to ensure that the therapy is helpful and effective for the client, and for this to be the case the client and therapist cannot be in business together or depend on one another for each other's social life or, most obviously, be sexual partners. In any of these circumstances, the capacity of the therapeutic relationship to be primarily focussed on the healing of the client would be undermined and eventually destroyed.

Though these boundaries are basic, they are obviously not enough to make therapy good therapy. If I have sex with my clients or make lots of money by investing in their businesses, it is very likely that I am a pretty unethical therapist. If I do not do those things, we have no idea of what kind of a therapist I am, except that I am not exploitive in those particular ways. There are, however, many ways in which a therapist can harm a client without ever breaking the most obvious rules. One of the most powerful of these is creating a climate of emotional dishonesty in a context in which the therapist has the authority to name reality, particularly emotional reality. This is a much more difficult kind of harm to discern because it is largely a matter of interpretation.

Empathy in the Therapeutic Relationship

The basic responsibility of a psychotherapist engaged in a process of interpersonal therapy is to create an ambience of accurate empathy. Empathy is the basic tool that therapists have to work with. No matter how kind, polite, soft-spoken, well-meaning, knowledgeable, or clever a therapist may be, if she does not create an empathic connection with her client, she cannot truly fulfill her fiduciary responsibility to that client.

There are a lot of things empathy is not. It is not sympathy, in which we feel for the other when she is in pain. It is not identification, in which we experience the other's experience as if it is our own. It is not intellectual understanding, in which we make cognitive connections with other things we know to enhance our knowledge of the other. Empathy is vicarious introspection, what Freud called *einfuehlung* (to feel oneself into another), to open oneself up so that the emotional experience of the other can resonate within us and then to pay attention to that experience as a source of awareness about the other.

Empathy is both the basic source of data in an in-depth therapy process—and the source of its deepest healing. It is within the ambiance of the empathic connection with a responsive caretaker that a child develops a vigorous, cohesive, and harmonious sense of self. The empathic responsiveness of the therapist is experienced in a similar way. Experiencing oneself as deeply and accurately understood is a vital and transformative component of the healing process.

Not all clients respond positively to an empathic therapist. For example, a sociopath might sever a therapeutic relationship upon discovering that his therapist was empathically attuned to him, and many other people have less clear-cut but profoundly ambivalent responses to the experience of being accurately understood. But that is the choice and the struggle of the client-participant in the therapy relationship, just as it is the adolescent's choice and need to ignore, reject, mock, or even, occasionally, embrace sensible parental care as part of the struggle for independence and the creation of a mature self. Whether accepted, rejected—or, more often, some complicated combination of both—it is the therapist's responsibility to create an atmosphere of empathic connection within which the client can grow and change.

One of the only checks and balances to the power differential in the therapeutic relationship is the client's unequivocal right to leave whenever she pleases. There are some exceptions to this—sex offender therapy, for example, where the offender chooses treatment over jail and premature termination means taking up residence in the local prison, or court-ordered therapy for abusive or neglectful parents. Most therapy relationships, however, are voluntary, and it is important for the therapist to be meticulous in protecting the right of the client to terminate the contract between them.

There are so many ways in which it is hard for a client to disentangle herself from a problematic therapy relationship (or even a therapy relationship which is just fine, but the client understands as problematic, or a therapy that is not what the client wants at a given time) that if she does get up the wherewithal to approach the subject of leaving therapy or taking a break, she should be given every opportunity to explore the issue freely without any pressure on the part of the therapist and with complete encouragement to act in her own best interests as she sees them, or even, simply, to leave without talking about it if that is what she wishes to do. Therapy should be a situation in which the basic rights of both participants are respected, and a very basic right of the client is to be able to leave when she wants to.

I have been speaking about the responsibility of the therapist to create an empathic connection with the client in a rather simplistic way, as if it were a matter of either accomplishing this task or not. Any therapist who has negotiated the deep and choppy waters of a long-term, dynamic psychotherapy relationship knows that this is nonsense. The degree of empathic connection a therapist is capable of creating in therapy differs considerably from one relationship to another and at different times over the course of a therapy process—indeed, often over the course of one therapy session.

The ability to open oneself to another human being, in such a way that their experience resonates within one, and then to use that resonance in the interests of that other person, is a basic psychotherapy skill that changes over the course of a therapist's career. A person in her mid-twenties, with a number of significant developmental tasks yet to negotiate, cannot possibly expect to have the same knowledge that she will have ten, or twenty, or thirty years later. And despite the experience, both personal and professional, that maturity brings, no therapist is ever a completely clear vessel for the use of her clients. Personal responses that block the therapist's ability to be empathic with her client are universal in the practice of even the most seasoned therapists. Some degree of countertransference is part of every therapy relationship. One of my colleagues, Catherine Fine, compares countertransference to the American Express card—she says we don't leave home without it.

As therapists we should be consciously developing an ever increasing level of comfort with, and awareness of, our countertransference responses to our clients. If we have not pretty well worn away our narcissistic sensitivities against knowing we are imperfect, significantly flawed human beings by the time we are relatively experienced therapists, this is a dangerous business to be in. When I come up against a therapeutic impasse, I routinely examine my participation in the relationship for countertransferential distortions that might be the source of the problem. If I cannot uncover anything of the sort myself and the problem persists, I take it to a colleague whom I trust to help me see what I might be blind to on my own.

If, even under these circumstances, I can find no evidence of problems of my own that might be blocking the process, this does not make me particularly happy. Problems of my own I have some control over; what I create I am quite likely to be able to change. If the impasse does not originate in, or is not being sustained by, my countertransferential blindness, then it is likely that what I have on my hands is a difficult situation, which time and patience and trying as many new things as I can think of may or may not be able to ameliorate. I much prefer dealing with my own problems to recognizing the reality that I may not have the power to help people make the kind of changes in their lives that I would like to see and that they say they wish desperately to make.

Such ongoing self-analysis and collegial accountability on the part of the therapist seems to me to be an essential component of an ethical psychotherapy practice. It is, however, demanding. I am disturbed by the increasing tendency to replace the demands of complex clinical and ethical analysis with prefabricated rules that override the particular contexts of our practice.

Rule-making as a Substitute for Complex Analysis

One of these areas, in my opinion, is our attempt as individual professionals, but particularly professional groups, to regulate therapist/client contact after the termination of the therapy contract. The feminist and humanist therapy movements seem to be participating with disconcerting zest in a left-wing form of conservative politics, designed to protect the incursions that we outlaws have made into the corridors of power by denying our heritage of challenge to the status quo. Crude legislative posturing sometimes seems to be replacing difficult analysis and dialogue. The result is the construction of the image of an "ethical professional," imposing it over the reality of a group of professions that have barely begun to wrestle in any deep and genuine way with ethical issues. This exercise serves only to protect the power of the profession rather than genuinely respecting and protecting the consumer from exploitation.

I see some of the more rigid positions about the boundaries of the therapeutic relationship as no more useful—and somewhat similar in terms of simple and unworkable solutions to complex issues— than the earlier "if it seems to work, do it; anything goes" framework and almost as likely to cover up rather than illuminate abuses of power in the therapy relationship. One example of this type of rigidity is a guideline that is increasingly commonly proclaimed in codes of ethics—"once a therapist, always a therapist."

Frankly, that seems like nonsense to me. That does not mean that I do not understand that in many cases, maybe even in the majority of cases in which individuals engage in a long-term, in-depth therapy process, that the emotional reality of the situation will be "once a therapist, always a therapist." To a substantial degree at any rate—at least enough to make the evolution of a friendship or a business or collegial relationship or a sexual partnership complicated and inadvisable and, indeed, unethical under some circumstances—many clients continue to experience themselves in a one-down power position vis-à-vis their ex-therapists. Some clients also want and need to keep open the possibility of returning to therapy with the same therapist after termination. For that to be a reasonable expectation, the boundaries of the therapeutic relationship must remain intact. In the majority of cases, at least in large urban areas, the issue of post-termination contact of a social nature rarely arises; most people do not particularly wish to become friends with their ex-therapist.

Creating a hard and fast rule, however, that forbids any such relationships once the therapy contract is terminated belies the wide variety of therapeutic relationships and limits the evolution of relationships in ways that might well be perfectly healthy and ethical in particular situations. Even, in my opinion, offering a specific time limit, like "no friendships or business or sex with ex-clients until two years after termination," though perhaps some protection against acting impulsively, is a compromise that solves neither aspect of the problem. If it is indeed impossible to create an extra-therapy relationship with certain clients that is as equal as any relationship can be in a patriarchal society, then it is not going to be a whole lot more likely that all of the factors that made it a relationship of significant power imbalance will fade away in the course of two years of non-contact.

It does not make sense to talk as if all therapy relationships between all clients and all therapists for all time periods under all circumstances have the same type of power dynamic and the same degree of imbalance. Quite some time ago, I was the client in a therapy relationship which, after a few sessions, I chose to terminate because I did not want to pay for a situation in which I experienced myself as the more powerful in too many ways to make it useful for me therapeutically. That does not mean that I do not recognize that there are some ways in which the therapist in any client/therapist dyad wields power that the client does not. As well as knowing that I was more grounded in my awareness of the dynamics of the therapy than this particular therapist was, I also knew that if I continued to engage in that therapeutic relationship, because of the nature and power of the therapy context, before long I would have developed a raft of intensely subjective feelings that would have drained my confidence and placed me in a vulnerable position vis-à-vis a professional whom I could not trust to use that vulnerability in my interest.

My dismay about the direction in which the professional community is moving in terms of solving complex problems like power with simplistic rule-making does not mean that it is my style to be particularly casual about boundaries. I started doing psychotherapy in a communal context in which I, my therapist, and my clients often saw each other in social situations or worked the communal farm together. I functioned as a therapist for five years in a child welfare setting in which home visits, police investigations, court appearances, and non-clinical interventions of all sorts were the order of the day. And I learned the hard way—through the work I could not do or that I started and could not finish—that wearing a few different hats makes doing in-depth psychotherapy very hard and sometimes impossible.

I have learned personally, painfully, and very slowly how extra-therapy contact with people can take the edge off the therapeutic project, and at this point in my practice I am inclined to be conservative about any extra-therapy contact with clients. I try to avoid social gatherings where my client(s) are present (or business occasions or teaching and/or consulting situations) because I have found that in many cases our therapeutic relationship limits the client's freedom to relax socially or conduct business objectively or learn freely—and limits me in these respects as well. I have also found that, more often than not, the struggle to engage in the dual relationship dilutes the therapy process big-time, and I do not get much satisfaction doing half-baked therapy.

In some cases, I might well forever try to avoid such extra-therapy situations with particular ex-clients, if it is my perception that emotionally the therapist/client affective intensity and power differential remain alive and strong in our interactions. I do not make such a choice because I consider that my clients remain my clients forever but because the relationship that evolves with certain ex-clients, as with other people who were never clients, is not conducive to an ongoing social/business/supervisory relationship that is useful for me and, probably, for them as well. This, however, is not a rule that I make; it is a practice that I consider I have a right and a responsibility to use my discretion about.

Therapy is a complicated and multidimensional endeavor. One of my most frequently invoked practice guidelines is "When you haven't a clue of what to do, don't do anything. When you don't know what to say, for heaven's sake, keep quiet." When in doubt, therapists should delay doing things they feel pressured to do—either internally or from their clients, colleagues, or all of the above—but uneasy about, and run, not walk, to consultation(s) with a trusted and experienced colleague. By catching countertherapeutic and/or ethically marginal dynamics before they become enacted and/or entrenched, timely and helpful consultation can save a great deal of headache and heartache for both client and therapist.

However, though a stance of caution on the part of a practitioner about impulsively acting in ways that are not standard practice ("This situation is different. No problem.") makes sense, imposing as a group, rigid and overly general rules that extend past the limits of the therapist/client contract is not a good solution to complex issues. Rather, this strategy enables, and indeed encourages, therapists to sidestep facing, theorizing about, and struggling with the issue of power in the therapy relationship—Who has it? What is its use? What happens when it is misused? It creates an atmosphere in which sloganizing and name-calling replace reasoned dialogue about difficult clinical, ethical, and political issues and where professionals are afraid to think important issues through for themselves and/or in communication with their colleagues because of fear of being labeled "unethical." It imposes an ideological structure on clinical work that is stifling to its creative possibilities and privileges conformity to the rules of the group (which, the history of psychotherapy illustrates, change substantially with every new generation of practitioners, and really more often than that) over the therapist's responsibility to engage in thoughtful exploration of the therapeutic process and relationship in all its complexity and specificity.

What troubles me about what I see as an increasing tendency to legislate post-treatment boundaries—not those dealing with the sexual, financial, or professional exploitation of clients currently in therapy—is that it creates an *in loco parentis* responsibility on the part of the therapist to a degree that is insulting in a relationship between adults. It is critical to acknowledge the dimensions of power in the structure of the therapeutic relationship. It is just as important not to become locked into a deterministic analysis in which dominant groups appear to be the only ones who can have individual agency, and subordinate groups are seen to be totally and forever trapped in structures of oppression. A useful critique demands the recognition of structures and agency on both sides of the equation in order to allow for resistance and change and to present the complexities of the sources of power and weakness in people's lives.

Decisions about what can and can't take place after the professional contract is completed should be considered by therapists in communication with challenging supervisors and peer consultation groups rather than be legislated by large professional protection organizations that have never been known for their ability to deal with complex situations in the interests of either their members or the general public. This does not mean that therapists should not be aware of the potential for exploitation in post-termination relationships of a social, business, or sexual nature, nor does it preclude clients or ex-clients taking appropriate action against a therapist if it is their perception that they have been exploited during, or after, therapy. Some therapists may wish to incorporate an absolute rule of "no post-therapy relationships with ex-clients," and clearly that is their prerogative. However, with little collegial discussion and no convincing empirical evidence, to declare by fiat that an everlasting and unalterable power differential is part of the essence of the therapist-client relationship is disrespectful to the relationship and both of its participants.

Most of my clients have no interest in any sort of relationship with me after we have terminated therapy. There are many clients that I would not develop a friendship with after they completed their therapy process, even if they expressed a desire to do so, because I would not experience it as a relationship of equals. It is my responsibility to be as rigorous in my exploration of the possible consequences of developing a friendship or a collegial or business relationship with an ex-client as I have it in my power to be. But reducing the therapy relationship to one of transference/countertransference disallows one of the most important and transformative aspects (or at least possibilities) of the therapy dynamic, the evolution from a relationship of unequal power in which transference is an important tool in facilitating the client's regression and consequent exploration and growth to a relationship of relative freedom from transference limitations.

Jean Baker-Miller, in her 1976 book *The Psychology of Women*, talked about therapy as a relationship of "temporary inequality" at a time when most feminist therapists were denying the depth and complexity of the therapeutic power differential. I think this is still a good way of thinking about it. In fact, a particular therapy relationship may not play itself out this way, and in many cases, transference has, as Laura Brown puts it, the half-life of plutonium. But it makes more sense to me to keep the door open for that kind of transformation than, under the guise of protecting the client, to order unchanging and unchangeable hierarchical power relations between therapist and client.

Sanctions like "once a client, always a client" are hegemonic, and they are created in the service of protecting the profession rather than protecting the client. They imply that the balance of power between client and therapist is, if not completely static, at least capable of very limited movement for the rest of each of their lives, and thus they patronize and infantilize individuals who contract for a relationship in which we are the helper, the wiser, the clearer, etc., for a specific time period only, not for the rest of their lives.

Many professionals, who do not take the prohibition of extra-therapeutic relationships and associations with all ex-clients as an absolute, make an exception in the case of sexual relationships. They would acknowledge that there are many areas in which discretion should be used. Sexual contact, however, is extricated from the realm of issues professionals must use their judgment about and prohibited absolutely, forever, under all circumstances.

It is important to emphasize that there are many—perhaps most— counseling relationships in which post-termination sexual contact would be unethical. For example, because of the nature and intensity of the long-term relationship that a highly dissociative trauma survivor usually has with her psychotherapist and the degree to which sexual abuse survivors are particularly vulnerable to revictimization, sexual contact with a client who has been treated for a severe dissociative condition—even long after the therapy was over—would likely be exploitive and therefore unethical.

It is incumbent upon the therapist to be aware of the possible dangers involved in post-termination relationships with ex-clients, and especially, perhaps, sexual relationships. I think, however, that this severing of sex from the possibility of a growing and changing relationship is a manifestation of the growing sex panic of some groups in the radical feminist movement and the feminist and humanist therapy movements, aligning them with the radical right in terms of sex negativity, misplaced scale,[7] and a disconcerting and dangerous degree of comfort with the defining, interpreting, and legislating of fit forms of desire and sexual behavior.

The rush to create rigid rules and regulations is understandable in litigious times like these. Such rules construct a comforting illusion of a guarantee of "no harm" in times when therapy is a very risky business to be conducting, and they create an anonymous, automatic morality for which no one has to accept personal responsibility. What they do not do, however, is as significant as what they do.

What global sanctions regarding post-termination relationships with clients do *not* do is deter sexual predators from exploiting their clients. Although we have seen important changes in this respect in the past five years, the vast majority of sexual abuse within the therapy context still goes unreported, and when allegations are brought to professional bodies or into a courtroom, the proceedings are likely to hold only a small percentage of perpetrators accountable for their actions. In the same way, overly general sanctions rarely deter professionals who, without conscience, exploit their clients or ex-clients, financially, professionally, or in a variety of other ways.

Significantly, this kind of dissociated rule-making makes it difficult for colleagues and supervisors to create an atmosphere in which confused and vulnerable (but not sociopathic) professionals who engage in sex (or other dual relationships) to the detriment of the client (either during the professional relationship or after its termination) would have been able to communicate their feelings, impulses, and intentions in supervision or peer consultation and expect to find a non-judgmental forum in which they could wrestle with the issue and possibly avoid acting in harmful ways.

Imposing overly general rules about the boundaries of professional relationships creates an atmosphere in which it is not conducive for therapists to explore countertransference and other personal issues deeply. Instead, they use professional doctrine or legal strictures as an escape valve that frees the therapist from that bottom-line and difficult responsibility that can never be accomplished perfectly. Ideology, under the guise of ethics hides the uncomfortable reality that any relationship, including a therapy relationship, is a balance of the good it does for the people involved and the harm it does, and there is no possibility of doing "no harm" ever, despite the inspiring and useful direction of the Hippocratic oath: *Primum non nocere.*

Contextual Variables

This kind of reductionism also obscures rather than illuminates the differences among therapeutic relationships (and other fiduciary relationships), neglecting to take into consideration contextual variables—such as race, class, culture, religion, gender, sexuality, ability, geography, etc., and the values and social conditions that may accrue to the client's and the professional's location along these lines—as well as a wide variety of personal variables. According to these standards, a mental health professional practicing in an isolated community in the far north of Canada (or a pastor in the same village) would find it impossible to conduct both an ethical professional practice and live any sort of life if the guidelines about extra-therapeutic relationships with clients and ex-clients (or members of congregations) are seen as absolutes.

If a rigid application of the "no dual relationships" proscription— or even the sort of relatively conservative application that I have been espousing—is absolutely essential to effective psychodynamic therapy, it would be impossible to treat clients in small, isolated communities in which there is an inevitable overlap of roles—or at least the results would be substantially compromised. The only study I know of that addresses this issue does not find this to be so.[8] Certainly before we assume it to be so, we need to do a great deal more research—talk to a lot more people—in a much wider variety of contexts. As Jean Charcot is quoted by his student, Sigmund Freud,[9] as pointing out, *"La theorie, c'est bon, mais ca n'empeche pas d'exister."* ("Theory is good, but it doesn't prevent things from existing.")

Cultural traditions in which the healers in a community are a part of the social fabric of that community must be respected (as well as challenged and explored when power dynamics are seen as exploitive by members of the community) rather than swept aside by professionals outside the community who feel confident that their standards of ethics have universal application. When I acted as a consultant to a Native Canadian social-service agency that provided therapeutic services to an urban Native population, one of the most complex issues was the development of boundaries protecting the therapy process that respected both traditional values of the integration of the healer within the community and the contemporary urban sensibilities of the workers, who had been trained in mainstream mental-health practice as well as through traditional Native teaching. Rigid rules about the practice of therapy that ignored the cultural complexity that was the lived experience of these workers and their client community would have been criminally insensitive to the goal of this agency and its workers—to develop culturally appropriate and creative services that combined traditional healing with mainstream mental-health practice.

The solution of including in discussions of ethical guidelines disclaimers globally exempting different racial or cultural groups from complying with strictures that are framed as mandatory for everyone else seems both patronizing and a case of sloppy thinking. The workers in this urban Native organization had to struggle to create a set of practice guidelines that made it possible for them to accomplish their particular goals with their particular group of clients. In that they share a struggle with every other responsible professional—the struggle to create structures that empower rather than diminish both the healer and those who seek healing by honoring the customs and values of both and being willing to offer challenge, both to themselves and, when necessary, to their clients.

• • •

This is a time when the pendulum has swung from deconstructing the boundaries of the therapeutic relationship to reconstructing them, sometimes in a rigid fashion that subverts the collaborative struggle that is the heart of an in-depth therapy process. The bottom line in terms of making a value judgment about whether a particular boundary in any relationship is useful, respectful, and ethical is its power to facilitate our capacity to reach out to other human beings, including our clients, in a grounded, passionate, and genuinely moral way. In order to do that, we need to be rigorous in examining the complexities of our relationships—including their shadows and their depths.

We are just beginning. We have been taking some of the most obvious first steps. We need to continue unlearning and relearning and reshaping the theoretical frameworks within which we practice and the structures of our communities so that we can be truly accountable to each other and to the most vulnerable among us. And we must struggle to create rich and complex theory about the healing relationship and wise and compassionate communities in which we can bear to know each other—not as us and them—but as we, as we work together in this struggle that is about the liberation of us all.

Notes

1. H. Wycoff, *Solving Problems Together* (New York: Grove Press, 1980).

2. H. Wycoff, "Radical Psychiatry Techniques for Solving Women's Problems in Groups," in *Psychotherapy for Women,* ed. E. Rawlings and D. Carter (Springfield, Ill.: Charles C. Thomas, 1977).

3. Jean Baker-Miller, *Towards a New Psychology of Women* (Boston: Beacon Press, 1976); N. Chodorow, *The Reproduction of Mothering: Psychoanalysis and the Sociology of Gender* (Berkeley, Calif.: University of California Press, 1978); Carol Gilligan, *In a Different Voice* (Cambridge: Harvard University Press, 1982).

4. Lerman, 1976; D. Carter and E. Rawlings, eds., *Psychotherapy for Women* (Springfield, Ill.: Charles C. Thomas, 1977); S. Sturdivant, *Therapy with Women: A Feminist Philosophy of Treatment* (New York: Springer, 1980); M. Greenspan, *A New Approach to Women and Therapy* (New York: McGraw-Hill, 1985); M. Ballou and N. Gabalac, *A Feminist Position on Mental Health* (Springfield, Ill.: Charles C. Thomas, 1985); L. Rosewater and L. Walker, eds., *Handbook of Feminist Therapy: Women's Issues in Psychotherapy* (New York: Springer Publishing Company, 1985).

5. Wycoff, *Solving Problems Together*.

6. R. Stolorow, B. Brandchaft, and G. Atwood, *Psychoanalytic Treatment: An Intersubjective Approach* (Hillsdale, N.J.: The Analytic Press, 1987).

7. G. Rubin, "Thinking of Sex: Notes for a Radical Theory of the Politics of Sexuality," in *The Lesbian and Gay Studies Reader* (New York and London: Routledge, 1983).

8. H. Beskind, S. Bartels, and M. Brooks, "Practical and Theoretical Dilemmas of Dynamic Psychotherapy in a Small Community," in *Beyond Transference: When the Therapist's Real Life Intrudes*, ed. J. Gold and J. Nemiah (Washington, D.C.: American Psychiatric Press, 1993).

9. S. Freud, "Charcot," in *The Standard Edition of the Complete Psychological Works of Sigmund Freud*, vol. 3 (1893–1899), trans. J. Strachey (1962) (London: Hogarth, 1893).

12 Barriers Not Withstanding

A Lesbianista Perspective

Mari E. Castellanos

THE ONGOING DISCUSSION regarding professional boundaries in ministry has largely taken place among individuals whose primary role is that of close observer. Ethicists, theologians, and pastors who counsel victims of clergy abuse are right in entering the debate. Other voices are needed however; namely, those of ministers themselves. This book seeks to widen the discussion in such a manner.

This essay is a contribution from the front lines. In the Latin American tradition of liberation theology this is secondary reflection on experience. It claims no expertise other than experience itself and prayerful reflection on it. Nevertheless, it comes from a perspective other than the one that has dominated the debate. As a Hispanic, feminist lesbian—a *lesbianista*, as I occasionally choose to name myself—I see some of the issues from a different angle. The following is an attempt to share this perspective.

The core of the problem is patriarchy and the ways in which those who hold patriarchal power exercise it. Any feminist observer will point that out. As we create new communities we do not need to replicate the structures of patriarchal power. We are not doomed to it. We can opt to put into practice the model of "discipleship of equals"[1] that we have been discussing for over a decade. The good news from the front is that this is indeed being done all over the place. Some of us have internalized the concepts of "mutuality" and "right relation"[2] and are committed to their implementation as we build communities of mutual accountability. How we do so will vary according to the needs of the specific communities.

The way in which "boundaries" have been so far described in the plethora of articles that have dealt with this issue over the past year conjures a vision of the Great Wall of China: big, heavy structures that are hard to move or change once in place. Nature offers an example of a different kind of boundaries: semipermeable membranes allow some substances to pass through the cell wall while keeping others out. In the case of living organisms this selection is done on the basis of molecular weight. Using this metaphor for professional boundaries allows us to be less rigid, to develop criteria that may vary from one community to another, as I hope to argue for, and to give the individual the opportunity to exercise personal judgment. It is my contention that a professional—whether pastor, therapist or other—who does not have good enough personal judgment to decide the appropriate amount of permeability of her or his boundaries is probably not fit to exercise the profession. While poor to mediocre pastors and counselors are far from scarce, this mostly applies to their skills, not their moral judgment.

This argument for flexibility does not extend to sexual involvement, which is always inappropriate within an ongoing counseling situation, both clinical and pastoral, where the dynamics of power are preordered and vulnerability is largely one-sided. The literature on the subject, and the abundant cases that make the newspapers, underscore the fact that it is not the absence of boundaries that have made clergy abuse of parishioners possible. A priest who has sexual relations with an altar boy is not drawn to it by any lack of boundaries. The book is full of rules against it; he just chose to break them.

Dual Relationships and Cultural Reality

Hispanics and other minorities do not favor doing business with strangers. While the most acculturated among us will do our shopping at large retail stores and supermarkets, the small "Ma and Pa" stores flourish in our "barrios" and communities. In some of our countries of origin the name of a business will reflect a relation, i.e., "Hijos de Juan Perez" might be a name used to build a business based on the good reputation of the owner's father. To do business with, or to otherwise engage in a professional relationship with, persons who are friends is considered desirable. That friendship could be considered an obstacle or a liability is culturally challenging, *una gringada*. After living in the States for over thirty years I still would much rather do business with a cousin of a friend than with a more competitive firm out of the *Yellow Pages*.

At the 1993 General Conference of the Universal Fellowship of Metropolitan Community Churches (UFMCC), Rev. Marie Fortune[3] argued against dual relations, that is, professional relations with persons with whom we may have personal friendships. This included, but was not limited to, clergy persons having friendships with members of their congregations. She and others who choose to are free to follow that criterion, but I and those who find it unacceptable should not be deemed less ethical because of it. At a time of serious moral dilemma I have sought the advice of an ethicist friend. I have done so and will do so again, because my friend is an excellent ethicist who happens to be my friend. I seldom seek the counsel of strangers. Similarly, the priest who baptized me, married my parents, and buried my grandparents, was a good friend of the family. Both he and my parents would have found any criticism of this dual relationship highly offensive. Our family physicians, a husband-and-wife team, were also close friends of my parents, regarded as family. Any implication that this could be construed as unethical or inappropriate would be so ludicrous to them and to my parents that it would simply be dismissed immediately.

Perhaps Anglo ethicists would do well to consider a variation of the old theatrical axiom, "Yes, but will it play in the "barrios"? I know that such objections to dual relationships will not play in Little Havana. I am afraid that in our increasingly litigious society, if a professional incurs liability in an abuse of friendship we will find fault with the concept of friendship and, consequently, we try to legislate the parameters of friendship. All of us who carry liability insurance against malpractice suits live with the constant awareness that our judgment is subject to another kind of judgment. There are good laws and good professional regulations in place to protect the vulnerable from abuse. This should remain so. When abuse takes place, the consequences should be swift and the judgment strict against those who commit a breach of trust, particularly sacred trust. It is precisely because of the moral seriousness of pedophilia, and of the sexual abuse of persons rendered vulnerable by the imbalance of power in a counseling relationship, that this issue should not be trivialized by attempts to extend the criteria in order to include arguable issues such as dual relationships. Ultimately, it is essential that we demythologize the roles of certain professionals. Pastors, physicians, and therapists are not gods, but rather professionals with a limited field of expertise, like engineers and accountants. Bringing pulpits down to pew level will go a long way toward eliminating abuse; much longer than attempting to regulate friendship.

Increasingly, clergy persons and entire congregations are coming out of the closet. That ministers sometimes are gay or lesbian may be an issue at denominational conferences but it is an otherwise mundane fact of life. The intolerance of homosexuality in most mainline churches has brought about the establishment of primarily lesbian/gay churches and communities of faith. This raises new and interesting challenges regarding professional boundaries for clergy. The self-identifying or "out" lesbian/gay community is simply not that large. Even in a large metropolitan area like Dade County, Florida, over a period of years an activist can come in contact with very large segments of the community. I sometimes joke that I pastor the entire lesbian community of Dade County, at least potentially, since I am the only "out" lesbian minister and have been so for many years. When a straight couple decides to get married, they have many choices of a celebrant. When a lesbian couple in Miami decides they want to have a Holy Union, chances are I am it. Similarly, in this tragic time of AIDS, I have done many—far too many—funerals and memorial services, including those of some well-known community activists. Additionally, I do a lot of presentations and workshops about issues of concern to our community. If I were single and looking for a date, I would be hard put to find a lesbian who shares my values and spirituality with whom I have not come in contact pastorally. This is not the same situation as that of a single heterosexual pastor. The minister at First Baptist can look for a date at Second Baptist and find a compatible stranger. The minister at a gay/lesbian Christian church has few options for fun and friendship outside her own congregation. The smaller the town, the worse the scenario that unfolds.

Creating New Models

Once again, the core of the problem is patriarchy. The lesbian and gay movement in the churches and other communities of faith offers a golden opportunity to build new structures. In repudiating heterosexism it is imperative that we also repudiate sexism, racism, and all the evils that thrive in a patriarchal setting. Sadly, this is at best done in a very superficial manner in most of our faith communities. Yes, organizations like Dignity[4] and the UFMCC have championed the use of inclusive language and have good records in areas such as gender parity. However, change must be structural, systemic actually. Repentance and conversion must reach and transform the foundations of our institutions. When I see a lesbian in a clerical collar, calling herself Reverend, I nearly lose all hope. A clergy person who accepts and/or adopts all the trappings of the patriarchy must therefore play by the rules. This includes the rigid boundaries that Rev. Marie Fortune advocates. You can't have it both ways. If you embody the "pastor-as-godself" model of ministry, then you must bear the consequences. Being god can be lonely, particularly for mortals.

There are other possibilities, however, that are indeed being enacted. It is simply a matter of ministers being willing to relinquish some power and of congregations being willing to claim their own power and assume responsibilities.

A recent incident illustrates the above point. A man came to me to discuss what had transpired between him and his pastor at another church in the town where he used to live. It seems this man was an employee at an establishment frequented by the pastor. This establishment was a "pick-up" place, about three miles from the church. Whenever the pastor patronized this establishment the man addressed him as "reverend." On one such instance the pastor pulled him aside and asked the man to stop calling him "reverend" because the pastor was "trying to get lucky" and being called "reverend" was not facilitating this happening. The man apparently had no problem with the issue of a Christian minister being in a bar with the objective of picking up a stranger for the purpose of having sex. Neither did the minister, ostensibly. The apparent conflict was over the use of the title "reverend." Without addressing the propriety or morality of anyone engaging in casual sex with a stranger, this story still raises some important questions. It's been suggested that the single gay minister should "go look" in the next town. It's been argued back that oftentimes that is an entirely unreasonable demand.[5]

The incident over the title "reverend" underscores part of the problem. For the minister in question, the title "reverend" is a permanent part of his name. He identifies himself as "Reverend Joel"—not his real name—practically always and everywhere. More often than not, he wears a clerical collar. Services at his church are structured in a traditional liturgical manner, with him wearing vestments and celebrating the eucharist. Everything about this man sets him apart. The title "reverend" means that he is due, or entitled to be treated with, reverence. This in turn means "a feeling or attitude of deep respect tinged with awe; veneration"[6]. Words are important. An object of veneration is subject to different standards than the rest of us. The message the man at the bar received was that either "reverence" is something one can put on and take off, or that sex and reverence are incompatible. The latter is highly problematic. Furthermore, the minister had no objection to this man addressing him by a title of deep respect, except when he was pursuing a sexual partner. Congruency and consistency between message and behavior are requirements for people who preach a renewed appreciation of sexuality as wholesome and holy.

Ministers have the option of presenting ourselves as we really are; namely, enfleshed spirits no different from anyone else and therefore subject to no greater standard of behavior. Alternatively, we can continue in the tradition of minister as reverend, pillar, person chosen by the Almighty to shepherd the sheep. Shepherds are subject to higher standards than sheep.

A minister can opt to be someone whose vocation is to serve, to walk with, to pay attention to a people; someone whose training is to do so by teaching, preaching, reconciling, sacramentalizing. The minister, alongside the nurse, the parents, the architect, the cook, the lab technician, and all of those who make up the congregation, is someone who is a part of, integrated with, not apart from. This is someone who empowers rather than who has power over. The issue of boundaries is about power, who has it over whom. In a model of ministry where power is more equitably distributed among all, where all are vulnerable, boundaries can be more like the semipermeable membranes of living cells. There is still serious caution required because so many people have been victims of abuse. This is a very serious moral responsibility, which all of us in the helping professions carry. We must always be aware that people perceive us to be powerful, even when we do not engage in power-over behavior. *Prudence* is always the first word. But we do not need to live in isolation. We can have friends in our congregations and, when appropriate, we can have lovers and spouses in our congregations as well.

Not one among us really knows how to be anything other than a faithful daughter or son of the patriarchy. We were brought up to look either up or down in our pastoral relationships. Feminists of every denomination have discussed this, and have sometimes implemented different models with varying degrees of success. Interestingly enough, it is perhaps fleeing from the most entrenched religious patriarchy, the Roman Catholic church, that the most experimentation and implementation has taken place. Inspired by the feminist liberation theologies and critical hermeneutics of Rosemary Radford Ruether and Elizabeth Schüssler Fiorenza, among others, women and men have pursued the development of the "Ekklesia of women," or what is now called "women-church." Women-church groups exist all over the country and in other parts of the world. Though varying in style and scope, these groups meet to celebrate their faith, to sacramentalize their lives, and to engage in justice making. One such group is Holy Wisdom Inter-Faith Community (IFC) in Miami.

One Case in Point

It began as an ordinary split, the kind that Christian churches sometimes experience. It was a matter of a strong disagreement between the pastor and the board of directors, backed by a considerable segment of the congregation, over the associate pastor. The pastor said, "she goes"; the other side said, "she stays." The pastor would not reconsider and after much struggle the congregation split. A minor tragedy in Christendom, albeit a very painful one for all involved. What made this one case a little different is that this is primarily a lesbian and gay congregation. Furthermore, those who left are mostly women and/or Hispanics, with a handful of Anglo men standing bravely in solidarity.

The controversial associate pastor, the author of this paper, is a Hispanic woman, a lesbian, a cradle Roman Catholic, and someone who has been deeply influenced by feminist and Latin American liberation theologies, as well as someone who has been involved in both the women-church movement, and the gay/lesbian movement in the churches. I had no intentions of starting a traditional parish for gay and lesbian people. Interestingly, a small community had gathered and bonded at the early morning sunday service at which I preached for three years. This was a community that was interested in issues of justice and liberation. Not surprisingly, a majority of them are women and Hispanics. Perhaps more interestingly, a number of them are not Christian or if so, not very traditional. It was a perfect opportunity for something new.

I did not covet the title "pastor." I did not want to be the church's CEO. I want to journey with a people, to do ethics and theology that are rooted in our own experience. Together I want us to celebrate life, to mourn our losses, and to proclaim God's liberation of God's people from oppression. I want to gather a liberating community; to offer sanctuary to God's gay and lesbian people, a place for healing and growth.

We are doing so. We are about fifty people that are quite literally building a church. We rented a warehouse space and have been busy transforming it into a community space. I am not very good at building, so I take directions from someone who is a general contractor when I try my hand at things from painting to cleaning to helping put up walls. We have very fluid boundaries. We have people who are responsible for many different things. I leave legalities to the attorney, computer decisions to the programmers, budget to the accountant, and acquisitions to the buyers. The poor musicians have to put up with me because I actually think I know something about music. I can preach, I can teach, I can do liturgy, and I can reconcile. Those are the gifts I bring, no better than anybody else's. Those are gifts that others also posses, something I try to recognize and nurture. We have been working by task force, staying goal-oriented, as opposed to establishing a board of directors. Presently, we are still small enough to hold business meetings open to all and with decisions reached by consensus.

I think I have the respect of the congregation and they have mine. Some of us became friends during the process of conflict and separation from the other church. We have relied on each other for comfort and solace. We are not only sisters and brothers but also comrades, *compañeros en la lucha*. My partner has been a part of it through it all. I wouldn't discuss my personal life from the pulpit if I had a pulpit, but there are a few people in the congregations who share my confidences, as I do theirs.

I don't wear vestments anymore, though I use my green stole from El Salvador some days because it holds a great deal of meaning for me. We need to discern what to do about deacons and others who are called to a priestly ministry. But the warehouse comes first. We'll do the ecclesiology later.

The gift of being an interfaith community furthers the challenge. I have been honored with the request to help celebrate our first bat mitzvah. Fortunately, I have some good rabbinical friends. We have celebrated the Seder at Passover and we gather for Shabbat once a month. We have welcomed folks from the Institute for Creation Spirituality, and some of our members regularly participate in a sweat lodge. I welcome all who want to journey together bringing about the reign of God. I do not wish to engage in any sort of religious imperialism, but rather I hope to be a catalyst in bringing together a vibrant community of faith. This is for me the imperative of the gospel: "To embrace the gospel means to enter into community, the one cannot be obtained without the other. The gospel calls into being the church as the discipleship of equals that is continually recreated in the power of the Spirit."[7]

By the grace of God, I am aware of the little and the vulnerable among us, those who image God to us most powerfully. The children ought not share the burden of the adults, thus we treat them with extra care and tenderness and we protect them in their innocence. When we do so they will grow to take their rightful place in the community of mutual accountability.

But we do not keep grown men and women separated by hierarchical structures. This new model of church we fervently pursue can only be attained if we overcome this structural-patriarchal dualism between lay people, women and men religious and clergy persons, which keep us divided. It is imperative that in this conversation about professional boundaries we clearly state that, as we vigorously protect the vulnerable among us, that we never, under any circumstances, blur the lines between the precious gift of friendship and the crime of abuse.

Standing at a Crossroads

In my country we have a saying: "Don't confuse magnesium with gymnasium." They are really not at all alike. We are at a crossroads in Christian history, in the unfolding journey of all of humankind. Paradigmatic shifts are necessary if our spiritual traditions are to have any relevance in the cultures of the new millennium. Adherence to values rather than regulations should be the norm for people who preach ethics and morality. Like magnesium and gymnasium, values and regulations are not at all alike.

The essence of the message that has been entrusted to us is the gospel of mutuality and inclusivity, the proclamation of the reign of God among us. Hierarchical structures no longer serve that proclamation well, if they ever did. We must systematically tear down walls, not erect boundaries that mimic them. Neighborhoods that build walls to keep crime out might work in the short term, but in the long run they further the alienation that fosters crime in the first place.

Let us not yield to the fear that some will abuse power. They will do so anyhow. We need to be a little bold and give up the privilege that comes with titles, the trappings of hierarchical office, and the fear of being vulnerable. There are choices to be made.

Friendship, intimacy, respect, vulnerability, mutuality and sharing of power, are necessary materials for building community, the "discipleship of equals," the reign of God.

Notes

1. See Elizabeth Schüssler Fiorenza, *In Memory of Her* (New York: Crossroad, 1983), epilogue, for discussion of this concept.

2. These two closely related terms are described by Carter Heyward first in *The Redemption of God: A Theology of Mutual Relation* (Washington, D.C.: University Press of America, 1982) and later in *Touching Our Strength: The Erotic as Power and the Love of God* (San Francisco: Harper and Row, 1989).

3. In her address, Rev. Fortune used the example of a physician misdiagnosing a friend because of insufficient objectivity.

4. Dignity Inc. is a national organization of lesbian and gay Roman Catholics.

5. After Rev. Fortune's address at the UFMCC General Conference, a long discussion ensued between her and a number of other ministers. It was her recommendation that single lesbian and gay pastors in small communities travel to other towns for their social outlets. This does not appear to me to contribute to an integrated life.

6. *Webster's New Collegiate Dictionary,* 1980.

7. Fiorenza, *In Memory of Her*, epilogue.

13 | Care of the Dying
Power Between, Power Under, and Powerlessness With as Means for Valuing and Balancing Boundaries and Mutuality

Bill Wallace

THERE ARE THREE essential properties of an effective presence with dying persons that inform the discussion about boundaries in helping relationships, particularly relationships of pastoral care and psychotherapy. In this essay, I will explore these characteristics and suggest how each one contributes to the boundary debate and the higher ground to which our dialogue aspires—better care.

Property One: Power Between

I remember having a what-do-I-want-to-do-when-I-grow-up conversation with a good friend who has AIDS. I was sharing with him my ambivalence about accepting a call to parish ministry. After a few minutes, he said, "One thing I like about having a terminal illness is that I do not have to worry about what I am going to do with my life. Instead, I am left to ask myself each day how I might, in the company of others, bless God."

Dying persons, like my friend, are much more likely to discover meaningful life in the immediate context of their present connections to lover, mate, friend, family, and co-workers. They are much less likely to search for personal well-being around the figurative bend where our frontier culture has promised the possibility of self-actualization to lie. Dying persons come to express what Martin Buber believed, that in the beginning was relationship.

Abraham Verghese, an infectious-disease specialist caring for persons with AIDS, and the author of *My Own Country: A Doctor's Story*,[1] said it another way while being interviewed about his book: "The people I encounter with AIDS are scooped off the pathway of life and find themselves in a crucible of meaning whereby every human emotion takes on exaggerated significance."[2] Dr. Verghese went on to say that the crucible of meaning to which he referred was the relationships through which the person with AIDS lived and died.[3]

So meaningful is their discovery of relationship as the essence of being human that many persons with AIDS are quick to say that the disease gave them the chance to live a more complete life. I recall a letter to a mother from her dying son. The son told the mother that she should not worry about whether heaven would be his reward in that eternal life was what he was experiencing now in the community formed through his illness.

The dying person's awareness of the saving grace of conviviality is expressive of theological and psychological tenets that challenge the belief by many that particular boundaries in professional helping relationships are heuristic, that is, essential to the creation and maintenance of an environment conducive to healing and growth. The theological tenet about which I speak is Martin Luther's understanding of *communio sanctorum*, the communion of saints.[4]

Luther reestablished the communion of saints in the world, and, therefore, erased the temporal and spacial boundary between earth and heaven. He understood the communion of saints to be all people, holy or otherwise, who participate together in Christ's adoring of them in the here and now. He opposed the medieval understanding of *communio sanctorum* as that future, heavenly company of the morally superior that the Christian, as *viator*, seeks to gain through good works on earth. In the *Smalcald Articles*, Luther, in speaking of how the gospel offers counsel and help against sin,[5] suggested a fifth way beyond the spoken word, baptism, holy communion, and the power of the keys to forgive; namely, *the mutual conversation and consolation of the [sisters and] brothers.*[6]

Luther understood that a foretaste of the eschatological end (aim and finish) of history is experienced in the present joy experienced among estranged persons in a mutual relationship of unconditional love. Such sisterhood informs and recasts the boundaries in helping relationships between the one who helps and the one getting helped. The helper no longer has the right, nor should she be audacious enough, to muster up a divine direction in which to point or prosper the one seeking help. What's left to the helper's rightful disposal is the courage she might have to accept the unconscious or conscious invitation given her by the one seeking help to stand together in the middle of whatever life situation is presented.

In doing this fifth work of the gospel, the helper's courage to *stand with* needs to be accompanied by a complementary capacity to shed herself of the dead skin of professionalism and step over the boundary of authority behind which she stands. The power over dynamic given to the helper by credentials, training, or charisma offers little to the one who comes to pastoral care or psychotherapy cracked open and poured into the bowl of meaning-making by the experiences of AIDS, depression, addiction, abuse, loss, and so forth. Persons seeking deliverance from these prisons, whether they know it or not, are looking for one shelter of truth among many shelters of truth; not the asylum of truth defined and dispensed by a professional in power over her, but the sanctuary of truth discovered in and as community with a fellow struggler. Truth, as Hannah Arendt suggested, is a dynamic, agonistic process of one person speaking, another listening and speaking in turn.[7]

The critical questions for the helper, then, are not what diagnosis of the soul fits, which treatment follows, and what outcomes can be expected. Rather, the questions are whether or not the helper can stand or muscle up to the eternal work of presence, mere presence (a bias toward mutuality), and whether or not she can be respectful of the power to bless and the potential to curse a soul so primed for encounter (a concern for boundaries).

Dying persons who seek help are the exemplary teachers of presence. For the situation dying persons bring to the helper is not something the helper can fix, chart a direction out of, or claim expertise in regard to. We all die and each person dies in her own way. One can see that the illness metaphor that permeates the trades of most helpers and prescribes the outcome of cure is of little value in the face of death, and, when followed, leaves the helper all thumbs. The helper, if she is to heal, must assent to the less fantastic metaphor of accompaniment. The climb up to the mountain of this metaphor is rugged and steep because few of the guilds within the helping professions give much credence to it. It can be a lonely journey with few markers along the way.

Dying is much like living, in that we are often embedded in situations that escape our strongest desire for and best attempts at reparation. Life-the-way-it-really-is has its way with us each day. As such, the ministry of presence among the dying shadowed by a metaphor of accompaniment is appropriate to practice with all who come to the healer for help. Furthermore, I believe this ministry and metaphor can be expanded into an effective ecclesiology. Presence with and accompaniment of one another is, I believe, the cornerstone of *communio sanctorum* as Luther understood it.

The psychological tenet I refer to is that promulgated by colleagues at the Stone Center at Wellesley College. They propose that the psychotherapist's management of a process through which psychotherapist and client identify with and understand one another is an experience of interdependent relatedness that makes well and models authentic living for a culture wrongly infatuated with independence and self-actualization. Their work on the value of mutuality in helping relationships and how a lockstep allegiance to rigid boundaries within them thwarts the healing process reflects what does and does not heal in a ministry to dying persons.

Judith Jordan's work,[8] in particular, grounded in object relations and self-psychology, illuminates a departure from psychoanalytic roots at two important places as far as boundaries and pastoral care of the dying are concerned.

First, while psychoanalytic-oriented psychologies acknowledge the value of understanding formed by unconditional love, they focus on the psychotherapist alone as an agent of it. As much as the client may receive from being the apple of the psychotherapist's eye, the client, because her value as a similarly loving agent is not grist for the therapeutic mill, finds herself not only bound in a relationship of disproportionate power but also caught in a dynamic that disregards her full humanity. Clients come to psychotherapy because they are dying, that is, being diminished in some way or another. Persons experiencing one or more of the many daily manifestations of dying are violated by care that draws a boundary around their freedom to live, to fully participate in a loving relationship.

This violation is at the heart of Carter Heyward's critique of her psychotherapist and their psychotherapeutic relationship in the book *When Boundaries Betray Us.*[9] In my opinion, Carter's psychotherapist, because she was ambivalent about her role and the parameters of it in the helping relationship, desperately clung to the tree of her theory, a theory that made paramount the premise that she was to be the sole loving agent in the relationship. The psychotherapist, by clutching to her theory, precluded Carter's desire and capacity to be fully human in the immediacy of the psychotherapeutic encounter, and, as a result, infantilized Carter as a person-in-the-making.

This need not have happened. If the psychotherapist had been centered on her allegiance to the traditional boundary that prescribes and constrains the psychotherapist as the sole loving agent, she probably would have avoided wounding Carter so severely. Had the psychotherapist delineated this thick boundary, rather than retreat behind it, she would have enabled Carter to better understand what the psychotherapeutic relationship could not be for her. Then Carter may have been able to decide against such therapy early on and from a position of greater safety and strength. Instead, the psychotherapist blamed, punished, and finally rejected Carter for the psychotherapist's own failure at maintaining this boundary within which she chose to work.

Second, psychoanalytic-oriented psychologies see the psychotherapist using her managed, one-dimensional, and, therefore, dissonant understanding of the client as that which, like a magnet and metal filings, coalesces the fragmented and fragile elements of the client's self into a unified whole better capable of loving and working, of being more sad than depressed. These more classical goals of psychotherapy, like medieval soteriology, are about the future attainment of personal salvation. The Marlboro Man of cigarette advertising fame and the Christian *viator* are more alike than unlike when it comes to matters of stature and autonomy.

Dying persons find both icons unworthy of devotion. For the dying person, salvation is experienced now in and as an interdependent, co-creating person in community; salvation, or wholeness, as something sought after by the achievement of a more cohesive, individuated self through submission to one who mainly values and practices the giving of unconditional positive regard has little appeal and less value.

In summary of property one, the pastoral and psychotherapeutic needs of dying persons create an unlikely collaboration. Luther's theology of the *communio sanctorum* and The Stone Center's ongoing work on mutuality, by locating the experience of the eternal and the attainment of wholeness in the here and now of loving interrelatedness, challenge the efficacy of boundaries in helping relationships that are established to move the one seeking help up this culture's holy mountain of the cohesive self.

The collaboration signals a guideline to be considered regarding boundaries in pastoral care and psychotherapy. Boundaries that limit loving to the pastoral caregiver or psychotherapist, which create a parental, power-over dynamic, might well be more lightly drawn. This allows the full humanity of the person seeking help to participate in the liberating encounter, the fashioning of truth, the extension of the heavenly realm.[10]

My experience with Martin represents lines more lightly drawn. Martin came to me, after the death of his lover to AIDS, for grief counseling. Over time, the parameters of the helping relationship softened. Martin became less a counselee and more a friend in Spirit.[11]

My most meaningful experience with Martin was near the time of his own death from AIDS. I picked up Martin from the AIDS clinic, where he had gone for a treatment to counteract his increasing loss of vision. Martin insisted on taking me to lunch. For two hours he coached my soul from the bench of his dying, a soul that had become wearied in a health-care position that was mostly about administration and marketing. The care and courage he gave to me that day became a foundation on which I built the decision to return to full-time pastoral ministry.

Martin's dying did not "excuse" our crossing of traditional boundaries. Rather, his dying poured us into the crucible of meaning and meaning-making of which Dr. Verghese spoke, a crucible that transcends and makes moot many of the established boundaries of pastoral and psychotherapeutic relating. I believe this crucible is the right container not only for care of the dying but for most helping relationships.

Taking down the one-way-street sign on the doors of pastoral care and psychotherapy when the impetus of impending death is not present calls for more from the helper than is prescribed by the pastoral care and psychotherapy professions. First, the pastoral caregiver or psychotherapist is urged to move beyond characterizing—and controlling—the affect in the room as transference and countertransference. Second, the healer lets the one seeking help have a figurative mirror in her hand as well, which enables the healer to be lovingly seen and shaped by the one seeking help. Consequently, she participates in the back-and-forth cueing of souls that ignites transcendence. Third, the healer acknowledges that she is witnessing and managing more than a window into the life of the one seeking help—the "as if" dimension referenced in the pastoral counseling and psychoanalytic literature; rather, she is experiencing life with the one seeking help in a way that new meaning about and for living fully is made together in the moment. In other words, life is lived in the community of the helping relationship rather than prepared for by it. For the dying, and, I believe, the living, the immediate moment is the most significant. Now is always.

Property Two: Power Under

I asked a young man in the last stages of AIDS what he considered to be the hardest thing about dying. He said that his friends no longer let him pick up the check when they went out to eat.

Rarely are dying persons afraid of death. It's the journey, not the destination, that is painful. The journey is about the increasing loss of agency over one's daily life, the mounting reality of not being able to live in the accustomed, desired, or required manner. Dying persons, therefore, often experience a spiritual crisis of powerlessness.[12] The suffering of dying persons is the relationship they take to, the meaning they make out of, such powerlessness. Accordingly, the orientation of pastoral care and psychotherapy with dying persons is to the loss of control over their lives, their resulting spiritual crisis of powerlessness, and the suffering they are experiencing because of it. The goal of such an orientation is the reclamation of previously established means of agency, the creation of new ones, and, finally, the sharing of grief regarding the ultimate victory of dying's slow, insidious, sure stripping away of life the way it has been known, experienced, valued.

To return to an aforementioned bias shared in the first part of this essay, living is dying; persons who seek pastoral care and counseling often are being diminished by situations beyond their control. Therefore, the orientation and goals of pastoral care and psychotherapy with dying persons are transferrable to most healing encounters. The question becomes, then, what can the pastoral caregiver and psychotherapist experience with the one seeking help to enable her to reclaim, create, and maintain agency while at the same time attending to the suffering and grief caused by the loss of agency?

The question is answered, in part, by reshaping the nature and shifting the location of boundaries in the helping relationship. First, we shall examine how traditional boundaries in the helping relationship rob the agency of the one seeking help, and, therefore, why they must be reshaped.

Within the healing arts of our society, pain serves a purpose. Pain indicates a need for help and motivates one to get it. Pain, then, is an agent of healing, which, because of its debilitating powers, simultaneously diminishes the agency of the one seeking health. Pain moves people to present themselves for help in less control than they were before their pain. For example, a parishioner waits to call the priest for an appointment when the shame of and fear about an abusive relationship gets too much to bear. A child asks for her allergy medication after the sniffles begin.

Hospice, with a charge to give dying persons as much control over their daily lives as possible, acknowledges how ineffective and unnecessary pain is as an agent of healing. Hospice asks physicians why they wait until pain becomes intractable before prescribing morphine. Hospice wonders why morphine can't be prescribed prior to the onset of pain so that the patient rather than her pain could determine her daily life. The result has been a revolution in pain control for dying persons. Doctors are learning to prescribe range doses, and pharmaceutical companies have developed slow-release morphine that enables a dying person to stay a few steps in front of her pain.

Pastoral care and psychotherapy, like pain control prior to hospice, impose the boundary of pain as an agent of healing, and, therefore, a *de facto* criterion for getting help. Such an imposition means that those who seek help are already out of control, and, therefore, in need of—and at the mercy of—healers aimed at restoring agency; the power-over dynamic is intact before the healing encounter begins.

Using hospice's insight as a model, prophylactic structures of pastoral care and psychotherapy can be designed to enable persons to more effectively navigate the pitch of their spiritual and emotional pain. By establishing prevention programs, they can give persons more agency over the situations of daily living and create less need for help. In practical terms, this means that pastoral caregivers and psychotherapists meet constituents prior to loss of agency and on their own turf—a relinquishment of control—with educational and informational programs. Given the present therapy-management model of parish ministry and the reimbursement game of psychotherapy, there is little motivation for change. Nonetheless, the need is great for it.

Another revolutionary aspect of hospice care has been the commitment to see dying persons as . . . persons. This is in opposition to Western medicine, which plays the Cartesian game of breaking down the spirit of persons into the matter of bodily function and dysfunction. As hospice insists, and Eric Cassell suggests, bodies do not die, people do.[13]

The dehumanization of persons by medicine's orientation to the accidents rather than the essence of their beings was brought home to me by Ted's shaming confession: "Well, Father Wallace, I failed my last chemotherapy treatment. I guess I'm now ready for hospice." To which I replied, "I wonder, Ted, if you might consider that the chemotherapy failed you."

Pastoral caregivers and psychotherapists, like physicians, are too quick to bind those who seek help with the rope of diagnosis and treatment. The boundaries of diagnosis and treatment are drawn in order that those seeking help may be broken down into manageable and comprehensible categories of meaning able to be examined and fixed. The one seeking help is de-mystified, and, therefore, discounted as a person for control's sake. The healer, by such reductionistic behavior, is able to stay perched above the more messy, unpredictable, indefinable phenomena aroused by any kind of relationship with her, particularly a mutual one. The healer clings to the power-over platform so as to maintain the respected and expected role of expert.

This scene reminds me of Kierkegaard's assessment of Hegel's historical dialectic. Kierkegaard said that Hegel had built a marvelous castle in which to place humankind only to leave out the privy, the place where Kierkegaard claimed to spend most of his time.

Healers who are bound to see the one being healed through the eyes of their models of the mind, emotions, and soul have too small a bucket in which to contain and celebrate the serendipitous material of the healing relationship. The idea of getting a larger bucket to catch as much of the uncontainable givenness of the healing relationship usually suggests to the healer a transgression of the boundaries of appropriateness. The bias of the healer breeds the sense of inappropriateness; the bias is that it is dangerous to remain open to experience that can't be understood and used for predetermined outcomes. Possibly. As we say in the South: "Where there is the biggest blackberries there is often the meanest rattlesnakes." Wisdom, though, suggests that it is better to pick with caution than to avoid the patch.

Another way of saying it: The unbounded material of a healing relationship is born of the God whose Spirit blows when and where she pleases. Inasmuch as the healer is able to wait expectantly for, and welcome the possibility of, a holy visitation in the midst of the healing relationship, the eschatological dimension of the healing relationship is preserved.

Dying persons erase another established boundary of the helping relationship in need of reconsideration; a simple but suggestive one. Rarely can dying persons come to a place for help and stay for the traditionally prescribed fifty-minute hour. Mostly they are visited on their own turf and for as long as they feel comfortable having company. Pastoral care and psychotherapy are taken to them. The privilege and task of boundary setting changes hands and whatever agency the dying person has is maintained and valued.

Where and how we meet persons for pastoral care and psychotherapy are rich symbols of authority and the boundaries drawn around it. The parish I serve has a hall with administrative offices on the third floor and only a doorbell at the locked front door to announce an arrival. The doorbell can't be heard three flights up. So, more often than not, I arrange times to meet them on the front steps. Moving out of my study and into an old and not particularly reliable elevator for the ride downstairs, along with the five- to ten-minute wait outside, is a ritual for which I give thanks. It creates a safer, more level field upon which the hurting, already compromised parishioner can better manage her perception of the priestly power through which I offer myself in the healing relationship.

Second, we shall consider how to redraw the boundary lines in the helping relationship so as to increase the agency of the one seeking help, thereby abating suffering and grief. The issue, in actuality, is not so much about how the boundary lines are redrawn, but who draws them.[14]

Hospice works to ensure that the authority to determine the course of care is released by the healers and assigned to those being healed. Expertise is relocated. Hospice does not serve as much as it places itself in the service of the dying person's expert sense of the situation and what it might take to soften it. Upon admission to hospice, the dying person displaces the physician as author of treatment and course of care. The primary hospice nurse and other members of the hospice interdisciplinary team serve as lieutenants in the revolution and daily resist the temptation to higher rank, the lure to take over.

In short, the power dynamic is turned upside down. The healer assumes a power-under position. The healer puts down her black bag and prescription pad and uses her now free hands to cup her ears to hear better and clean her glasses to see better. The hard and continuous work of discernment begins. Inevitably, what the healer discerns about the desires and needs of the one being served contradicts her "better" judgment. The powerlessness of the dying person becomes the lived experienced of the healer. An empathic connection is made that well serves a healing relationship based on mutuality. More about that in the third section of this essay, "Powerlessness With."

The thought of pastoral caregivers and psychotherapists allowing and enabling the one seeking help to draw the boundaries of the healing relationship seems mind-boggling and, if nothing else, inviting of chaos.

The question, though, is whose chaos? Ours. Is our chaos about the loss of control? I think so. Further questions arise from the healer.

What was I trained for if not to guide and direct the healing process? By what authority does the one seeking help define issues, establish goals, and measure outcomes? How will I know what works and if it is working? All questions about power and who should have it.

Pastoral caregivers and psychotherapists are trained and equipped for penetrating and nuanced seeing of the lives and situations of those seeking help. I wonder, though, if we also are called to respect and trust the capacity of the ones seeking help to be seers into the healing relationship's appropriate manner and creative momentum. I'm not sure; but if my hospice experience pertains, I think so.

Anyway, I ask myself and colleagues, particularly my partners in ministry, some relevant questions. Are we ordained more to serve those seeking help or heal them? Service is about supporting the agency of another. Is it safe for the one seeking help to establish the ground rules of the healing relationship? Well, I imagine healers are at least as good, and probably better, at honoring the boundaries set by those seeking our help as we are at transgressing the ones we establish. Finally, are we sinning against the Holy Spirit by not remaining open to being moved and changed by God's visitation in the person and power of the one who seeks healing from us? This is the question I was left to ask after Carter Heyward's psychotherapist, in *When Boundaries Betray Us*, refused Carter's invitation for relationship deeper than her psychotherapist's model of the mind and emotions allowed.

Property Three: Powerlessness With

The single most important factor in being a healer of the dying is the ability to remain present in the midst of profound powerlessness. What do you do when what you want to do, need to do, is not done? What do you do when there is nothing that can be done? That's the rub.

Palliative care, the science of managing the symptoms of terminal illness, can be taught to any moderately competent clinician in six months or less. Presence in the midst of another's despair about dying, and one's own anxiety at not being able to do a god-damned thing about the dying, can't.

I'm not sure if the capacity to keep one's feet grounded and heart open in the hurricane of dying is a gift one has or a skill one learns. Probably both. I do know that the hospice professional, if she does hospice work effectively for any length of time, has to practice what Shirley Holzer Jeffrey, a grief counselor, called heroic helplessness.

Heroic helplessness is when the caregiver faces the limitations of her ability to make well and chooses not to sprint back to a job on more solid ground, that is, intensive care or home infusion nursing. She stays put after hitting, several months into the job, what I call the hospice wall. She comes to terms with the fact that her helplessness, finally, is the most she has to offer, the precious source of empathic connection that fades unhealthy distinctions between healer and healed. She comes to understand Will Campbell's definition of where two or three are gathered: "The church is one cat in one ditch and one nobody of a son-of-a-bitch trying to pull her out."

The pastoral caregiver and the psychotherapist who risk allowing the ones seeking help to set the boundaries of the helping relationship, and thereby establish a power-under position in relationship to the ones seeking help, experience a powerlessness not unlike that of the hospice professional. They are called to the aforementioned heroic helplessness and to the critical awareness that their helplessness is the blessed tie that binds them to the ones seeking help, the bond that makes them more like than unlike them. Powerlessness with the ones seeking help is a seam stitch in the fabric of pastoral care and psychotherapy grounded in mutuality.

Maintenance of mutuality grounded in powerlessness with the one seeking help is mostly about resisting the temptation to regain power. The pastoral caregiver and psychotherapist are tempted to step out of the thicket of powerlessness under and with the one seeking help and step back over the boundary of professional authority, thereby regaining control of the helping relationship; that is, they move from a position of power-under and power-with to power-over. Usually the shift is manifested in pastoral and psychotherapeutic busyness. We try to do something with or for the ones seeking help. In so doing, the vital center of the helping relationship, empathic connection, is lost.

I'm reminded of Jesus' night in the Garden of Gethsemane. He took his best friends with him and asked only that they watch and wait with him. They were so anxious about not being able to do something for their teacher and friend that they fell asleep; not once but three times.

The pastoral and psychotherapeutic challenge is not to fall into the sleep of anxious activity out of fear of powerlessness, but to watch and wait with those who invite us to be present with them in their forests of despair, and to accompany them through forbidden forests in which they do not want to travel alone.

The three essential properties of an effective presence with dying persons that were illuminated above—properties that pertain, I believe, to all healing relationships—inform the discussion about boundaries and mutuality by means of five suggestions for consideration. While the suggestions may seem unorthodox, they represent the conventional wisdom of good care of the dying.

One, the healer's boundary of professional authority, which sustains the healer's power-over position, is abandoned for a mutual relationship. The lines between healer and healed lessen or dissolve. Each party is simultaneously object and subject, discovering and making meaning together about the situation at hand. Both are sanctified, that is, changed through the relationship for a fuller life in community.

Two, the boundary of the healer's objectivity as the sole loving agent in the helping relationship maintained for the purpose of moving the one seeking help toward a more cohesive and sturdy self is abandoned. The one seeking help is allowed to be a loving agent. Consequently, the goal of the helping relationship shifts from personal salvation/wholeness to deeper relatedness.

Three, the boundaries of the healing relationship are redrawn. Suffering is not a precondition for care. Suffering, when presented, is not tightly framed by the healer's model of the mind, emotions and soul. Suffering is not attended to solely on the figurative and literal turf of the healer.

Four, the healer's authority to define the boundaries of the healing relationship is abandoned and handed over to the one seeking help so that the agency of the one seeking help, lost to the situation at hand, is restored.

Five, the healer, subject to the boundaries established by the one seeking help, experiences a loss of agency and crisis of powerlessness that provides an empathic connection with the one seeking help. A context of mutuality is created upon which hope is born.

Notes

1. Abraham Verghese, *My Own Country: A Doctor's Story* (New York: Vintage Books, 1994).

2. Dr. Verghese made this remark in a lecture given in Boston on June 7, 1995.

3. A vivid and moving account of the crucible of meaning about which Dr. Verghese speaks is expressed in Reynolds Price's poignant novel *The Promise of Rest* (New York: Scribner, 1995).

4. Paul Althaus, *The Theology of Martin Luther* (Philadelphia: Fortress Press, 1966), 294–303.

5. Sin is understood here in the more Protestant sense of estrangement, what Paul Tillich referred to as our separation from the Ground of Being, self, and others.

6. Theodore G. Tappert et al., eds., *The Book of Concord* (Philadelphia: Fortress Press, 1959), 303.

7. Patricia Lewis Poteat, *Walker Percy and the Old Modern Age* (Baton Rouge and London: Louisiana State University Press, 1985), 23–24.

8. Judith V. Jordan, Alexandra G. Kaplan, Jean Baker-Miller, Irene P. Striver, and Janet L. Surrey, *Women's Growth in Connection* (New York and London: The Guilford Press, 1991), 81–96.

9. Carter Heyward, *When Boundaries Betray Us* (San Francisco: HarperSanFrancisco, 1994).

10. For further analysis of the participation of the one seeking help as a loving agent, see John Patton's work, *Pastoral Counseling: A Ministry of the Church* (Nashville: Abingdon, 1983), esp. 30–32, 167–69.

11. By "Spirit" I mean the shared awareness between Martin, a Jew, and myself, a Christian, that our relatedness was deeper than we would want to name with the names given to us by the categories of religion or psychology. We were aware that we were being held by a dynamic experienced as holy and mysterious. For a particularly Christian assessment of that about which I speak, see Charles Gerkin's *The Living Human Document: Re-visioning Pastoral Counseling in a Hermeneutical Mode* (Nashville: Abingdon, 1984), 55–75.

12. Bill Wallace, "Pastoral Care for People with AIDS," *The Christian Ministry* (Jan.–Feb. 1989): 14–17.

13. See the Preface to Eric Cassell's book *The Nature of Suffering and the Goals of Medicine* (New York and Oxford: Oxford University Press, 1991).

14. Wallace, "Suffering, Meaning, and the Goals of Hospice Care," *The American Journal of Hospice and Palliative Care* (May–June 1995): 9–13.

14 | Epilogue

Katherine Hancock Ragsdale

"Some of the major disasters of mankind [sic] have been produced by the narrowness of men with good methodology."[1]

It is impossible fully to reckon the stakes in this argument without an excursion into epistemology—the study of knowledge itself. The defining question of epistemology is: How do we know what we know? or What is the nature of that which is known? Empiricists will say that reality (a real world) exists to be discovered. The point of our study, theorizing, etc., is to understand more fully the reality that exists in spite of us. Radical social constructionists will say that we construct reality. The act of coming to know, the meaning we make of our experiences, creates the world.

Warning: Trying to hold on too firmly to either of these polar opposite theories will prove so counterintuitive as to make you crazy.

Feminists have long understood the dangers of radical empiricism. That's the theory that tells us that the world is as it is as a fact of nature—an act of God—and there is nothing we can do about it. Men hold most executive positions because men are more powerful and better suited to intellectually demanding labor than women—that is the nature of the sexes. More whites than African Americans go to college because whites are smarter—that is the nature of the races.

Such empiricism is alive and well. Recall, for example, the fuss raised by *The Bell Curve*. But we who have had such arguments used to control us—to keep us in our places—too often, know better. We have seen that when we look at the world with new eyes, we see new things—and, as a result, the world changes. Note that I am not saying merely that we come to see the world differently but that the world *becomes* different.

However, the very feminists who have demonstrated so clearly the faulty logic and dangerous consequences of a strict empiricism have also begun to identify the pitfalls of radical social constructionism. To contend that there is no reality to be known, or that our inquiries (our attempts to know) shape reality so completely that it changes as fast as we can see it, is so counterintuitive as to be paralyzing and crazy-making. It leaves us, finally, with nothing to say.[2]

The trick, of course, is to abandon the patriarchal proclivity to reduce complicated questions to either/or propositions. It is not the alternatives (empiricism and social constructionism) themselves that are defective but rather the notion that they are alternative, rather than complementary, visions.[3]

What, then, does all this have to do with discussions of professional boundary issues? Simply this: Belief in social constructionism (to any degree) causes the stakes to skyrocket. Belief in empiricism (to any degree) drives home the immediacy and urgency of the problem.

If one believes in principles of social constructionism, it becomes apparent that the work we do, the decisions we make, will have an impact that far exceeds the span of our lives and the reach of our imaginations. How we behave in the world, the choices we make, the conversations we enter, influence the essence of that world, create the meaning of being human, and, in some sense, create the world itself.

At the same time, we know empirically that lives are being touched and shaped and, yes, harmed—right now. And we must, therefore, not fail to act. We must respond by working together to create trustworthy relationships—even in the face of all our disagreement about what such relationships would look like.

But we must be cautious lest in our fervor to acknowledge the vulnerability of women (as a class) and those in pain in our society and to, therefore, protect them from the victimization that so often accompanies vulnerability, we create circumstances that lock even more nonprofessionals (clients, patients, laity, women) even more firmly into positions of less respect, less power, and more vulnerability. Even if we could ensure that these powerless and vulnerable people would no longer be victimized by professionals engaging in sexual misconduct (and we can't), we may still have victimized them in a perhaps even more profound way by cementing their status of inferior power, by ignoring, and so eroding, their ability to be simultaneously victims and resisters, simultaneously seekers of help and agents in their own lives.

Theories of sexual misconduct and standards of practice, our ideas about boundaries and vulnerability, the assumptions that undergird our decisions about what is and is not ethical and efficacious practice, will shape and redefine the helping/healing professions. They will determine how we protect, or otherwise relate to, those who turn to us for help. But they will also shape and redefine what it means to have (or not have) power, the meaning of pain and vulnerability, and the degree of human agency accorded to each of us in our various circumstances.

It would be easier if we were not required to balance the considerations forced upon us by both empiricist and social constructionist insights. We could agree to protect people now with no fear that so protecting them will lead to a steady erosion of agency for the less powerful, the nonprofessional, for generations to come. Or we could focus on the world we hope to create without having simultaneously to respond to the perils of the world we live in now.

But we cannot ignore either side of the balance, for lives are at stake either way. And so we do the work of ethics, weighing the various epistemological and practical considerations; balancing competing needs, interests, and costs; negotiating our way through a web of interconnected issues and theories; continuing the conversation.

Notes

1. Alfred North Whitehead, *The Function of Reason* (Princeton, N.J.: Princeton University Press, 1929).

2. Or, as Donna Haraway puts it, "We end up with a kind of epistemological electroshock therapy, which far from ushering us into the high-stakes game of cre-

ating public truths, lays us out on the table with self-induced multiple-personality disorder." Donna Haraway, "Situated Knowledges: The Science Question in Feminism and the Privilege of Partial Perspective," chapter 9 of *Simians, Cyborgs, and Women: The Reinvention of Nature* (New York: Routledge, 1991), 186.

3. Haraway goes on to say, "I think my problem and 'our' problem is how to have [simultaneously] an account of radical historical contingency for all knowledge claims and knowing subjects . . . [and] a no-nonsense commitment to faithful accounts of a [real] world, one that can be partially shared and friendly to earthwide projects of finite freedom, adequate material abundance, modest meaning in suffering, and limited happiness." Ibid., 187.

Contributors

Kasimu (Garth Baker-Fletcher) is associate professor of ethics at the School of Theology at Claremont, California. He is the author of two books, *Somebodyness: Martin Luther King and the Theory of Dignity* (Fortress) and *Xodus: An African-American Male Journey* (Fortress).

Ronald G. Barton is senior minister of the Community Church of the Monterey Peninsula in Carmel, California. He is co-author, with Karen Lebacqz, of *Sex in the Parish* (Westminster John Knox) and other articles. While on the staff of the Northern California Nevada Conference of the United Church of Christ, 1979–90, he developed Guidelines and Procedures for situations involving allegations of clergy sexual abuse. He has served as a consultant to many regional and national church agencies and judicatories, and has taught courses at several theological seminaries.

Susan Baur, Ph.D., is a writer and a licensed psychologist. She is the author of books and articles on the history of science, psychology, and chronic mental illness. Her recent works include *The Dinosaur Man: Tales of Madness and Enchantment from the Back Ward* and *Confiding: A Psychotherapist and Her Patients Search for Stories to Live By*. She is currently working on *Risky Business: Love and Sex in Psychotherapy*. She lives in New England.

Mari Castellanos, a Cuban American, is a lesbian feminist activist, pastor, and theologian. She has held local and national leadership positions in the feminist and gay/lesbian movements in the churches, particularly within the Roman Catholic church. Castellanos's work has included a five-year appointment to the Dignity Task Force on Sexual Ethics, extensive national coalition work in Women Church Convergence, and several pastoral appointments in local churches. She holds a master's degree in theology from Barry University and is currently pursuing a D.Min. Castellanos is the founding minister of Holy Wisdom Interfaith Community in Miami.

Marie M. Fortune is executive director of the Center for the Prevention of Sexual and Domestic Violence in Seattle, Washington. She is a pastor and teacher, a practicing ethicist and theologian, and the author of numerous books and articles, including *Sexual Violence: The Unmentionable Sin* (The Pilgrim Press), *Keeping the Faith* and *Is Nothing Sacred?* (Harper San Francisco), and *Love Does No Harm* and *Violence Against Women and Children: A Christian Theological Sourcebook* (Continuum).

Miriam Greenspan is a psychotherapist and consultant in private practice. Her book *A New Approach to Women and Therapy* is a pioneering work in the field of feminist therapy. She is currently working on her second book, *Healing through the Dark Emotions: The Alchemy of Sorrow, Fear, Anger, and Despair.*

Beverly Wildung Harrison is the Caroline Williams Beaird Professor of Christian Ethics at Union Theological Seminary in New York, where she has been on the faculty for thirty-two years. A Presbyterian laywoman, she is the author of *Our Right to Choose: Toward an Ethic of Abortion* (Beacon) and *Making the Connections: Essays in Feminist Social Ethics*, edited by Carol S. Robb (Beacon). Her current writing project focuses on capitalist spirituality, the political economy, and class.

Carter Heyward, an Episcopal priest, is the Howard Chandler Robbins Professor of Theology at the Episcopal Divinity School in Cambridge, Massachusetts. She is the author of a number of books and articles, including, most recently, *Staying Power: Reflections on Gender, Justice, and Compassion* (The Pilgrim Press) and *When Boundaries Betray Us: Beyond Illusions of What Is Ethical in Therapy and Life* (Harper San Francisco). She is currently writing a book on Jesus.

Sally A. Johnson is a partner in the Minneapolis-based law firm of Faegre & Benson. Her practice focuses on representing nonprofit institutions including private schools, colleges, seminaries, youth-serving organizations, and religious institutions. She is an active Episcopalian, serving as chancellor (general counsel) to the Episcopal Diocese of Minnesota, a delegate to the national conventions of the Episcopal church, a member of the national Standing Commission on Constitution & Canons and Publications Committee, and a member of local boards of Episcopal-affiliated organizations.

Karen Lebacqz, Ph.D., recently returned to the Graduate Theological Union in Berkeley, California. Co-author with Ronald G. Barton of *Sex in the Parish*, she is the author of several books and numerous articles on sexual ethics, professional ethics, and bioethics, and is the editor of Pilgrim's forthcoming *Sexuality: A Reader.*

Leng Leroy Lim, a native of Singapore, received his A.B. in public policy and international affairs from the Woodrow Wilson School, Princeton University, and his master of divinity from Harvard Divinity School. A deacon in the Episcopal church, he is assistant chaplain at UCLA, and a health outreach worker to the Chinese community with the Asian Pacific AIDS Intervention Team.

Katherine Hancock Ragsdale is an Episcopal priest, consultant, and senior associate of Leader Resources. A former executive director of Common Cause/VA, and staff officer at the national offices of the Episcopal church, she is currently the national president of the Religious Coalition for Reproductive Choice.

Margo Rivera, M.Ed., Ph.D., is a psychologist and assistant professor of psychiatry at Queen's University, Kingston, Ontario. She is co-director of the Personality Disorders Program at Kingston Psychiatric Hospital and director of Education/Dissociation, a community organization dedicated to disseminating information about child abuse and severe dissociative conditions to professionals and the general public. Dr. Rivera has published and lectured widely—in Canada, the United States, and Europe—in the areas of trauma, psychotherapy practice, and post-traumatic dissociation, and is the author of *More Alike Than Different: Treat-*

ing Severely Dissociative Trauma Survivors (University of Toronto Press).

Fredrica Harris Thompsett is academic dean and Mary Wolfe Professor of Historical Theology at the Episcopal Divinity School in Cambridge, Massachusetts. Her most recent books are *Courageous Incarnation: In Intimacy, Work, Childhood, and Aging* (Cowley Publications) and *We Are Theologians* (Cowley Publications). She is currently working on two writing projects: a volume on tradition and change in the Episcopal Church, and an edited collection of writings from Asian, African, and Latin American theologians from member Churches of the Anglican Communion.

Bill Wallace is an Episcopal priest and rector of Emmanuel Church in Boston. For almost two decades he has specialized in the care and counseling of the dying and bereaved and the administration of hospice programs. A graduate of Lutheran Theological Seminary in Columbia, South Carolina, he received his clinical training at the William S. Hall Psychiatric Institute of the South Carolina Department of Mental Health and the Center for Pastoral Psychotherapy of the Georgia Baptist Medical Center. He is a practicing spiritual director on the staff of Episcopal Divinity School and at the Monastery of Saint John the Evangelist, both in Cambridge. He has published numerous articles on hospice, AIDS, grief and bereavement, and spirituality.

Traci C. West is an assistant professor of ethics and African American Studies at Drew University Theological School. She is an ordained United Methodist minister who has served in parish and campus ministries. She pursues a commitment to work on issues related to the intersection of race, gender, and intimate violence in academic, church, and community settings.

Index